~ **Radical Señora Era** ~

Radical Señora Era

Ancestral Latin American Secrets
for a Happier, Healthier Life

ANN MURRAY DUNNING
and CHRISTINA KELMON

Kensington Publishing Corp.
kensingtonbooks.com

DAFINA BOOKS are published by

Kensington Publishing Corp.
900 Third Avenue
New York, NY 10022

All Kensington titles, imprints, and distributed lines are available at special quantity discounts for bulk purchases for sales promotion, premiums, fundraising, educational, or institutional use. Special book excerpts or customized printings can also be created to fit specific needs. For details, write or phone the office of the Kensington Special Sales Manager: Attn. Special Sales Department, Kensington Publishing Corp., 900 Third Ave., New York, NY 10022. Phone: 1-800-221-2647.

The DAFINA logo is a trademark of Kensington Publishing Corp.

Library of Congress Control Number: 2025936282

ISBN-13: 978-1-4967-5131-7

First Kensington Hardcover Edition: October 2025

ISBN-13: 978-1-4967-5132-4 (ebook)

10 9 8 7 6 5 4 3 2 1

Printed in the United States of America

The authorized representative in the EU for product safety and compliance is eucomply OU, Parnu mnt 139b-14, Apt 123
Tallinn, Berlin 11317, hello@eucompliancepartner.com

Dedicated to the magical señoras and doñas who influenced my life and raised me: Mercedes, Margarita, Maria, and Carmen Luz, an even older generation I never met: Eva and Blanca and Yayita, the new generation of radical señoras: Eva and Andrea, and all of our *hijitas*.

—*Ann Murray Dunning*

For Matt, my steadfast anchor and greatest champion, who supports me in every wild and daring dream. For Margaux, my free-spirited muse—may you always dance through life untamed and full of wonder. And for Elizabeth, whose unwavering strength and love have shaped the radical woman I am today.

—*Christina Kelmon*

~ Contents ~

⋍ Foreword ⋍

I AM A clinical psychologist, and in my line of work, I offer culturally responsive mental health services, with particular attention to intergenerational trauma. I have even written a bestselling book about it, *Break the Cycle: A Guide to Healing Intergenerational Trauma.* So, what does this have to do with being in your señora era?

To explain, let me tell you about my favorite señora era ritual. I love to incorporate my tea ritual into everything I do: my TV interviews, podcasts, even some of my work with clients. What some people don't know about my love for tea is that my Dominican grandmother used to make lemongrass tea and have moments where she would sit down and sip her tea mindfully. My mother also practiced this same exact ritual. My tea ritual is how I am now honoring my intergenerational señora era, and I am doing so with these wise women in mind.

Teas were a favorite of our ancestors because they are powerful remedies. They taste delicious, sure, but many teas have actual healing properties within them that can help us to feel physically better and calmer. What's more, when we slow down the tea-making process and make it a mindful team moment, we have an opportunity to actually create a wellness practice within our tea breaks. It's truly a win-win for our mental and physical well-being.

Being in your señora era means mindfully slowing down how you're living life, just like that. You automatically slow down when you start a new knitting project, take the time to make some delicious tea, create a señora morning walk ritual, work in your garden, even put on your favorite podcast while you clean the house. It's a natural way in which we regulate our stress level to what's happening around us, especially if we're experiencing particularly challenging times. Our ancestors knew to do this instinctually, but those of us who have had those beautiful traditions severed by migration, forced assimilation, and a host of other reasons haven't had the privilege of regulating ourselves and honoring our need for slower-paced moments.

We find ourselves in an era where we are reclaiming what it means to be a woman of color who lives in peace and harmony. We're resurrecting all kinds of stress-relieving and mentally healing practices that our mothers and their mothers and their mothers have used for generations to subconsciously regulate themselves emotionally. Even something as simple as *limpiando la casa* on a Saturday morning—with some salsa music by Celia Cruz and El Gran Combo, a *balada* from Juan Gabriel or Luis Miguel, or even a *merenguito* from Johnny Ventura or Las Chicas del Can playing in the background—is something that we grew up witnessing and we're conditioned to do ourselves.

Forming dance circles was another practice the women from our ancestral past did to heal and find joy. They would surround the person who was believed to be struggling and in this way help them release the pain and stress that was causing them to feel weighed down. Sitting back in their rocking chairs and having meaningful conversations with a *vecina* or a *prima* was their way of doing talk therapy with each other for generations. These rituals were so baked into our culture that they weren't even considered healing practices at all, but just a natural way of life.

We may have switched from playing La India or Selena to listening to audiobooks or indie or house music, but the benefits of this ritual are still there—we release tension from our nervous systems while creating a sanctuary in our homes. It's all very therapeutic and healthy for us. We're transforming and claiming these practices as our own and seeing how they can continue to be a form of self-care for our generation. That reclamation and intentional emotional regulation are beautiful ways in which we can honor our Latine roots while tending to our emotions.

This is why I was so excited to hear about this new book project about being a Radical Señora, where we reclaim these beneficial ancestral practices to create a new way of stepping into a lovelier, slower-paced era of our lives. We are taking our softness back and holding it tight, so that it can liberate our lineage and help us feel the tenderness we deserve. Whether you're emerging into adulthood and want to have a guidebook for how to mindfully create a higher quality of living while retaining some of your ancestors' wisdom, or you already have integrated well-established routines into your daily life and just need soothing new rituals to add as you head into the new, uncharted waters of womanhood, this book, inspired by the women that came before you, is sure to bring a great deal of surprising joy.

> —Dr. Mariel Buqué, Afro-Dominican, Columbia
> University-trained psychologist, intergenerational
> trauma expert, and the author of *Break the Cycle:*
> *A Guide to Healing Intergenerational Trauma*

⁓ Introduction ⁓

THINK BACK TO the best, well-rested day you've had over the past year. A day when your mind felt calm, the tension melted off your body, and you felt really rooted. You weren't stressing out about much, like you're probably doing right now while reading this book. What if you could feel that way more often simply by introducing some familiar, easy routines into your life? And what if an essential part of feeling this way meant just changing the way you look at mundane, everyday things, like work, for instance?

I know, I know. You've heard all of that before. No doubt you have read a small library of books, watched countless YouTube videos, and listened to many podcasts about creating a happier you. How boring! What if the secret to feeling a little happier has been with you all along, hidden in the memories of the daily routines of the señoras in your family tree? That true magic is in your great-great-grandmother's typical Saturday: the smell of sizzling *asado* barbecue; the scent of fresh *pan amasado* baking in the clay oven out back; the sound of chickens clucking in the *huerto*, maybe a donkey braying, or dogs barking off in the distance (in Spanish, of course); and the faint sound of a radio playing in the background. Can you imagine how calming it would feel to have just a tiny bit of that feeling every day?

I spent the past three years learning more about my homeland of Chile and building a business alongside my bestie, Christina Kelmon, who is a cofounder of Vamigas, our Latina wellness and skin-care line, and a third-generation Mexican American. Together, we stumbled onto something we never expected to find in a million years: that time-tested slow-living routines and habits from the lives of our grandmothers, great-grandmothers, and beyond just may be the secret sauce to bringing back a little bit of joy and well-being in our lives.

Although I came here when I was in elementary school, I have very vivid memories of living in Latin America. Being Chilean in the US has always been just part of my identity, something I never thought much about daily. When I launched a beauty brand with Christina that was rooted in Latin America, and particularly Chilean beauty secrets, I started to think more mindfully about the country of my birth. While doing research on Chilean biodiversity as we dreamt up new skin-care formulations, I began to read about the daily lives of Chilean women. I dove deeply and went down a research rabbit hole of useful herbs, fascinating homemade beauty creations, practical home and garden ideas, and history.

At the same time, there were big changes in my life. The routines and habits that had helped me in my twenties and thirties were no longer sustainable or working for me. I was in a completely new environment as a first time (and older) mom, no longer able to rely on my career as my identity crutch. Seeking reassurance and a sense of serenity, I turned to the rituals and routines of my homeland, and before long they became part of my daily life.

This was what had been missing from my life all along. I became completely hooked on Chilean señoras of the past. I wanted to learn about all the hacks my great-grandmother had for daily life, such as what she baked and what she planted out back, and do them all myself—with a modern spin.

Listen, we know how you've been feeling over these past few years. You're overworked, burned out, overscheduled, and possibly drowning underwater. The last year especially has been very dark for many. For starters, your employer is undervaluing and underpaying you. You're coming home exhausted, only to impulsively blow half your paycheck on "wellness" cures pushed by shiny-haired influencer moms from Utah with big hats—people you can't actually relate to.

There's something truly magical about exploring the daily lives of señoras of the past and incorporating aspects of those lives into your own, for instance, by starting a garden, growing your great-grandmother's favorite herbs, and using them to make a delicious tea. Just imagine the high you'll feel in discovering a secret recipe that has been hidden in your family tree and maybe even in raising a couple of chickens, if your HOA lets you, that is. This is what the señora era is all about.

It took Christina and me two decades of being stuck in a toxic girl boss culture, where we were obsessed with work and brainwashed by Silicon Valley and Wall Street wizards into believing that our work was our identity to the point where we honestly thought being very busy boss babes, being on call practically 24/7, was the most important thing in our lives. One day, right after the entire world turned upside down in 2020, we found ourselves burnt out, disillusioned, feeling unhealthy, and without the one thing that had once defined us: our careers. Oh, and we were in our forties and were brand-new (and very anxious) moms. The only thing that hustle culture had given us was morning anxiety, panic attacks, and a dental guard for nighttime teeth grinding thanks to stress.

It's a major feat to make it big in whatever industry you're working in or, at the very least, be on your way up the ladder. Since many of us are immigrants, or kids of immigrants, we tend to get so preoccupied with being high achievers that we don't realize we're doing it at the expense of our lives, family, and well-being until one day we wake up twenty years older, asking ourselves, *Where the heck did my life go? And why does this not feel right?*

Make no mistake, worshipping at the altar of hustle culture is not going to save you, and neither are those boss babe influencers who try their best to sell you on their propaganda. And buying things online that you really don't need won't, either. We're now fully convinced that the secret to having a life that makes you feel good simply means living more slowly and intentionally, like your *abuelas* did, by embracing this fun little meme called our señora eras.

Some of you are reading this and perhaps thinking, *I'm not an old lady yet! I don't want to be in my señora era! Does that mean I won't have any fun?* It's a natural reaction to have, one that Christina and I also had at first. We may have been resistant to shedding our old lives as overworked boss babes in the beginning, but eventually, we came to our senses and embraced the opportunity to change our way of living. Allow me to share with you how adopting a señora era mentality made our lives better, and why it has zero to do with sitting in a rocking chair or never going out again on Friday nights.

Christina and I were lucky to enter our señora eras together. This happened after a decade of becoming cogs in San Francisco's finance and start-up worlds—the birthplace of hustle culture, where sleeping under your desk was an *aspirational* goal to strive for. We then partnered up to jump into an industry we thought was all about balance, self-care, and wellness—the beauty industry. We created a skin-care brand that launched at major retailers and was featured in hundreds of media outlets, from *People* magazine to Oprah Daily, *Allure*, Today.com, *Elle*, and *Good Housekeeping*. In time, the business was making nearly one million dollars in revenue (not profit!) and expanding to Target, Whole Foods, JCPenney, Nordstrom, and other retail venues. We basically built it from scratch and made it blow up.

There we were, busy collecting small business wins, happy as clams, when we came to the horrific realization that being a small business owner has its own version of toxicity: big corporations copying ideas from tiny brands, celebrities jumping on the bandwagon and stealing market share, scammers looking for an easy buck. It was like a never-ending toxic spiral, one that we weren't prepared to deal with. We began to encounter one obstacle after the other. For a while there, it felt like the world was against us after giving us so much good news.

Do you know what got us through all the mayhem? Going all in on our señora eras and finding joy in little moments of señorahood. For me, it took planting and cultivating a whole vegetable garden and getting some hens to force me to find joy outside of work and create work/life balance. For Christina, it meant completely leaving behind toxic habits she had learned early on in her career and being true to herself. Our lives ended up looking a lot like what our grandmothers and great-grandmothers were doing at our age, except with more hashtags.

One day, when we started to talk about this on TikTok, the reaction was *wild*: We got six million views and over fifty thousand TikTok followers, and hundreds of thousands of Latinas became our friends. Would you like to know why our sisters came in droves? Because they were all feeling the same way we were. They were sick of hustling harder only to feel the same sense of "meh," to *not* feel rooted in or anchored to their cultures, or to feel the acute stress of trying to be really good at work and at home. They all felt isolated and restless, or they fell into the trap of allowing work to become their identity, without getting much back in return. They felt something beautiful was missing in their lives.

In retrospect, we even angered some women, who seemed to misunderstand completely what we were trying to say. In response to our videos, sometimes there were comments or emails like, *Oh yeah, okay. I'll just quit my job and starve, thanks.*

This big misunderstanding was that the señora era concept was never about quitting your job and moving to a rancho or a farm. For us, it boiled down to adopting the mindset of living life intentionally, slowly, and creating boundaries between work and life. If you're working hard and still not feeling good, making enough money, or getting much benefit, stop right there. Hit the **PAUSE** button and take a deep breath. Tell yourself that you're not going to get much more out of yourself by just working harder. You're only going to hurt yourself. Your self-esteem should not be based on what you do for work.

In our first video that went viral, for every angry comment, there were a thousand positive ones, such as "My dream!" "My *abuelo* raised chickens and always had fresh eggs. I really want that, too." "This is amazing! I want in!" "I'm moving in!" "You found me!"

They were also coming to us because something fascinating started to trend online during the pandemic, something that had actually started brewing a few years earlier. The hashtag *señora era* was being used by millions of people on TikTok, a social media tool that was heavily used by Latinos. The word *señora* describes a woman of a certain age who does housework in the morning, drinks tea in the afternoon, and goes for leisurely strolls around the *vecindario* (neighborhood) afterward or during a break at work. In a relatively short span of time, we connected with tens of thousands of *amigas* online during a dark moment in history, when people needed to feel healthy and at peace, hear something positive, connect with others, and know more about their culture. The pandemic also made people re-evaluate how they wanted to spend their days, and realize there was so much more to life than work. They were interested to hear about how the señoras of the past lived, about their soothing home-life routines, from baking to beauty to collecting delicious herbs for tea, all passed down from generation to generation. In my case, much of this señora wisdom was lost when a branch of my family tree moved to the United States and settled in Los Angeles. In Christina's case, this happened a few generations ago.

As the authors of this book, we'll share with you how we reclaimed those rituals, so that you'll realize just how important it is to slow down, create balance in your life, and start to feel real purpose. We are planning to do it in a very modern way. One of the other critiques we received when we started sharing these ideas is how the concept of the señora era is too anchored in the past and ignores the long history of injustice, disempowerment, and gender inequality in our homelands, and the world, for that matter. Though the señora era is rooted in a Latin America of the past, the Radical Señora Era is modern. It's a state of mind that promotes using the tools that señoras of the past used, far removed from the problematic ways that women throughout history have been told they were unequal and with an empowered point of view.

Christina and I are both still learning to embrace our inner señora eras. Our lives are not perfect, and we won't claim that we have discovered the true meaning of life or something like that. Our lives, especially as moms, are messy, chaotic, and filled with more awful or exasperating moments than we care to admit. Sometimes we feel terrible, or bored or annoyed with the world. Embracing our ancestors' practical habits has simply given us a tool set for how to deal with the crappy parts of life—and the current state of the world—a little better.

Here's what we aim to accomplish with this book. First, we intend it to be a slow-living guidebook featuring personal stories as well as a Latin American history book. We are going to help you achieve a higher degree of happiness and better state of "wellness" by showing you how the señoras of the past lived. If you are a history buff and are trying to live a slower life to feel a little bit happier, this book is for you.

Next, we're gonna help you navigate the next few decades of your life, because whatever stage you're in, you can harness the power of señorahood to age joyfully and gracefully in a modern-day era that basically doesn't honor women past their thirties. Finally, we will help you reconnect with your roots so that you feel less lonely. Your señora era is your time to heal, a time when you connect the dots and figure out what's working for you and what's not. It's where you make amends and even reconnect with loved ones, living and deceased.

By the time you're done reading this book, you'll know how to plant a garden or expand yours to include herbs from your family's homelands, make the same rose water your great-grandmother made, blend teas, grow your own tomatoes and potatoes, create less waste, make your own low tox cleaning products for your home, or start your day off right. Any of these habits have the added benefit of making you feel more calm and your days more peaceful. You'll accomplish this while learning to leave work outside your home and your identity. Because if there's one thing we are sure of these days, it's that the señora way of life is the antidote to a modern world full of nonstop bad news, anxiety, loneliness, poor health outcomes, and uncertainty.

These secrets have always been in your family tree, but this knowledge was forgotten, and this got us off track. The time has come for all of us to travel into the past, find these secrets, and bring them back into the present. Make a cup of your favorite tea or *cafecito*, grab a blanket, and sit back. Welcome to your wonderful Radical Señora Era.

—Ann Murray Dunning

What the Radical Señora Era Is:

- A way to live your life as well and as stress free and calmly as possible with the tools you already have
- A strategy to help you live a more joyful life
- A way to connect with your ancestors, whether you're an immigrant, first or second generation or beyond, whether they're living or no longer with us
- A way to have a more grounded life, no matter what is happening in the world or in your life
- An easy, slow-living playbook
- Learning beautiful, motivating and fun habits from señoras of your family's past.

What the Radical Señora Era Is Not:

- A solution to all your problems: If you're not feeling okay, consider talking to a therapist. No matter what wellness influencers tell you (even those doctors on YouTube), you cannot cure yourself by just being more positive.

- A #tradwife book: We're not trying to bring back the past, or reinforce outdated gender stereotypes. We're bringing a little bit of the past back to us in a modern way.
- A homesteading book: This book is about Latin American cultural traditions, which intersect a lot with other cultural traditions, histories, and rituals of great-grandmothers, like those who practiced a homesteading lifestyle. We think everyone would be happier and healthier if they borrowed some of their great-grandmothers' traditions, creations, and rituals. In this book we teach you a little bit about starting or expanding your garden, and erecting and optimizing your own chicken coop, but this book isn't about homesteading. It's also not a recipe book.
- A midlife-crisis book: This book does not delve into the many challenges of being a woman entering midlife. It's for everyone who wants to balance work and life and prioritize self-care.
- A *curandera* book: Though some of our ancestors' rituals were influenced by herbalism and other practices of Indigenous cultures, Christina's and my ancestors weren't *curanderas*. If you have *curanderas* in your family line, we encourage you to research that further, because it's beautiful.
- An Indigenous knowledge book: Our families and yours were mestizo and *castizo* families, products of colonial intermarriage (and possibly even sexual violence) between Spanish and Indigenous people.

Christina and I have Indigenous ancestors. (My great-grandparents were from the Aymara community in Chile.) However, we didn't grow up in those cultures, and we don't want to benefit from cultures that are not familiar to us or take advantage of them. We want to honor the traditions of the women in our ancestral lines–including those of Indigenous women–by resurrecting and embracing some of them, but we won't go beyond that, and we don't pretend to own them.

- An advanced gardening book. We're just giving you the basics, to get started quickly, and a few tools to expand your knowledge.

CHAPTER 1

Stepping into Your Great-Grandmother's Era

Just the Good Parts

IMAGINE THE ANXIETY that comes with knowing that millions of people have seen your face online.

One of Christina and Ann's videos had just gone viral on Tik-Tok, and the comments began pouring in immediately, one after the other, arriving nearly every second. Some accused them of telling Latinas to be lazy or to quit their jobs. Others said there was nothing wrong with hustle culture and how dare they imply that they should not work hard.

Is this some kind of cult? one asked.

Some comments were just mean-spirited and criticized their Latina-ness, or their garden.

The text overlay on the video simply read: *If you're a Latina who wants to plant a garden, enter your señora era, and leave hustle culture behind, be our* amiga.

They even got an email message from a woman who told them that what they were doing was very wrong. **Why do you think that?** Ann emailed her back, surprised at her randomness.

Because you shouldn't be elevating these women from the past who were doing nothing special. They have nothing to teach us, she replied.

All Ann and Christina were doing was telling Latinas to slow down if they wanted, to start a garden, maybe drink a *tecito* on the patio. *The horror!* Why was the simple idea that Latinas should be allowed to rest so confusing or rage-inducing that it made people start fights in the TikTok comment section and send angry emails?

This is what went down. One morning Ann woke up to find one of her TikTok videos had blown up overnight. At the time her bestie and cofounder, Christina, had a sad little TikTok profile with just a hundred followers, and they used it for their small business, a skin-care line called Vamigas, which they had created as newborn and toddler moms stuck at home during the pandemic. In the video, which took Ann just five minutes to shoot on her phone the day before, she was walking through her garden beds, wearing her oldest, tattered sun hat, an ugly pink pajama top, and no makeup. Unlike most viral videos at the time, this was definitely *not* an aesthetic moment by any means, though the song playing in the background was Álvaro Carrillo's timeless ballad *"Sabor a mí,"* sung by Eydie Gormé and Los Panchos.

That morning Christina and Ann were both in the middle of the usual morning kid chaos in two different cities in California. Upon realizing that the video had gone viral, Christina called Ann in a panic. "Ann!" she said. "What the heck did you do?"

"Nothing!" Ann replied.

"I thought *you* did something!" Christina insisted.

They were so confused that Ann was sure this had to be some kind of prank, hack or, worse, a TikTok mistake, and that they would have to give all their followers back. But the views kept going up and up. At first, there were thirty thousand views, then a hundred fifty thousand, and then three hundred thousand, and ultimately, the count reached half a million in just a few days, with fifty thousand new followers. You have never felt true anxiety until complete strangers on the Internet start yelling at you.

Though there were the mean ones, most of the comments were incredibly energized, like **Please take me with you! I have found my people!** and **Teach me!** There were even some who asked Ann what her address was so they could come over and start working in her garden. That week there were messages and comments at all hours of the day and night, mostly from older Latinas, but some were in their late twenties and wanted to get a head start on their señora life.

There was something so powerful about sharing this simple idea that reading it made some people feel really good and others *super* uncomfortable. What the heck was it? It's almost like they had tapped into a secret network of millions of Latinas who felt just like them. They were tired of pushing hard, of the constant grind, of "stressed out" being their default mode, of the anxiety from worrying about what fire they had to put out next. In the journey for that elusive American dream, they were putting health and well-being last, after caring for others.

Christina and Ann were part of a broader trend: a group of Latinas who had done everything that was expected of them—graduating from college; using student loans, which they were still paying off; spending decades building careers in industries that sometimes paid them just cents on the dollar. Some of them had found themselves in a boys' club that wasn't very friendly to women. Others had clawed and sacrificed their way up the corporate ladder, just to find that once they had babies, they weren't given much leeway to be both a present mom *and* employee. So, many of these Latinas dropped out of the work-force and launched side businesses, thinking this would help them have work/life balance. But then they found themselves working themselves to the bone.

Like Christina and Ann, these women wanted to step out of this never-ending cranking machine and tap into another type of life, one you might find in stories about your great-grand-mother who was an herbalist, or in the slow, calm routines of your *abuela*, who seemed to have perfected the art of protecting her peace while also putting in a good day's work. But Christina and Ann wanted to do this in a more modern way.

They were completely cut off from what used to nourish women in their homelands, providing them with simple joy and happiness: community and family, plants and herbs, wholesome cultural foods, a project that fired them up without getting in the way of their life, and calming at-home rituals. They just wanted to find some peace and balance. What was so wrong about that? Why should they have to be constantly struggling?

As it turns out, a lot of Latinas wanted this. A 2024 PEW Research study found that more than half of Latinas feel the push and pull to provide for their families, while 75 percent say they feel the constant pressure to also succeed at their jobs.[1] This work/life problem is familiar to women everywhere who are trying to be good at all things at the same time. *News flash, you can't do it all.*

This hustle culture we seem to be trapped in doesn't help, either. Over the past decade, we have been fed this lie that rest is for the weak. They tell you that to survive, you've got to work all the time, have multiple side hustles, or think about your company above anything else in your life. If you're not thinking about work all the time, then you're doing something wrong and you have to work harder.

Somehow, hustle culture has permeated every industry. Our cultural heroes are the personification of the hustle; they have million-dollar cars, twenty or more beauty brands, and their own Hulu shows, where they say things like "Get your (expletive) ass up and work!" Except they're also people with generational wealth who have never had to work a single regular job in their lives. They make you think that you, too, can reach that level of wealth—but only if you hustle hard enough.

At one time in their lives, Christina and Ann absolutely lived for this hustle. They *boss babed* the hell out of their twenties and burned the candle at both ends during their thirties. They read Sheryl Sandberg's *Lean In* and the favorite of finance bros everywhere, *How to Win Friends and Influence People*. They followed all the coaches and gurus, and it freaking changed their lives. They leaned in hard, had zero work/life boundaries, and the only thing that made them happy was making more and more money. They got a little weird. Ann and Christina thought the corporations they worked for were their families, while almost ignoring their real families. They thought life was about trying to make millions. Then one day they realized that all this sacrifice hadn't been worth it, and that there was another way, which they had totally ignored. The way of their *abuelitas*.

Where did they go wrong?

When worlds collided!

Over the past four years, Christina and Ann have collectively gone through some really anxious times and have felt the effects of worldwide issues that had started bubbling up to the surface long ago. It was a moment when a few troubling elements began to intersect. People were suddenly not very happy. In 2011 the

UN began issuing what's called the World Happiness Report, a ranking of how happy countries are based on citizens' self-reports. The most recent report is kind of a canary in the coal mine. The US has been completely bumped out of the top twenty happiest countries. What's more, the percentage of US adults diagnosed with depression is now ten points higher than just a decade ago. These trends started largely before COVID, and we all know the pandemic, the economic fallout, and things like long COVID have made mental health issues critically worse.

You may not even feel depressed—just bleh. Maybe you just haven't felt like your old self in a long time. In his book *Languishing: How to Feel Alive Again in a World That Wears Us Down*, author Cory Keyes writes that there is a space between mental illness and mental health that is called *languishing*, and it is where you're not clinically depressed, but you're not thriving, either. Instead, you feel numb, perhaps from seeing no meaning in life or from completely lacking any warm, trusting relationships. You're just not feeling the good emotions. Keyes points to the pandemic as a time when many people began feeling this way, and it hasn't improved much since. Many of you may be shaking your heads in agreement as you read this.[2]

As a result of this collective languishing, our generations—Gen X and millennials—started talking more about self-care, wellness, and alternatives to hustle culture. The concept of self-care was first developed by poet Audre Lorde and Black activist Angela Davis. It was an idea that called for people to consciously practice rituals that helped them feel healthier, mentally well, and rested, while they put in the work in their communities. We're not talking bubble baths here, but soothing practices for the body and the mind that work to reinvigorate you.

Latinas have our own spin on self-care, and it's things that are largely familiar to us in our home. It's practicing our beauty routines or taking a calming walk, because that is what we have memories of our *abuelitas* doing. It's cooking the *sopita* you remember from when you were growing up, or making an *asado* for your extended family and your friends. It's starting a balcony garden, watering your plants, knitting, sewing, or studying herbs. We generally aren't buying that eighteen-hundred-dollar-a-year gym membership. We Latinas want to do things that remind us of beautiful moments tied to family members who are either still here with us or resting in peace.

However, we also aren't the greatest at taking care of ourselves. Dr. Yasmin Davidds, an organizational psychologist, the founder and CEO of the Latina Global Executive Leadership Institute at USC, and the author of *Graciously Assertive: How Becoming a Better Human Makes You a Better Leader*, thinks that one of our greatest strengths is also something we don't use on ourselves.[3]

"I've worked with many Latinas throughout the years. We have this superpower where we are very loving and kind. We use it for others, and especially our mothers and our kids," she told me. "We don't, however, use that superpower on ourselves. We are the worst at self-care because we think it seems selfish to us."

The solution, she said, is to "reframe this superpower as an understanding that if I am not well now, I am not well for anybody."

We also collectively started yearning for the *campo*. The explosion in work from home jobs and the feeling of being confined in your apartment led to a migration from the city to more rural and suburban areas, where you could get more space for your money. The popularity of living in the country started growing again after decades of rural population loss. For Latinos, the dream of our homelands and the *terrenos* (this concept of the acreage owned by your ancestral family) has always been important to our identity. To us, this might look like wanting to leave the city, go back to the *terrenos*, and live the slow, quiet life, just like our ancestors did.

Christina and Ann also saw pushback against hustle culture and blowback for the workaholism of the past few decades, which was rooted in the idea that hard work above all else would bring you happiness. They counted over three hundred articles critiquing this idea over the past year, with many calling this way of thinking toxic because it doesn't take into consideration environmental factors—like poverty or racism or lack of access to higher education—that might make someone who is working their hardest unable to succeed.

Latinas are now getting master's degrees and other advanced academic degrees at a faster rate than other groups, they are making a killing in such industries as marketing and real estate, and they are making inroads into industries once led by the kids of the wealthy, like tech and finance.[4] But we're realizing that once you reach some of the career success you've always dreamed about, you may feel like you're languishing, rather than enjoying the happiness you thought you'd find, and like life is a little bit more complex and multilayered than you expected.

It was also the fact that many of us millennials and Gen X Latinos have been approaching midlife and not seeing ourselves represented in the mainstream culture. Hollywood, the media, and brand marketing teams have largely ignored topics relevant to modern Latinos over the age of thirty, except to talk about our health and risk factors or the habits of Latino boomers or members of the Silent Generation. You hear about funny things like *chancla* culture, which isn't really familiar to Gen Xers and millennials anymore.

These were all ingredients of the *sopita* that created the señora era phenomenon and made so many Gen X and millennials besties want to embrace their señora eras, which meant being thoughtful about creating a life that is slower paced and peaceful. We were all entering or moving through midlife together, mourning our lost cultures and the grandparents left behind, while trying to figure out why we had worked so hard to move the needle ever so slightly. In many ways, embracing that we were entering our señora eras allowed us to approach this new stage of life in a positive, joyful way, and to stop feeling guilty about luxuriating, resting, and not taking life so seriously.

So why is being in your señora era so radical?

The pandemic hit the Hispanic community particularly hard. We had nearly the highest rate of death due to COVID, second only to Non-Hispanic Native Americans.[5] Many families in our communities lost elders, leaving some without *abuelitas,* who were the matriarchs of the family, or *tíos,* who took care of everything. The post-pandemic economic slump left many Latino small business owners up a creek without a paddle. It's a radical thing to look for calm and joy during and after such unimaginable loss and economic instability. Our community has been through a lot these past few years.

What's more, recent shifts in policies and national conversations around immigration have created a rise in anti-Hispanic sentiment, creating uncertainty for both immigrants and long-standing Hispanic communities. Additionally, the pushback against diversity, equity, and inclusion (DEI) initiatives has led many to be suspicious of those Latinos who are successful.

These challenges have reinforced negative stereotypes and misunderstandings and is making it much harder for our community to be at peace.

There is scientific research that shows how highly Latinos value working hard. In one study,[6] for example, 75 percent of Latinos said that most people will find success only with hard work, compared to just 58 percent of the general population. This is true for first-, second-, and third-generation Latinos. If you find a problem that you can't solve at work, you likely have a tendency to keep at it, so much so that you end up spinning your wheels, just creating busy work, and stressing yourself out. It's not very useful to put in a lot of effort without achieving anything or working without getting anything back in return.

Our ancestors instilled in us a relentless drive for hard work, but we now live in a world where many companies are salivating to take advantage of a work ethic like that. Bosses and employees at the typical company just don't value taking time off like they do in other countries. For example, 30 percent of all American workers get zero PTO, and 52 percent of all employees say they work during vacation or other time off.[7] A recent Harris Poll found that 78 percent of North Americans eighteen and over don't use all their time off and half of workers are "afraid" to ask for time off, while 60 percent don't fully disconnect when they're on vacation.[8]

During the time when many Gen X and millennial Latino/Latinas were starting to enter the workforce, dominant themes were hustling and boss babe-ing. In 2018 the Rachel Hollis book *Girl, Wash Your Face* was the soundtrack for boss babes everywhere and turned into a bestseller. Talking about how you, and only you, are responsible for making your life better, the book makes no mention of how family connections and generational wealth give many people a running start. That mindset told you that all you had to do was to work your butt off, and everything would fall into place.

Many of us read authors like Rachel Hollis, and we hustled harder, figuring maybe one day we'd get paid what we were worth. However, that final payoff moment didn't come for too many Latinas, and all we were left with was a job that underpaid us and an overwhelming amount of student loans (Latinos are the most overloaded with student loans right now).[9]

There is an abundance of opportunity in the United States and Canada, compared to other countries, but some companies may not have your best interests in mind. Women are underpaid overall, but Latinas make just fifty-seven cents for every dollar paid to non-Hispanic men. And sometimes companies try to get away with not paying them at all.

Working harder on its own isn't going to fix that. Sometimes it's the system that also has to make changes.

Ann has a terrible memory of her job search as a young USC grad student. She had three interviews over the course of three weeks at a trendy, mission-driven shoe start-up. Interestingly, this company is still in business. She got offered a full-time marketing internship with the start-up, which could have been life changing in terms of her career growth. Then she got the offer letter: full-time hours and zero salary. Oh! Don't forget to add an hour each way commuting to and from her house. *But think of how much work experience you'll get!* Imagine expecting a student to work full-time with no paycheck. Like, who can even afford to live like that? Maybe a very small percentage of the population—but especially not Latinas with student loan debt.

In her groundbreaking book *Rest Is Resistance: A Manifesto*, author and activist Tricia Hersey goes against this cultural idea that productivity is the one and only measure of self-worth and says that reclaiming rest is more an act of resistance against a relentless demand for labor and productivity.[10] Hersey, who is speaking to Black women in particular, promotes things like naps, meditation, self-care, and rest for a more balanced life, collective healing, and community support. You could say that the señora era is the Latina's way of reclaiming the rest and relaxation that were forgotten when our families moved far away from our homelands. We need work/life balance and simple rest now more than ever, during these chaotic last few years.

It's a radical thing to say, "I need work/life balance as much as anyone else in this country, and I will not be taken advantage of under the guise of hustle culture or the false belief that it will solve all my problems. I can work hard, but sometimes hard work can't fix a broken system or faulty belief patterns, so I have to take care of myself and my well-being first while I'm climbing the ladder."

Latinos have it economically harder than others. At the time of this writing, the average Latino family's median wealth is $60,000 versus non-Hispanic White families' $188,000. That's a big gap, and it adds up over the years. There was a lot of work discrimination that Latinos faced in the past, and that's still prevalent today. Historically, Mexican Americans were systematically left out of the workforce. Christina has deduced that the reason the Mexican side of her family started a family restaurant business is that one hundred years ago, there were very few jobs for which Mexican Americans were allowed to apply. So they had to make do and work very hard, perhaps much harder than the general public. *It's a radical thing to want to take time off or care for yourself when generations before us have worked so hard to achieve what we have in this country, often beating insurmountable odds.*

It's even harder if you're a mom! Or a single mom! Not only do you get paid less than men for doing the same work, but you're undervalued, overworked, and working overtime for little pay. Many workplaces can be super inflexible for moms, and that makes it really hard for us to do even basic things, like take care of our little ones when they're sick. In fact, we're just now hearing about workers who were pregnant moms and got laid off during the post-pandemic economic slump.

You very well might be a mama who is trying to balance work with managing a household, organizing your kids, making meals in the evening, and not losing your mind. It's a radical thing to prioritize putting yourself first sometimes, and giving yourself the proper care that you need to feel rested and refreshed, without always thinking of what's best for the company. After all, this will make you a better caregiver. *What's best for you*, amiga?

Well-being shouldn't be expensive or hard to attain. That's why our Radical Señora Era philosophy is to find things from our great-grandmother's *ranchito* or backyard garden, kitchen or home that will also make us feel good. They're easy things that are usually low cost or even free. We'll talk about these in this book. *It's a radical thing to have our own unique version of well-being and self-care that doesn't even require a credit card.*

Lastly, what embracing radical señorahood really means is that you're welcoming slow living. Señorahood shares many ideas with slow living, a cultural movement that's rooted in the Slow Food movement, which started in Italy and was all about promoting traditional ways of cooking, from start to finish. Slow living is about doing less, embracing minimalism, and enjoying everything the slow, traditional way. Sometimes people call it living "the soft life."

In fact, it was the general public's fascination with "slow living" that made sourdough bread baking and gardening go viral during the pandemic. People wanted to live more mindfully and be more grounded. However, in our community, slow living generally *isn't really a thing*. Like, you don't tell your bestie, "Wow, this month I'm really trying to practice more slow-living techniques." Instead, you might say, "I just entered my señora era, and I'm kind of here for it." Then you'll also make sourdough bread and start a balcony herb garden, just like *abuelas* used to do.

Exactly who are we talking about when we say "señora"?

We'll get into this more later, but señoras are all kinds of women in your family tree. Your *tías* were señoras, and so were your grandmothers and great-grandmothers. Their neighborhood *comadres* were señoras. There were the señoras who worked at the *mercado* where your own family shopped every Thursday morning. Let's not forget the señora who worked at the bank and said hello to all of the customers.

Señoras worked inside and outside the home. There were señora *jefas* and señora small business owners way back then, too. Christina's great-grandmother was the *jefa* of a Mexican restaurant in the San Francisco Bay Area, and Ann's paternal grandmother was a *jefa* of her own hair salon for many years.

Though women in Latin America primarily worked in the home during the pre-1950s era, modern señoras began to work outside the home. In 1990 the percentage of women in the Latin American workforce jumped from 18 percent to almost 30 percent. They initially held traditionally female jobs, such as nursing and teaching. On top of that, they came home and still performed a lot of the labor that was needed in the household, for example, helping the children with their extracurricular activities. They also helped their community through charity work and their churches.

Ann's maternal grandmother was a kindergarten teacher, but she also picked up the kids from school, helped them with homework, and project managed the home and the school schedule. Some years she also volunteered at the local YWCA to help women who were in need. Her señora era consisted of *once* (Chilean teatime, a version of our elevenses), strolls to the *mercado* and later to the beach where she lived, an afternoon with music or a book, and evenings listening to the radio (which were basically early podcasts).

Why some parts of the señora era are problematic

The señora era isn't all unicorns and rainbows. Sometimes we get angry comments from people who say that this state of being is just privilege, or that all we're doing is telling Latinas to stop working and keep their butts in the kitchen. Once we even heard that we're advocating the "tradwife" lifestyle, which opens up a whole new can of worms.

Guess what? We agree! We can't talk about señoras without also speaking about the very challenging parts of being a woman through Latin America's history. For example, in our homelands, they talk about machismo, meaning a very specific, exaggerated, often misogynistic type of masculinity, one that has hurt the women of Latin America in many ways. There is also something called *marianismo*, which is the idea that a woman's place is in the home, that she should at all times be passive and home- and family-oriented.[11] This means she did not have the free will to choose what she wanted for herself, a choice we are lucky to have today. This was all baked into the life that the old-country señoras lived, and it was normal and common to them. They knew nothing else.

Machismo's collateral damage throughout history has meant that some Latin American women endured physical or financial

abuse and *infidelidad*. Just ask your *tía* to tell you about that
neighborhood lady who came to her home claiming one of the
primos was the secret father of someone's baby. You'll hear many
stories like this—and worse—if you go digging in your family tree.
Those telenovela stories weren't created out of thin air.

There's also the class issue. When we talk about señora routines, we're referring to women who were able to afford to stay
at home or hire help. Not everyone had that luxury. Ann's and
Christina's grandmothers and great-grandmothers had that mid-
dle-class privilege, but many of their friends' ancestors did not.

Their *abuelas* were also nonIndigenous Latinas (except for
Ann's paternal grandmother). You may have an Indigenous ancestor, too. We now know that Indigenous people faced severe
persecution in their homelands. These tribes are still around,
and they have experienced centuries of generational trauma
due to experiencing genocide and being forcibly removed from
their homelands.

To be a Radical Señora also means that we want to understand
the dark side of our ancestral past, the very complicated history
of machismo, *marianismo*, class inequality, and racism, while holding space for those señoras who didn't have any power.

What's more, enjoying the routines and rituals of señoras
doesn't mean you believe that a woman's place is in the home.
It's wherever the heck she wants it to be. Ann desires to be in
her gardening era, and she also wants to own her own small
business. Christina wants to be home with her daughter, but before that, she was on the stock market trading floor, making
some cash money. Both women are also Latina angel investors.
You might be a big-time *jefa*, but you can still be in your señora
era. Avoiding hustle culture doesn't mean you have to quit
your job and live in the freaking *campo*. It just means that you
don't want to work for little pay and no promotion, and at the

expense of your mental or physical health or family and relationships.

A Radical Señora is whatever she chooses to be, as long as she approaches it slowly and mindfully and from the point of view of her own well-being. It's a mindset removed from what you do for a living, who you love, and whether you have a family or live by yourself.

The Radical Señora Era is also inclusive. It's for everyone: working moms, stay-at-home moms, ranch moms, dance moms, single ladies, women, men, non-binary people, LGBTQ folks, all ethnicities, Christian moms, atheist moms, vegans, CrossFitters, Pilates girlies, entrepreneurs, artists, small business owners, retirees, and the list goes on and on.

If you are a Radical Señora who has privilege or feels blessed, you may want to give back to another señora, for instance, by buying as much as you can from minority female-owned small businesses, by giving and donating to Indigenous organizations, or by becoming an angel investor so that you can support small business founders. When you consciously decide to support your own community, you are actively helping create generational wealth within it, and you're creating happier señoras, to hopefully make this world a better place for everyone.

South American vs. Central American señoras

Ann is a Chilean immigrant. She arrived in the US when she was elementary school age. Christina, her business cofounder and coauthor of this book, is third-generation Mexican Ameri-

can. From the little that she's been able to piece together from
her ancestry research, Christina's ancestors likely came to the
United States about one hundred years ago and set up shop as
a family-owned Mexican restaurant in the San Francisco Bay
area, where they thrived and their American story began.

As you can see, Christina and Ann are both considered
"Latinas," even though their backgrounds could not be more
different. That's the case for all Latinos in the United States.
They are first-generation immigrants, second- to fourth-gen,
and multi-hyphenates; and some of them speak Spanish or Span-
glish, and others don't speak Spanish at all. They all vary across
incomes, educational attainment, and level of acculturation.
Some of them are very connected to their roots, and others
aren't (and there is nothing wrong with either one!). It's important to Christina and Ann that as they share these stories,
histories, routines, and ideas with you, you also differentiate between South American, Central American, Spanish Caribbean,
and Mexican señora habits. It's very rare for our cultures to be
differentiated like this, but it's really important. Sometimes you
will hear about the señoras from Ann's Chilean ancestral past.
Other times you'll hear about what Christina knows about her
family's Mexican background.

We hope that you see now that to talk about how to use our
señora eras to live a happier life, we need to explore the history
and the "why" of our ancestral señoras. This is why we say that
our señora eras are so much more than aesthetics or gorgeous
home decor and that we're not just going off on random tangents
for funsies. It's an entire movement that can change your life.

There is a silver lining to our video accidentally going viral.
Thanks to that upside-down day, we have since built a huge
community of Latinas who love things like gardening, plant life,
homesteading, keeping chickens, and living life like our great-

grandmothers, all with a side of comedy based on the Latino experience. We have over seven million views, over one million
likes, and many viral videos having to do with slow living, our
señora eras, and the *ranchito* life.

CHAPTER 2

Hustle Cults
to Señora Era

ANN GHOSTED HER family and got lost in hustle culture—and it was all thanks to Sheryl Sandberg.

It all started in the first decade of the twenty-first century, when she was an entry-level junior executive in a new industry called digital marketing. It was a time when there was no such thing as TikTok, a video app called YouTube was just starting to trend, and some of us were still blinging out our MySpace pages. She was a first-generation, immigrant, San Fernando Valley kid from a blue collar family, just trying to figure out her place in the business world.

Ann was working at agencies that helped big movie studios and food brands connect with bloggers, decades before marketing turned into the influencer cottage industry that it is today. She was doing everything she had ever wanted—writing, blogging, and immersing herself in online communities. She was even writing a column for a popular magazine belonging to the Condé Nast stable, one of the biggest publishers in the industry.

Ann felt a little bit like a digital Carrie Bradshaw, laptop in hand, gliding her way around the LA scene. Okay, maybe a much younger, poorer, more Latina version of her. She had made it! Or had she?

What changed things for Ann was when one day one of the friendly admins at her job discreetly asked her to go down the street and grab a juice with her. It was a little weird, because they had never gone out for drinks together before.

"I shouldn't be saying this, but you're getting paid much less than you should be," Ann's coworker said in a near whisper while looking around the shop to make sure no one could hear them. "None of the women around here are," she said. She, as an admin without any client management duties, was actually making more than Ann because she was a good negotiator. "You should really ask for a raise."

This honestly came as a shock to Ann. She was making more money than her parents had when they were young adults—and new immigrants—in the United States, and so her salary seemed just fine to her. In fact, Ann's parents had looked at her first paycheck, and it made them very happy and proud. She was so appreciative of every job she took, and she strived to be a diligent and hard worker. Ann busted her butt double time, sometimes even on weekends, to make the bosses happy and help meet her team's monthly goals.

Ann had done everything to make her immigrant parents proud. She had graduated from UCLA and had even got a master's degree. But even after getting this fancy degree, she wasn't making much of a dent in her student loans, and living in LA was so expensive. During her twenties, she eventually had to move back in with her parents. Ann realized that she didn't have the same negotiation and salary skills that some of her colleagues had, some of which had been taught to them by their

American-born parents, who were used to the corporate game. This is a common problem that immigrants, people of color, and poor people face when they start to rise up the ranks.

According to 2021 research by McKinsey & Company, in which they analyzed data from the Bureaus of the US Census and Labor Statistics, Latinos are underpaid by nearly three hundred billion dollars annually.[1] Foreign-born Hispanics make just $31,000 per year, compared to the $39,000 US-born Hispanics make. Contrast this to the average $53,000 a year salary that non-Hispanic white workers make. A big reason for this income gap is the lack of representation in higher positions. The study's models found that 50 percent of this gap in some occupations like STEM, law, medicine, and accounting can be attributed to this.

Negotiation skills are another big reason for this income gap. When your parents are first-generation Americans and work in a factory or with their hands, they don't know how to navigate the business world, and you often have to figure out your financial life and first job all by yourself. Ann's parents had college degrees and had had advanced jobs back in Chile. In this country, her parents worked manual jobs because the university degrees of immigrant people aren't recognized easily in this country, and so people often end up having to start their career all over. Either way, she never had the same guidance about career growth and negotiating her salary that her friends whose parents were lawyers or finance executives had. Kids of undocumented parents or parents who never finished grade school face even steeper hurdles.

One summer afternoon in her parents' backyard, while baking in the hot valley sun, Ann read a book called *Lean In: Women, Work, and the Will to Lead*, written by then-Facebook COO Sheryl Sandberg. She finished it that same weekend.

Sandberg's book opened her eyes to the problem that was the women's wage gap. In the book, she advocates "leaning in" to your career, which means really petitioning for that promotion or raise, while doing everything in your power to be included in the room where the decisions were taking place. Sometimes that means stepping up with confidence, saying yes to all the urgent deadlines, and taking on all the hard projects. Really showing your boss that you're in it to win it by outworking everyone in the room and being proud of it.

The book also opened up a world to Ann that she had never known existed. There was a forty-nine-square-mile region in Northern California where people who created all our tech tools lived. They were developing the tools that we all used every day. They were changing the world in real time, in this region called Silicon Valley.

Lean In planted this seed in her head that she had to go there and be in that "room where it happens." When Ann shut the book, she could see herself as a CMO of a big start-up company. She pictured herself wearing pantsuits like Sheryl Sandberg, sporting a neat little Sophia Amoruso bob, and being the "wing woman" for some big tech CEO. All she had to do was work harder and outwork everybody around her in the Bay Area.

Then, in a moment of kismet, an opportunity opened up for her to move there: A friend offered her a position. Ann couldn't pass this up. She told her parents that she would be gone for only three months, to try things out. They told her not to worry about them. "*No te preocupes por nosotros*," her mom told her. But Ann could tell she had *ganas de llorar* and would probably start to cry the minute she left, as she'd done when Ann left for graduate school.

Ann packed everything she had into her old, white Toyota truck and drove out to her new city. She had drunk all the

Lean In Kool-Aid and literally leaned her way in all the way to San Francisco.

Though she wasn't technically in tech, Ann was given a front-row seat to the start-up and tech cultures. This was the era of peak Silicon Valley, when companies were IPOing left and right, and everybody was a founder. Those were the days when you would go to a start-up party, and everyone would tell you they were developing an app. You heard the most amazing and also the most useless app ideas.

Ann was a true start-up fangirl. It was so easy to get caught up in the excitement of the city. Back then, you could walk by the offices of a browser you used, drive past the app that powered your mom's favorite game, go to massive glitzy parties in Palo Alto or Downtown San Francisco hosted by your favorite taxi app, with unlimited food and booze, or maybe even go on a date with a tech founder who happened to have been on Bloomberg that week.

Her life was a lot of fun. She became a member of The Wing, a woman-owned coworking spot that was custom built for millennial boss babes. Ann would arrive early in the morning, grab fresh juice from the café, then head to a desk nestled in millennial pink tones and work among some famous female company founders. After, she would go have drinks at a cool Latina-cofounded private club called the Battery in San Francisco's financial district, where you were likely to see influential people, from the founders of Google to Mark Cuban and Beyoncé.

She rubbed elbows with some of the most famous billionaire venture capitalists in the world. Here the celebrities weren't on TV; they were the guys who had invested in Facebook or Twitter before they got big and, as a result, were reaping the benefits. There were billion-dollar deals being made wherever she went—at coffee shops, at the tennis courts, in the booth behind her while she sipped whiskey, in the bathroom stall next to her while she peed.

The closest she had gotten to this level of wealth back in the San Fernando Valley was when her mom would pack them all into the car at 5:00 a.m. to drive her dad to Beverly Hills, where he worked with a construction crew building a 123-room "manor" for a huge Hollywood producer. Her dad told the family that the guy wanted to build the house with fourteen bedrooms but had only two kids.

"Why does he want so much house?" her mom once asked.

He joked, "When you start making crazy amounts of money, some people tend to get a little loco."

There was a darker side to the start-up space: complete ownership of your time. Companies out there were known to pay a lot of money to employees, in addition to giving them major stock benefits, plus throwing in other special perks. But the thing is that many of these were all benefits meant to keep your butt in the office—and sometimes working way more than you should.

Management at some offices even made it an unofficial requirement to work weekends with no added pay. These companies offered "flexible work," which in reality meant that your boss wanted you answering emails no matter where you were, 24 hours a day, 7 days a week. Many employees take lower salaries in exchange for stock options, only to see them become worthless when the company fails or restructures. What's more, the beer kegs, free snack fridges, and "meditation rooms" were offered but everyone is too busy to use them. Employees are constantly told that "we're all family here," only to be laid off via email at 3 a.m. when profits dip. Entire teams are wiped out overnight, with no warning, as a "cost-cutting measure" to keep investors happy.

In this industry, it was a flex to say that you hadn't taken any of your vacation days or to say that you were getting three hours of sleep each night. It was like people were *leaning in* out there, but on steroids. One now infamous CEO was known to even encourage employees to sleep at the office.

There was nothing inherently wrong with the tech and start-up space—it wasn't all that different from traditional corporate culture. The problem was the toxic environment that had taken root within it.

As a result, this created a culture where work/life balance was nonexistent. When you signed a contract to work at a start-up, you were often signing over your life, your nights, and your weekends. There was not much of a boundary between your personal self and your work self, and your career was the source of your greatest accomplishments. There were many companies doing good things, and some really cared about their employees. But those were far and few between in Silicon Valley.

There was also a lot of inequality. Many of these companies were run by very lucky twentysomething dudes, kids of elite parents whose friends invested in their companies. Brilliant innovators who were women or gay or poor or had a disability found it much harder to raise money and launch a company. What's more, it was hard to break through if you didn't look the part of the typical founder. The number of Latina and Black women entrepreneurs who have raised one million dollars or more is now at 350. Back then it was under fifty.

This hustle culture era also gave rise to epic disasters, like Theranos, the "Pharma Bro" debacle, WeWork, NastyGal, and the FTX crypto grift. Even convicted fraudster Anna Delvey had a start-up. One of Ann's startup acquaintances was even wanted by the FBI for alleged fraud. There were a lot of people trying desperately to make a name for themselves. Hustle culture was an effective method of making a lot of money, but it was also really good at making people lose their sense of self, personal values, and true-life priorities. There was something not quite right with the culture that this industry had accidentally created. In fact, a 2017 study found that a hustle-like mentality creates a mindset where people are hyper-focused on themselves and their well-being, and this increases the likelihood of their immoral behavior.[2]

Unreal amounts of money flowing made people a little loco indeed.

Christina's Finance District Girl Boss Era

Right across town, before Ann even knew she existed, Christina was girl bossing it up on the forty-ninth floor of a building in San Francisco's financial district. You would often see her crossing the street to get to work in a wrap dress and kitten heels, with a trench coat for the cold San Francisco mornings. Christina, who is half Mexican American, was raised by her mom, alongside her three brothers. The family had suffered a tremendous loss early on—her father, whose family was originally from Oaxaca, was lost to an illness when Christina was very little. Her mom had worked her butt off to provide for all four of them, and this had always been the primary driver for Christina's ambition. She had seen her mom work hard all her life and had sworn to herself she was never gonna let her down. Many have observed that this was the reason she was always looking to outwork the hardest-working person in the room. At certain times in her life, that drive has turned into her downfall.

Christina was one of the few women on the trading floor and, in the mid-2010s, the only Latina among a sea of finance bros. It was a world that had once been foreign to her: taking black cars everywhere, doing multimillion-dollar trades for clients, meeting the CEOs and CFOs of some of the world's biggest tech companies, taking conference calls with money managers for Apple, Cisco, Oracle. After a few years she was able to move up from the trading floor to venture capital and have her own office, and she went all out to design it. She even got a new wardrobe to match the vibe. It was the type of career everyone her age longed for. By her late twenties, she was making more money than her ancestors would have ever dreamt of when they came to San Francisco from their homelands.

It was truly her ancestors' dream, except soon it would become her worst nightmare.

Ann's Stuck in Her Struggle Era

After she had spent nearly a decade in the city, work became Ann's entire identity. She now owned a one-woman PR agency and had carved out a good reputation in the space. The hottest companies sought her out to do their marketing, and she was in the stage of her career where she didn't really need to pound the pavement. Maybe Ann wasn't the CMO of some fancy company and didn't have the "bob" like she had originally dreamed, but she'd found a career where she had job freedom, a really good salary, and had become her own boss.

So, how did it feel?

Ironically, owning your own business means you're working harder than ever because your success—and livelihood—rests entirely on your shoulders. Anxious that she could lose her business in a heartbeat, she would work very long hours, often starting to answer emails as soon as she woke up, and finishing right before bedtime. There was no slowing down at this stage.

Ann was constantly ill at ease. At night, she would stay up, wide awake, until very late, her mind spinning, heart pounding, and her thoughts spiraling out of control. Her laptop would be on the moment she woke up in the morning until she took it to bed at night. She nervously ate her breakfast while in the Uber to work. Her weekdays were a blur of meetings and emails. She loathed weekends because it meant she had to go out with friends and miss out on time when she could be rushing to catch up for Monday. She had stopped working out and walking, so basically out went her only self-care routines.

Mondays were horrible. She'd wake up with anxiety in the morning, because she was terrified of upset clients and the first thing that would come to her mind was what emails were in her inbox. On her way to work, she'd start to feel nauseated and sweaty just thinking about the day ahead.

Everything Ann did was rushed. She went from one meeting to the next, speed ate through lunches and dinners. She talked a mile a minute. To save time, she had stopped doing things that made her feel good, much less taking care of herself, like scheduling preventative medical appointments. Ann went years without having a primary care doctor.

Within a year of arriving in San Francisco, she had started to feel bloated all the time, and started getting really heavy periods and bad menstrual pain, which was not normal for her. They were so bad that once she stained a chair with blood at work, even though she was wearing a heavy tampon *and* an overnight pad. "I'm so sorry. I'll pay for it," she told her then-boss, mortified, looking down at the bloodstain on the cushion of the very expensive chair. Thankfully she had a very kind boss who told her not to worry about it.

Her doctor just put her on the pill. "You need to have more balance. It seems like you're working too much and not taking care of yourself," she said to Ann. When she did some testing, she found a lot of gnarly fibroids and suggested that Ann's hormones were all out of whack. Ann also had developed GERD. Sometimes she felt like she was so mixed up that her brain wouldn't work properly. Still, Ann would leave her doctor's office, rolling her eyes so hard she thought they would pop over to the back of her head. *I don't have time for this*, she would say to herself.

Worse yet, Ann went MIA on her family. At first, she would take the bus back home to LA once a month, but the busier she got, the further apart those visits got. It was like the more money Ann made, the less she saw them. She stopped texting her mom every day like she used to. She missed so many of her sister's milestones, such as her niece's birth. When she visited, she was always in another land, telling her family to be quiet because she was working or answering emails. Holidays back home were not a time to relax or have fun; they were just a change of office scenery. She completely stopped going to Chile to visit her last remaining grandmother, during what turned out to be her last few years before becoming very ill. Family is really important in Latin cultures, and so it felt like this was a major failure. Ann will never stop regretting her absence.

Though after years of hustling, Ann had some nice disposable income to play and travel with and had even started investing in start-ups, she felt like slowing down was unimaginable. It's like she had become scared she'd lose it all if she did. Plus, her entire sense of self-worth was tied to her work—it felt like her job title defined her entire identity.

Wait, was she in a cult? It sure felt like it sometimes.

This way of living could not have been more different than what she remembered life being like back home in Chile. Work there was just something you did to pay the bills—not your entire identity. You left your work at the office, and you spent the afternoon relaxing and making good food with the family. Weekends were spent at Grandma and Grandpa's house, at an *asado* at one of your cousins' houses, or at someone's *parcela*. People took whole weeks off for the 18th of September, the country's Independence Day. After a decade of hustling, Ann had turned into a person her ancestors back home would probably have a really hard time understanding.

Christina Can't Stop

Several years had passed, and Christina had reached the career zenith she had always dreamt about. After years of paying her dues, of getting up at 4:00 a.m. and rushing to the office to be ready for Wall Street's opening bell, she had really made it. But something felt off. She knew from the get-go that she had signed up to work in a cutthroat industry that was still really old school. The industry then was a testosterone-fueled boys' club, where you were exposed to sexist jokes, hard-charging people who had a lot of money at stake, and others who had egos the size of Texas.

There were some things she put up with that she knew weren't right. Sometimes she felt like she wasn't treated like a human and was downright disrespected. There were times when she was sent emails with disturbing images, including graphic pics, mostly to get a rise out of her. There was a crazy amount of booze at the happy hours and at the conferences, where you would see that some companies had hired professional models to entertain the investors. Sometimes she would even see people trading cocaine at general industry parties. Lunchtime was spent at the fancy French restaurant downtown, where you might be eating right next to the mayor. Over lunch, you and your colleagues might find yourselves staring at the bottom of two bottles of red wine, and then you would drag yourself back to the office. It was the old-school finance way.

There were many occasions when she was asked to be in uncomfortable situations. One time, she was woken up by a phone call at midnight from someone who thought it was appropriate to tell her to be ready in twenty minutes, because a big-time investor had requested that she immediately hop on his private jet and entertain him on a trip to New York. She refused, knowing she had been asked because she was the "office Latina" and they needed an exotic face. She too often felt tokenized, sexualized, and "othered," and she started feeling a sense of dread going into work, because she felt almost like the industry mascot.

But she prided herself on being someone who did not give up easily. When there was any obstacle in her path, she just tried harder. Maybe she just needed to work longer hours, get up earlier, hustle harder, and outwork everyone in the office. She even started changing herself to fit in more, because maybe that would help people see her as more of an equal. She started wearing more neutral, understated clothes, anything to stop people from thinking of her as the token Latina. She changed so much that she started to blend in with the furniture. She was exhausted all the time, was irritable and would feel nauseous every time she walked into work. She'd wake up with such overwhelming thoughts about another workday, it caused her to become paralyzed with panic. She had many mornings when she couldn't get out of bed, and she would linger there, frozen with anxiety.

One evening she called her mom. "I have no clue what's going on, but I feel like I'm dying." Her mom rushed over and took her to the hospital, where she was diagnosed as having a panic attack. This was more than burnout; this was an anxiety disorder, worsened by an industry that she had absolutely started to loathe.

What was this feeling of dread and fear, and why had no one prepared her for this? Why did she think she could dig herself out of this by just working harder?

One day, she felt the final nail hammered into the coffin.

Her office had hired a very successful, powerful and semi-famous older woman whom she admired, a woman with an impressive thirty-year career in business. Everything about this woman was incredible, and she was someone Christina had really admired. But as soon as this woman walked out of the office, the jokes started: awful, sexist comments by the most senior finance bros about the way she looked and dressed, clearly alluding to the fact that she was "past her prime" and that her clothing wasn't on trend. Her colleagues couldn't care less about this woman's accomplishments. She was just a woman past her "prime" who didn't belong there.

Is this where I'm headed? Christina asked herself. *Hustling hard through the next twenty years in this industry, only to still be reduced to my age and my appearance?*

That weekend she walked to the San Francisco Museum of Modern Art, as she often did. It was one of the rare things that gave her joy during those days. There she was, surrounded by so much peace and beauty. She walked among Matisse's work *Paysage*, from 1903, and the humongous Mark Rothko paintings. She paused to stare at *Frieda and Diego Rivera*, from 1931, the couple looking back at her from a time long ago. She wondered what Frida Kahlo, who was her favorite artist, would do if she were in her shoes. She pictured her painting in her quiet studio space in the Blue House. Frida had actually lived in San Francisco for a bit. As she strolled, she thought about the way these museum walks made her feel. She would always temporarily forget about her never-ending anxiety.

As Christina walked out of the museum that day, she burst into tears, because she knew what she had to do. She gave her two weeks' notice the very next day. It was like a weight was lifted off her. She was never going to let any job, or industry, make her feel miserable about life and terrible about herself. She applied for and got a job doing what brought her the most joy: working at an art gallery in the city, despite a huge pay cut and zero knowledge of the art world. This meant she would have to dig into her savings and live off credit cards for a while, but she didn't care. She wanted to be surrounded by that same beauty that had inspired her to change her path in life.

She had found her señora era early.

Latina Struggle Eras and the Hustle Culture Trap

The last twenty years have been a remarkable moment for Latino and Latina excellence. Our communities have grown in terms of wealth, small business creation, home ownership, and more. The college graduation rate for Latinas skyrocketed from 5 percent in 2000 to a whopping 20 percent in 2021, and there's been a nearly 300 percent increase in Latinas with master's degrees.[3] Hispanic workers are in more management jobs, have faster salary increases, and are starting businesses at record rates. More and more Latinas are entering a wider array of industries, from finance to technology, health care, real estate, hospitality, and marketing. They're also heavily represented in positions in law enforcement, IT, insurance, firefighting, public relations, nursing, and the physician's assistant professions.[4]

With this success, our wealth is growing, too. Between 2013 and 2022, Hispanic families' household wealth tripled, hitting $63,400 in 2022, up from $20,000 in 2013. Though still low compared to other groups, this is significant growth. What's more, one in five Hispanic adults are now considered part of the affluent group in the US, with particular income growth in the younger generations.[5] Nearly 50 percent own their own homes. "The exponential growth in Hispanic wealth and homeownership over the past two decades is a testament to the resilience and determination of our community," according to Sara Rodriguez, chair of the Hispanic Wealth Project. "We are optimistic about the future as we strive for even greater economic empowerment."

Organizations like the Hispanic Wealth Project support the continued prosperity of Latino and Latina entrepreneurs and homeowners, and networks like Hispanics in Philanthropy and L'Attitude Ventures, and Pipeline Angels, are funding Latino entrepreneurs, small business owners, and nonprofit organizations.

Yet as we celebrate incredible growth in our communities and career lives, we need to be mindful of the trap of the "hustle culture" mentality, which often targets our community in particular because we are proud hard workers. We are more likely to take on multiple jobs and work more than forty hours a week.[6] While ambition is the cornerstone of success, what many elite performers have also discovered—and are not sharing with the rest of us—is that prioritizing well-being and self-care is also critical. Why doesn't anybody tell us that we have to take care of ourselves, too?

Christina and Ann had picked up some really bad habits that were clearly unsustainable. They felt productive only if their schedules were full of back-to-back meetings. When they tried to sit still, their brains would go into panic mode. They needed to feel they had multiple projects—or multiple jobs—going on at the same time. That dopamine hit of accomplishment was always in their mind. It's almost like they wanted to feel like they were still fighting, no matter how good things were. Somehow, they equated struggling—or hustle culture, or whatever you want to call it—with their sense of worth. A big part of their self-esteem was now tied to their work.

So, where did this come from?

Latinos may get stuck in a scarcity mentality largely thanks to the way some of us saw our parents hustling to survive. This happens when you believe things like money and opportunities are finite. You have a constant feeling of fear that there isn't enough to go around and that you're one step from losing it all.

If you're first- or second-generation Latino, chances are your parents struggled. You saw them working multiple jobs or getting up at five o'clock in the morning, doing a two-hour commute, working with their hands, working at a fast-food place, taking care of other people's kids, digging trenches, or working in the fields. They may have been single moms, responsible for the family's livelihood, and filling the role of two parents, but somehow making ends meet. There was no time to rest. Taking care of their health and wellness wasn't a priority for them, because *your* health and wellness were. This is why they were always working—and not because they were workaholics or because of a passion for personal fulfillment. They simply had to put food on the table. This means that if you remember them always working during your childhood, you've got to give them grace.

Our families quite literally invented their own version of hustle culture, because it was a necessity to survive. They had to invent ways to make enough money to keep their family healthy and happy, often taking extreme measures—without any tools to cope with the stress. Christina Montoya Fiedler writes in an article for *Parents* magazine that immigration status, moving to another country, and finances push immigrants to learn unsustainable ways to cope, like putting in very long workdays and doing too many things at once.[7] It's as if we immerse ourselves in work as a way to escape the deeper challenges we face.

While writing this book, Christina and Ann sat down with Dr. Vanessa Milagros, therapist, mental health advocate, CEO and founder of Exhale Family Therapy, and first-gen Afro-Latina. They asked her whether Latinas were more likely to fall for the trap of overworking, hustle culture, and burnout. As a fellow first-generation American, she has an insider's perspective on how our immigration experience plays a role in our mental health and how even birth order is important.

"The 'hustle culture' is not anything new to most Latinas, because that was very much ingrained into the cultural dynamic of raising a young Latina woman," she told them. "We tend to see this specifically more with the eldest daughter, where she is responsible for not only raising herself but also her siblings, and at times even raising her parents. So, by the time they go out into the real world, the hustle culture is all they know, and on some level, it does bring comfort in familiarity."

"There are also times where this phenomenon is extremely damaging for Latinas," she said. "For instance, it is very difficult to unlearn the idea that resting means uselessness."

In her book *Break the Cycle: A Guide to Healing Intergenerational Trauma*, Dr. Mariel Buqué writes about the theory of intergenerational trauma response, where your parents' trauma gets passed down epigenetically, so that whatever was your parents' way of dealing with stress is likely your strategy, too.[8] It's very likely that the stress your parents were feeling during their immigration journey or other difficult challenge has affected how you deal with—or don't deal with—stresses you face today.

Though you may be stressed out about a project deadline, while your parents were stressed about losing their savings, you may have the same type of overwhelming feelings.

If you're a child of immigrants, your parents also did a great job with you. The children of immigrants simply do better in life. People who are born to immigrant parents, for example, have a greater median wealth than their parents and are also more likely to become entrepreneurs than the general population, launching both small businesses and Fortune 500 companies. In addition, immigrant residents who arrived in the US in 1990 and before were shown to have a greater median wealth versus people who were born in the US.[9] So, by being the child or grandchild of immigrants, you're automatically on the right track!

But here is where things start to get a little wacky. Even though you may feel like you've made it, you may still be carrying the scarcity mindset, which you learned from your parents. You still feel like you have to sacrifice whatever it takes to keep the streak going—even if you're technically living a life that may be exactly what your parents envisioned for you. According to Dr. Buqué, this may be related to a special kind of trauma.

"Immigration trauma is one of the most understated traumas that we have in this world," Dr. Buqué told us. "It disrupts and disconnects families. It creates prolonged grief and despair for everybody that's impacted. For many of us, it leaves us with a low sense of self-worth and the belief that we don't belong, or imposter syndrome." This likely applies to many immigrants, given the fact that some may have left their country to flee things like crumbling economies, cartel violence, wars, dictatorships, a communist regime, or natural disasters.

Being an immigrant kid, or a child or grandchild of immigrants, may have impacted you in ways you don't notice. It's almost like survivor's guilt, where you feel guilty for being able to have perks your parents could not, like working cozily from home, having unlimited vacation time and great stock options, or making a great income. This survivor's guilt may have also led you to overwork your way to the top—sometimes unnecessarily.

What Hustle Culture Is and Isn't

There's a huge gap between overworking and working hard. One is working to get ahead the healthy way, and the other is working hard and consuming hard, grinding and working at all hours just to feel busy, letting people push you around, trying to be the richest, best, most successful person in the room, doing things in order to get richer that go against your values, and letting your job get in the way of physically and mentally taking care of yourself and allowing it to disrupt your personal life in the quest to be "perfect."

Yet our communities still confuse the two concepts. Many people misunderstood us on our viral video, where we talked about leaving hustle culture behind. Many of these women just weren't seeing the difference between working and allowing work to take over your life, or between doing "good enough" work versus an all-or-nothing mindset. Before this scarcity mindset hijacked our lives, our ancestors worked normal hours, then came home and had a nice, joyful life with their families. They had very clear boundaries between the personal and the professional.

It's sad to live in modern times, when people think the only way to exist is to work at the expense of your well-being, and when you get yourself so caffeinated and so worked up about work that the only emotions you feel are anger, exhaustion, and terror.

How did we get here?

The Case Against
Hustle Culture & Perfectionism

Studies have consistently shown that Latin American cultures look at work in a very unique way. In our homelands, there is a strong separation between the work self and the personal self, and hustle culture doesn't really exist. Restaurants and cafés close for an afternoon break in Latin America and in most parts of Europe. People everywhere take longer vacations than Americans in the US. Can you imagine how amazing you would feel if you could peace out from work for one month without feeling guilty?

US Americans haven't always been about the hustle. There was a time when their lives and routines were pretty similar to those of your ancestors. In her *Business Insider* article titled "How Hustle Culture Got America Addicted to Work," Aki Ito states that early US Americans worked in jobs like farming and balanced work with napping, drinking, and having big meals with their families.[10] There was no boundary between work and life, because it was all just life, accented by bursts of work. The modern concept of work and having a schedule began in the 1800s, when people started to work in factories in return for a salary.

The workplace started to change again in the 1960s, Ito writes, when people started seeing work as self-expression and as a way to change the world (think *Mad Men*). US Americans started to glamorize working long hours and having less leisurely time, while their European cousins—our ancestors included—still approached work in a more traditional way. In fact, Ito's article cites a study in which US Americans and Italians were asked how they felt about someone who worked long hours. Americans saw the person as "rich," whereas Italians saw them as "poor." That is very telling.

This is when the modern concept of "hustle culture" took hold, where people "lived to work" instead of working to live. This idea then infected every industry. We're now at a point where US workers have been found to value hard work over things like self-fulfillment, marriage, patriotism, religion, and even tolerance for others.[11] The United States has become the culture of "conspicuous busyness," where you are considered productive based on the number of hours worked and it is cool to say you are always busy.

US Americans now work hundreds of more hours each year than their European counterparts, but they don't necessarily get more work done.[12] Some Nordic countries, which have the shortest workweeks in the world, don't actually get less work done. They merely get the job done in less time, because they know how to work smarter since they have to log off at 4:00 p.m.[13] Some of these countries also have a better social safety net than we do, which means their citizens don't have to worry too much about things like proper access to health care, and moms get several months of paid maternity leave. When you have to make more money to pay off medical debt, you'll work your butt off, no matter what.

If you haven't noticed the vibe shift lately, hustle culture is well on its way out. The word *hustle* now tends to be associated with cringy online scams trying to separate you from your money, and Gen Z is pushing for an end to this toxic type of work culture, which is unattainable and unsustainable.

Dr. Yasmin Davidds tells us that we got used to an aggressive hustle culture mentality at work, "where you just heard the commands 'Do this, and do that!' But the fact is that people don't respond to that anymore. People respond to feeling that they're cared for, inspired, listened to."

What's more, in the years after the pandemic, there were unfortunate massive layoffs at many companies. This was a time of mass disillusionment for people who at one time or another believed that their workplace was their family, when in fact companies were trying to get them to work more for the same amount of pay.

A 2023 study by consulting firm Deloitte found that 70 percent of executives were "seriously considering quitting for a job that better supports their well-being," and many workers wanted "human centered" leadership that prioritized their own well-being and were not afraid to show their vulnerable side at work.[14] That's the future of work. Modern companies are just now starting to wake up to this fact, though some brands are very in tune with their employees' health and wellness, as well as their work/life balance.

The pandemic also expanded the definition of workplace, particularly due to the availability of working from home. People started to realize there was a lot more to life than what happened from nine to five.

Perfectionism is another instigator of hustle culture. In his book *The Perfection Trap: Embracing the Power of Good Enough*,[15] Thomas Curran, a social psychologist and expert on perfectionism and mental health, lays out how pursuing perfection can lead not only to burnout but also to depression, anxiety, and low self-worth. Perfectionism, he argues, is just a tendency to want to avoid failing or being judged by other people, and modern culture pushes this on us by stressing hyper-achievement and constant optimization—of your health, your career, and your entire life. This is basically just a trap, leading you to never feel like you're good enough. Instead, Curran says, the key is to embrace the idea of being "good enough" and to work on compassion toward yourself, resilience, and seeing the beauty in imperfection.

Yet many Latinas are experts in perfectionism, and that is in part due to the unique pressures to honor family expectations and be the first in the family to succeed, especially for first- or second-generation kids who come from an underprivileged background. Latinas face unique pressures to succeed academically, in their careers, and at work, and they even put a lot of pressure on themselves to keep a perfect home. Although these characteristics are helping them move up in the world, they are also tied to such afflictions like anxiety and depression—and loneliness.[16]

Think about it this way. Can you picture your great-grandmother putting all this pressure on herself to make millions and have a perfect home? No. She did good enough in her garden, good enough at her job, and then she sat down to rest on the patio with a cup of tea to talk to her *comadres* or spend time with her family. Think about it like this: You've got to find a way to succeed in life in a way that's not harming you in the long run.

The Radical Señora

The Radical Señora is the enemy of hustle culture, perfectionism, and a scarcity mindset. Your ancestors knew intuitively that work and life are completely separate worlds. This is what inspired Ann and Christina to name the post hustle stage the Radical Señora Era, because it beckons you to abandon the outdated idea that your identity is completely tied to what you do for a living, to having a perfect life, and to sacrificing it all to be a "boss babe." It's about learning to look at hustle culture—and people who pressure you into it—as just a dumb and unnecessary cultural artifact of past decades.

This is an era in which we are reclaiming our right to calm and rest and are taking back our personal lives. It's a realization that we don't have to sacrifice it all for work and that we can push back on workplace policies that are hurting us. It's a need to be "good enough," instead of needing to always be the best ever.

Of course, alongside this personal pivot, we need to push for policy change that helps shrink the wage gap between women and men and that make the workplace kinder. This cultural hustle attitude is not serving anyone but the bigwigs who own the corporate conglomerates.

This doesn't mean you've got to stop being ambitious. It means finding a way to climb the ladder of success without losing your peace in the process. In fact, you'll probably do your best work and grow in your career much more mindfully and strategically when you come at it from a peaceful mindset.

Thinking like a Radical Señora means not tying all your self-worth to what you do at work and never ever feeling guilty about protecting your peace. It's that exact moment when you leave your scarcity mentality behind and call yourself number one. The world won't end if you don't answer that email, and work will still be there when you come back and check your inbox on Monday. Your personal peace is invaluable.

Entering Our Señora Boss Eras

In many ways, their beauty line was a result of this pull Christina and Ann felt toward a calmer and slower life. They wanted nothing more to do with systems in which hyperproductivity was all that mattered. They knew there had to be a way to be productive without getting lost in work, or letting it run your life.

They had met thanks to Pipeline Angels, a women's angel network, where they learned how to become angel investors. Together they invested in women founders, particularly those starting Black- and Latina-owned businesses. They had bonded over drinks, two burnt-out Latinas who were disillusioned with their girl boss eras and who finished each other's sentences. They were so passionate about the same things. One of these was how ridiculous they found the fact that Latinas had been ignored in the packaged goods space. What brands were even trying to target them? They were also starting families at around the same time. Ann was going through IVF, and the experience taught her there was a huge need for Latina clean beauty.

Why don't we start a beauty brand honoring our homelands? Christina texted Ann one day, when she was in Sonoma for her birthday. Ann didn't want to at first, because she knew nothing about the intricacies of personal care products or running a product-based business. But Christina was ever the persistent pitchwoman. So, they started planning their new beauty business, Vamigas, in late 2019, during the second trimester of Ann's pregnancy, when she was getting ready to go on maternity leave.

The work that goes into starting a beauty brand is pretty boring, and pricey (you're looking at something like a fifty-thousand-dollar start-up cost). At first, you're mostly dealing with creating the LLC, bank accounts, and a website, making sure you're legally protected and ready for taxes. The fun part was the actual product formulations. Christina and Ann did a lot of testing of different formulas and selecting what types of products they wanted, and they dove into learning as much as they could about how the sausage is made.

They wanted to approach this business differently than how they had handled their careers. No more of this boss babe, perfectionist mentality keeping them in a constant state of panic. Alongside building a brand, they wanted to create a work culture that was peaceful, that didn't get in the way of their family life and personal time, and didn't end up controlling their lives. They made a pact that if things ever got too overwhelming, they'd quit.

However, this didn't mean they weren't giving it their best effort. Ann took crash courses in product formulation. She bought a stick blender and learned how to make lotions and butters from scratch in her kitchen. She made good-smelling exfoliants and scrubs and her favorite, a simple beeswax body balm you could use for anything. Her favorite moments were when her ingredients turned into a delicious whipped moisturizing hand or face cream. Christina and Ann would geek out about finding out what was actually in fragrances. They tested about one hundred different soap scents and designs and ended up with boxes on top of boxes full of soaps and a house that could smell like roses one day and oranges the next.

For Ann, playing with skincare formulations made her calm and made her happy when she was stressed out with work. During the darkest days of the pandemic, when things seemed to be getting bleaker by the hour, or when being home all day every day with her six-month-old made her feel overwhelmed and overstimulated, Ann knew she could always count on giving the baby to her husband or her mom, putting on an apron, finding her stick blender, and making some dreamy formulation.

Christina was in her element when she was designing their website and labels and figuring out the look for their bottles. She decided on clear bottles and a signature tint, which contrasted with the bone-white labels and gold lettering. She did the logo herself—a gorgeous gold-toned sun setting on top of mountains. Their main product, Chilean rose hip oil, was in a beautiful bottle with a bright red color, and the face oil was a rich amber, which an *Elle* magazine editor later said was like a "setting sun." It's like Christina was naturally gifted to create beautiful things.

This new business was just a slow, beautiful project that made Ann and Christina feel happy and helped them find calmness during the challenging days of being a mom in the early days of the pandemic.

By the way, Ann hasn't completely left behind her startup hustle era. She still collaborates with exciting, up-and-coming technology companies but now prioritizes life balance, ensuring she never again sacrifices her health and well-being for her career. She loves what she does for a living, but *familia* and well-being always come first.

CHAPTER 3

Work Like a Señora

THOUGH CHRISTINA AND Ann launched their skincare and wellness company with a señora era ethos, they still had that Latina relentless drive. Their launch made a big splash because theirs was one of only a handful of amazing Latina-led beauty businesses. There were a few Latina-owned beauty brands that had come before this new batch of brands, but this was the first time that a group of businesses felt like a movement. It seemed like all the elements were there to create the perfect "L-Beauty explosion," the Latina girlies' equivalent of K-Beauty (the popular Korean Beauty trend). Still, it didn't happen overnight. They spent many months planning the launch, with Christina dealing with vendors, pulling strings, getting good deals, negotiating, and sourcing the best and highest quality ingredients from Latin America. They refused to cut any corners or use problematic ingredients that were ecological disasters, sourced unethically, or may be bad for your health.

It took them a year to get back on track after the pandemic hit, and they finally hit the press in April of 2021. They got a fantastic article in the well-respected and influential beauty-industry magazine *Beauty Independent*, followed by one in *Forbes*, and many more write-ups followed, including on websites PopSugar, Refinery29, OprahDaily.com, then in magazines like *Elle* and *Allure*. They even secured some awards, grants, and an Ipsy partnership. Thanks to that press, they were able to get the attention of such retailers as Nordstrom and Thirteen Lune, which had a relationship with JCPenney, Anthropologie, and others. However, they had their eye on one retailer in par-ticular—Target—and eventually were able to get a foot in the door through their accelerator. Then came Whole Foods, which was another dream retailer because of their steadfast commit-ment to sustainability and founder-friendly business practices.

Though their brand seemed to be everywhere in those early days, Ann and Christina did it in a way that didn't interfere with their daily lives. This is when the señora era concept came about: Christina joked that they were in their señora eras, be-cause all they did during the early days of the pandemic, while they were home, was play with herbs, make soaps, clean the house, and drink tea on the patio while FaceTiming alongside their babies. During this time, Ann also heavily got into her plants and gardening. They'd go for walks, which they called their señora walks, after seeing everyone on TikTok talking about "hot girl" and "Latina" walks during the summer of 2021.

It's like they were relearning how to live a normal life, one that was slower, less frantic, and allowed them to spend more time with their families. Finding calmness was not in the rush of a trade, but in the little moments of enjoying a sweet-smelling fragrance, the taste of some new flavorful tea, the act of watering your plants. When work got stressful, they forced themselves to step back and not let it ruin their entire day. It felt like the whole world was waking up to this new, slower era of living.

It was around this time that Ann left the city and moved her family to a small country town in Southern California to do what she knew she should have done long before: come back home to her family. She and her husband found a house that had a beautiful little *huerto*. It reminded her of the orchard in her great-grandmother's home in Quillota. They were close enough to her family that she could visit them and host them for *asados* on the weekends. This single decision improved Ann's life exponentially because it meant getting back that village everyone talks about, which is so important when you're a parent. Moving from a big, bustling city to the *campo* was a change she never expected to make, since she always saw herself as a "city girl."

Though they were living life like true señoras, Christina and Ann weren't slowing down on the career front. If anything, feeling calmer and happier inspired them to launch new projects, but more quietly. They started an angel investing syndicate—which is a "club" of sorts that invests together—with another bestie from the Pipeline Angels network, Lisha Bell, who was a brilliant technologist at PayPal. Their community funded and supported technologies that solved major problems for parents.

Ironically, sharing this idea about slow living and the señora life on TikTok was what made them go viral—not product videos. The TikTok video was all about leaving hustle culture behind and entering your señora era, and they ended up with six million views and over fifty thousand followers, who were seeking the same things they were. Ann and Christina received so many questions weekly from their new followers that they had to create a weekly newsletter to answer all of them and keep their community organized.

Yet something started to shift after a big burst of media attention. Yes, they got scooped up by some of the country's biggest retailers, were profitable from year one, and were able to start paying themselves pretty quickly. But in year two, they were robbed by a con artist, were victims of a home invasion, made a couple of enemies, and lost a lot of money. When you're a business owner and peoples start to sense that you're beginning to see even a teeny amount of success, there are people out there that will try to take advantage. It's a well-known reality that no one in the business community likes to talk about—but if you're a founder, be prepared, because it's bound to happen to you.

One big crash came after another. They started to face business challenges because they didn't have enough cash flow to put millions toward ads, because they weren't raising millions in funding. Plus, the economy was tanking, the beauty industry was changing, and people were buying fewer products. Even big retailers were feeling the burn. Eventually, indie beauty brands started shutting down one after another, creating a wave of uncertainty across the industry. To make matters worse, after ending their partnership, an online retailer that once featured their beauty line suddenly released a strikingly similar product. It was essentially the same ingredient from the same location! But there was nothing they could do about it, because there are very few protections for founders when dealing with bigger corporations.

Next, Christina and Ann got a huge bill they hadn't anticipated, one that was more than either one of them could have ever imagined, because of a mistake in a retailer's sales projection, and it was a major blow to their bottom line. It turns out many brands experienced similar problems, and it cost them their business. And just to make things even more *fun*, the beauty industry was suddenly overrun with celebrity skincare and makeup lines that competed with indie brands. Because, you know, what the world *really* needed was another A-lister's innovative take on moisturizer.

Then someone—a random individual who they later found out was a professional at targeting small businesses—set their sights on them. It was a typical shakedown operation using legal loopholes, and the perpetrator had done it before. It was a hard blow for the ladies. There was a major loss of money involved, lawyers, and months of figuring out exactly how much of a hit this meant for their company. They were so crestfallen at the realization that there were people in this world who wanted to harm you just because they were hard up for money. The final nail in the coffin was right after they got a big press headline in which they talked about how much money the business was set to make that year, which was a huge mistake: Christina came home from vacation one day to find her home had been burglarized. Money and important and irreplaceable family heirlooms had been stolen by some lowlifes. They both had a sinking feeling it was because of that article. Lesson learned: Never talk to too many people about how much money your business is making. Also get a large, angry guard dog and an angrier lawyer.

How did they survive this emotional roller coaster? By leaning into their señora eras even more.

Here are a few of the things they learned along the way:

Radical Señora Boss Lesson #1: Avoid the busy trap

Ann absolutely loves looking at her calendar and seeing no appointments anymore, but there was a time in her life when this would have given her a panic attack. Both she and Christina had felt a need to fill their entire calendars with meetings. Some meetings were very necessary, especially for finishing important projects, but others could have just been a simple email.

They think this made them feel important and like they were showing people who worked with them just how valuable they were. Yet there is no need to do this if you're showing value—and results—through your work. Having back-to-back calls won't make you a busy boss babe or a tech CMO or a beauty founder; it will just drain you. If you edit your calendar and avoid busy work for the sake of busyness, you'll give yourself so much time back. This is time you can spend organizing your day, meal prepping, working out, doing things that can make your day better, or working on a project with a deadline early on, so that it doesn't creep up on you.

Here's what you do. At the start of each week, go through each of your calendar invites and ask yourself, *Is this a call or an email?* If it's an email, send a quick note to cancel the call, and then go over everything you would have mentioned or asked during the call. If it must be a phone call, limit the calendar invite to thirty minutes or less. From now on, when people request a meeting, just send them an email explaining what you want them to know. Don't even bring up the meeting—just send them what they need to know. You'll end up with more time to get your actual work done, more mental space to create higher-quality things, and you'll become more efficient. Your brain will have more time to process.

Avoiding the busy trap also means saying no to events that will make your schedule harder. Early on, Christina and Ann were being invited to every business event in California and receiving all the media invites. They wanted to accept them all. The problem was that they were trying to balance being small business owners with being parents and keeping the house from falling apart. They had to be choosy. Christina was the first to say no to things that would have made their lives much harder, because she had more experience at this Mom thing than Ann did.

"Just focus on the core things that are most important to our business goals," she would say. "Forget about the extra stuff." This meant saying no to some really fun events and nice people, but in the end, it kept them laser focused on revenue, and it helped them avoid small business burnout, which you'll feel if you are trying to be everywhere at the same time. Just focus.

Radical Señoras guard their calendars like a pit bull. Now, don't you dare send me a calendar invite. Just send me an email.

Radical Señora Boss Lesson #2: Grow your business mindfully

Some lessons Ann and Christina learned were thanks to some of the mistakes they made while running Vamigas. Having a beauty business—or any business—is really hard, but on social media, all you see from brands is the fun stuff: the winning, the events, the awards, and the media attention. If you're considering starting a business, you'll need to keep in mind that you'll encounter problems that you could have never planned for. Being positive, feeling like a badass, and pulling the "*jefa* moves" are sometimes not going to be enough to get you through. In fact, toxic positivity sometimes makes things worse. Christina and Ann got into some retail relationships that didn't really work. They weren't profitable for them or, worse, drained their bank accounts. They took them on because they thought they could do it and were really confident in things turning out well.

One of the things they should have done differently is to manage how fast their business was growing. The two women had a lot of ups and downs and many growing pains while building their business. During the "ups," they said yes to everything that came their way. They now know they should have said no a lot more. Instead, you've got to slow down and create mindful, planned growth momentum that can be easily managed, so you don't end up like a runaway train. Some growth is sustainable, and some isn't.

Christina and Ann are not against all forms of hustling. Hustling is well suited for short bursts of important projects such as when facing looming deadlines. Dr. Davidds also talked to them about the importance of controlled hustle when taking care of important projects, almost like controlled burns.

How do you use hustle energy in your favor?

"Set boundaries and become very clear about how you intend to regain your energy," Dr. Davidds told the ladies. "What depletes your energy and what reenergizes you. If it's an important project that you need to take care of, use guardrails to set strong boundaries around your project. There's no way one can balance everything at the same time. It comes in seasons."

To opt out of hustle culture means to grow your business mindfully and not recklessly. If you have a project with an important deadline, you buckle down and devote dedicated time to the project and sprint as hard as you can to complete it.

The Radical Señora grows her business with an eye toward the future and knows that with the good times also come the bad ones. She's motivated, and she's a dreamer, but she knows her limits and is never afraid to say no to a project that may be too big or unwieldy for her. She's also ready for anything that may be thrown at her.

Radical Señora Boss Lesson #3: You don't have to fit in at work

Ask any woman who is in her señora era, and she will tell you that she cares so much less now about what other people think of her. She's also no longer afraid to make people talk. Ann and Christina think that comes with a few decades of experience dealing with people and the business world, but señoras are particularly good at it. Do you remember how daring and bold your great-grandmother or grandmother was? They probably wore what they liked and were never too shy to negotiate or complain at the *mercado*, especially when they felt as though they were being shortchanged. They gave zero cares if anybody looked at them weird or thought they didn't belong there, because they knew they did. Now, that's fierce!

It was mentally draining for Christina to go into the office every morning and try to fit in with those finance guys. Changing the way she dressed, toning down her personality, going to uncomfortable events when she didn't want to were all ways she made herself try to fit into this mold of being someone who was successful in that industry.

Dressing well to create a professional image at work is one thing, but changing who you are to make others happy is really just people-pleasing, which can be very emotionally damaging. Writer and psychologist Maytal Eyal says bottling things up is terrible for our physical health, too, with women now accounting for about 80 percent of sufferers of autoimmune disorders, which she suspects have roots in how we deal with this problem.[1] In fact, Harvard researchers found a link between censoring oneself and depression, and a University of Pittsburgh study showed that hiding your true emotions and avoiding conflict may increase heart disease risk and may even elevate the risk of premature death.[2]

In her thirties, Christina began to care less about what others thought and was gentler with herself around expectations. She cherished her authentic self and is now teaching her daughter never to change who she is to fit into any spaces. If someone doesn't think you fit in, slowly plan to leave that place and find a better cultural fit. Life is so precious and short. Why spend it on places or groups of people with whom you don't align? The señoras of your family tree would have rather given away their *terrenos* than be in a room that didn't want them in it.

The Radical Señora Era is a time of confidence. It's draining to hide your authentic self, and it's really fulfilling to have a work-place that accepts and loves you for who you are. The more fulfilled you feel, the more you're likely to perform at your best, because you feel cherished for your authentic self, and you're not embarrassed about people seeing the real you. When you allow yourself to be real at work, you're bringing really unique perspectives and ideas to the workplace. This diversity can spark limitless innovation and creativity in anything you do.

A Radical Señora is always unapologetically herself.

Radical Señora Boss Lesson #4: No, work is not you

Repeat this over and over again: "I am not my work, and my work is not me. My entire sense of self-worth is not tied to my business. I am more than what I achieve at the office. I am more than the revenue that my business generates or the press my brand gets." Ann's entire identity had become wrapped up in her work, so when she had a baby just as the pandemic hit, part of her world fell apart, leaving her struggling to figure out who she was. Without work, what made her happy?

When you're first generation, sometimes you learn a bad habit. You start to place your self-worth in things that allow you to achieve goals or be productive, because you want to make your parents proud of you. So, you may become hyper attuned to beating the odds at all costs. Because you'll stop at nothing to win (and rightfully so!), you'll work as much as you can, no matter the personal cost. It's an excellent quality to have in the cutthroat business world, but this can easily turn into a lack of boundaries between your personal life and your business life.

Your parents didn't have a problem separating their work lives from their personal lives, because they didn't have that problem. They couldn't work from home. You can't take manual labor or fast-food work home with you. When they came home from work, they didn't have to think about a big presentation at work or that big conference call that's coming up. They were done for the day. What you're doing is new to your family.

That stuff creeps up on you, and you don't see it coming. It starts by you saying yes to taking work home with you or working on weekends—without pay. That one weekend of work turns into many others, and then you wake up at the end of the year and realize you haven't taken any of your vacation days and you feel frazzled, unmotivated, unhealthy, and unhappy, with nothing to show for it. What's more, you're not getting paid much more, and you don't have the promotion.

If you're a parent, your home life starts to suffer, and your kids begin to see you less and less. These are years in your kids' lives that you will never ever get back. Look, it's fine to work some weekends to prepare for a big pitch meeting or to make a presentation as perfect as possible. And it's okay to pull a late night to meet a deadline. This is the way to get ahead! However, if this starts to happen too often, it will become a habit, and your boss or team will get accustomed to it. They'll always remember that you're the token staff person they can give their extra work to, because they see that you're okay with consistently working weekends or late nights. It's completely okay to say no to consistently bringing work home with you.

Christina has this talent where she can easily make her home life and family a priority. She hustles like the best boss babes on the planet, but when something coincides with family time or her baby, she draws the line like a mob boss. If things have to get pushed, they will, because nothing is more important to her than the *familia*. Ann is glad she knew Christina before having her baby, because she wouldn't have known how to navigate the challenges of being a working mom without first seeing her friend in action. Now she knows her weekends are sacred family and personal time.

Her philosophy? Business deadlines can wait a day. Your baby's first words or first steps will never happen again, so always be fully present for them. Waiting a weekend won't matter much. Deadlines can be pushed if you have an emergency. Lean out, my babies!

Radical Señoras know that they're more than what they produce at work.

Radical Señora Boss Lesson #5:
Set clear boundaries

The idea of "setting boundaries" always sounded foreign to Ann. She never paid much attention to its importance until she met Christina, who taught her that it was the key to being happier and more balanced in whatever you did. Setting boundaries means that you're communicating right off the bat what your expectations are and what you don't tolerate—in a diplomatic way, of course.

When it comes to work/life balance, for example, you might set the boundary that people don't contact you when you're on vacation. Some of the women at the PR firms where Ann worked were especially good at this and had fierce work/life boundaries. For example, you didn't find them consistently working on the weekend—they were with their families.

The importance of setting time boundaries is critically important to Latinas, because we might see it as not working hard enough. "Developing a healthy understanding of how to implement boundaries within their relationships, friendships, and careers does not mean they are abandoning their responsibilities," Dr. Vanessa Milagros says. "But rather that they are implementing healthier dynamics that can increase their happiness, self-love, and ability to love without enabling others."

At one point, when Vamigas started growing too fast, it began taking over Ann's and Christina's family lives. It disrupted family dinnertime or took them away from their children's nighttime routine or got in the way of back to school. Sometimes the deadlines were stressing them out so much that it would put them in a bad mood around their families, who couldn't have been more supportive of their small business.

So, Christina and Ann set in motion a series of Señora Rules to help keep each other in check when one of them might be overworking. First, they created *"Chisme/Copucha* Only Tuesdays,"* setting aside one day in the week to not talk about the business. During this day, they are just besties. They may talk about what's happening with Selena Gomez, the new Netflix shows they're watching, or the crazy new brand that just launched. Usually, they are pretty strict with each other, because they both break this rule a lot. If one of them starts talking work on a Tuesday, the other goes, "Remember, *chisme* only today! Sooo did you see the Kardashian news? And did you see the new *Bridgerton* season is out?"

Another area in which to set boundaries is in the use of social media. Ask any mom who also owns a small business, and she'll tell you that you can't work two full-time jobs and do them both well at the same time. This is especially important when it comes to the pressure of social media. Being a small business owner these days means you're also forced to become a part-time content creator, which takes up a great deal of your time. Since Ann took ownership of their marketing channels, she was tasked with creating some of the content that would go out on their social media pages.

Some videos that she made tanked, while others got thousands or even hundreds of thousands of views, comments, and likes, which turned into a real dopamine boost for her. When they got millions? It felt like a drug. At one point, it got kind of addicting to try to figure out which videos were going to be the winners. Ann had to start setting time limits when she shot content, because she couldn't be recording while also trying to make sure her little one wasn't putting bugs in her mouth or petting *campo* mice. Another problem was figuring out just what the ROI, or return on investment, was for these videos, meaning how many products did the content actually sell? Some of the videos that got the most views moved very little product, whereas some of the more boring content moved a lot. Christina was always there to remind her that their job wasn't to make cool content, but to build a brand and sell products.

Luckily, a secondary benefit of their videos was that they accidentally created a community of really good amigas.

You're gonna have to resist spending every waking moment on your phone, shooting content, because you feel like that's what all the other brands are doing well. This is only going to take away from your free time with your family. You've got to keep laser focused on what's more important for both you and your brand. Do more of the content that's actually helping you reach your goals and leave the rest for some other time when you're free. Keep your free time free, not spent on your phone.

If you work in an office environment, you might create a boundary where you're not answering emails after hours all the time, and if you have to work on a weekend, make sure you're being fairly compensated, either by getting overtime or by accruing personal time off every day that you work extra.

Radical Señoras create a fierce boundary between their work hours and personal time, and they should have no regrets about that.

Radical Señora Boss Lesson #6: Learn how to quit

Are you unhappy at work? The señoras from your family tree would tell you to go change that. Move somewhere that makes you happy and where you have a team that treats you kindly. There is no use remaining somewhere you don't like, with people who don't treat you well. Christina tried even harder to create a work environment fit, but that led only to a breakdown.

The problem is that unless they have a lot of savings or a trust fund somewhere, most people can't quit right away. So, plan it out. Sit down with a pen and paper and maybe a small glass of wine or tea, or whatever makes you happy, and write out the type of job that you feel would make you happy. Think about the environment that you would love. Is it working from home? Or do you love getting out of the house and going into an office, where you can talk to your coworkers? Is it a workplace that values wellness and community?

Then draw up a six- to twenty-four-month game plan for how you're gonna get there, while saving some money, paying off bills, and filling in any skills gaps you may have, to help you really kill it at your next position. Then track the date on your calendar, and on days when you're feeling particularly miserable, think of the fast-approaching deadline and how much happier you'll be at your next job. Sometimes it will be very hard, and you may need to take classes to upskill or learn something new that will help you land a better job. But there is always a better job out there, one that will treat you better. Never feel like you're stuck at your job.

There were moments early in Ann's career where she hated it. She dreaded going into the office each morning, and she'd feel literal pain deep inside her bones. The only things that would keep her going were friends she had made in the office and a great boss whom she was learning a lot from. Sometimes Ann stayed too long, when she knew she wasn't needed anymore. Sometimes she'd overstay her welcome and then get laid off because she wasn't making many sales. But she stayed for no reason and sometimes only because she felt bad to leave her boss hanging.

Ann has a very special memory of the first time she realized she could just leave a job that wasn't a good fit. She was in her twenties and lived in LA. She came home particularly depressed because she'd had a miserable day at work. She brought out a nice bottle of wine and watched *Jerry Maguire*. Then she decided right then and there, thanks to Tom Cruise, that she had bigger goals, and that in order to meet them, she needed to *learn how to leave*. She took out her laptop, looked at the calendar (this was back when you didn't have a calendar on your phone unless you were rich, LOL), and designated a date as her deadline for leaving the job. Ann gave herself until X date to find a new position elsewhere. That meant she had to start researching, interviewing, and making things happen. That decision ultimately led her to San Francisco, altering the course of her life forever.

Of course, Ann will be the first to give you the advice many of our immigrant parents offer us, and it is still very good advice—never leave a job without having another one lined up, unless you're being discriminated against or abused at work. In that case, lawyer up!

Being a Radical Señora means you do not owe anybody any favors, so stop feeling bad about wanting to find a place to work where you're actually happy. Perhaps you're afraid to ask for a raise or the higher-ups aren't treating you very well, and you want things to change. Stop asking for crumbs. You're talented, skilled; they hired you because they needed you, and they value your work.

A Radical Señora doesn't stay where she isn't happy. The End.

Radical Señora Boss Lesson #7: Your company is not your *familia*

Our backgrounds and cultures make us especially prone to being *too loyal* to a workplace. Your parents very likely looked at jobs as gifts from the gods and probably told you never to leave your position, but ask them and they'll tell you of the many times when they were unfairly fired, suddenly laid off or, worse, not even paid for their work. The sad fact is that though you're loyal to people who hire you, your boss will almost never be loyal to you over the company. It's tough to hear this, but once a company gets big enough, you're no longer "like family." You're just a part of a machine that was put there to help the company make money.

Many companies love to say, "You're part of the family!" but they never really mean it. Understand that people who need something from you (your time, brain, and effort) will do and say things they know will make you stay. Some may mean it.

Others are just B.S. artists. Some workplaces may truly want to be warm and supportive and offer a family-like environment, but when budgets are cut, management teams have to answer to the call of investors, and so it's every person for him/herself. Yet other companies will give you all the perks you could ever want, but that's strategically meant to keep you in love with your company. You should never fall blindly in love with your company. It's not even personal–just business. But you've got to protect yourself.

In your business or work life, find or set up an environment where it's impossible to be pushed around. Choose people, communities, networks, and clubs that will guide you and support you. This will give you the confidence to stand up for what is truly in your heart, and you will be able to listen to where your soul wants to guide you. Also, always research the environment before jumping into any job, because this will help you avoid bad situations. To do this, you'll have to become an expert at due diligence.

Radical Señoras guard their hearts in the workplace.

Radical Señora Boss Lesson #8: Pull up another *amiga*

If you have gotten far in your career, one of the most rewarding things you will ever do is to help a woman who is a version of you a decade ago and maybe even has a dream similar to yours. As you'll read in Chapter 4, señoras of your family tree helped others by volunteering at a nonprofit or at their church, or they also gave a helping hand to other moms.

Christina and Ann started investing in women business founders right around the time they met each other. Run by the remarkable Natalia Oberti Noguera, Pipeline Angels is a place where you can learn how to angel invest and then give money to a woman-run start-up. Christina and Ann met so many amazing founders, and they got to give money to some of them through angel investing. There really is no better way to make an impact than by putting your money where it's really needed and helping an *amiga* build a new company and hopefully eventually reach her dreams.

Angel investing isn't a huge undertaking, and you don't have to be a multimillionaire to do it. People see the Sharks on *Shark Tank* and think you have to invest hundreds of thousands of dollars in a fledgling business. Did you know that you can invest as little as one thousand dollars? The investment range for the types of networks we are in is one thousand to ten thousand dollars. The way it works is you invest with a group of other people in a particular company, so the group might invest one hundred thousand dollars in a company. At Pipeline Angels, Ann and Christina learned that business founders like them—immigrants and Latinas and other people of color—tend to lack the "friends and family" checks, which most founders are able to rely on when starting a business. Remember those checks that Elizabeth Holmes got when she first launched her start-up, checks from, like, her neighbors and her dad's friends, who happened to be some of the biggest investors in Silicon Valley? Yeah, most of us don't have those connections. Checks like the ones angel investors will write are stand-ins for friends and family rounds, which these founders lack, and could make the biggest difference in the world for them.

If you can't be an angel investor, find an organization or a nonprofit where you can mentor women in your field and where you can set your own volunteering hours. You'll help them by giving them advice on things like how to break into your industry or how to work your way up the ladder.

Ann and Christina also started the Latina Founders Club so that they could give advice to fellow founders, and create a place to share useful resources. It was another way for them to give back to their community.

Radical Señoras are mentors to amigas, *and this is how we create more Radical Señoras in the world.*

Radical Señora Boss Lesson #9: Don't do things because you think you should

Being a business founder and maybe even reaching nearly a million dollars in revenue doesn't mean that you're rolling in the dough. The reality is that you usually have to wait awhile to reach profitability. Christina and Ann were very lucky in that they reached that in year one, but they didn't really start paying themselves until year two. Most of the money ends up going back into the company and creating products. That means that in those first few years, or until your company can afford it, you don't take any pay. Even once you do, there are some moments when you have to stop paying yourself, because the company comes first. That is the reason why many business founders raise funds, usually millions of dollars. That keeps the company going, helps them create new products, and pays for marketing, like advertising and digital initiatives, which helps them make more sales.

When Christina and Ann launched Vamigas, they got a lot of early meetings with investors because they were in a really buzzy crop of Latina beauty brands launching at the time. They seriously considered it and were really close to taking investment, but something kept telling them to wait. They just didn't feel ready yet. They even got a really exciting major funding opportunity that was beyond their wildest dreams. But something kept telling them to wait. The truth of it was that they really didn't want to give up control of their company. They were worried that a funding round would keep them afloat for only a year, and that would force them to keep running after more rounds. Another issue was that once you accept outside funding, the focus inevitably shifts to a hyper focus on profit margins—driving pressure to produce goods as cheaply as possible and create new products as fast as possible.

Fundraising is the right thing to do for many companies. But Ann and Christina were toddler and preschool mamas, and their days were already hectic. They didn't have much time to do anything, let alone travel the country and raise millions of dollars. So, they grudgingly passed up the equity opportunity. Maybe one day this will change, like when their babies are more grown up, but for now this is right for them in this era.

That's what being a Radical Señora is all about; not forcing yourself to accomplish something only because it's what you think you should be doing or because you feel FOMO (fear of missing out). Being successful has many different definitions, and it seems as though over the past decade, this has gotten murky. One definition has won out, and that's that of the boss babe, who sets out to break world records, outcompete, and make cash hand over fist. However, in the past few years, this definition has gotten pushback for its focus on unrealistic or superficial ideas of what success really is.

A señora does things because she wants to, not because she thinks she should.

Radical Señora Boss Lesson #10: Work smarter and optimize everything

Christina and Ann also fell into the trap of conspicuous busy-ness, where you felt productive only if you had back-to-back tasks, meetings, and a mile-long to-do list. If you are a millennial or Gen X Latina and come from another country or have immi-grant parents, this mindset will particularly resonate. The problem is that if you actually were to measure how much work you've done, it actually wouldn't be much at all.

In his book *Slow Productivity: The Lost Art of Accomplish-ment Without Burnout*, author Cal Newport argues that productivity is a cult, and that we're overwhelmed with useless meetings and the obsessive need to "look busy."[3] Newport pro-vides a manifesto that encourages modern workers to focus on quality over quantity of work and on deep work and meaningful tasks, rather than on just being busy, by doing things like set-ting goals that are realistic, being better at prioritizing your tasks, and creating moments of rest during the day (not after). This ironically allows you to set up your workplace to be the most balanced and productive workplace you've ever been in.

There are obvious changes you can make to enhance your productivity, like prioritizing tasks that give you the most value for your output, figuring out what's taking up most of your time and seeing if you can cut some of that out of your schedule, giv-ing up being a perfectionist, and more.

The Radical Señora doesn't do things just for the sake of doing them, and she doesn't do busy work, which is an empty pursuit. She figures out what she's doing that isn't getting her any results and cuts it out of her routine. She also doesn't allow others to control her time. For example, she doesn't take calls or Zoom chats lightly. She also isn't easy to catch or book. Her time is important, and anyone who wants to get on her calendar better have a good reason.

Use technology tools to make your work more streamlined and efficient. Efficiency, not overwork, should be your objective. For Ann's public relations business, she uses technology tools to manage clients and get them away from email, and the latest CRM tools to streamline her communication with media. You need a good process to create a calm workflow that works for you and not against you.

The Radical Señora optimizes processes wherever she can to make everything she does count.

Radical Señora Boss Lesson #11: Remain authentically you

Vamigas launched alongside a group of really bold, beautiful, and colorful Latina-owned brands. They all remain very true to their cultures and this is reflected in certain elements of their brands. Each of them has its own brand DNA that is its signature. Sure, they are all under the "Latina/Latino" umbrella, but each represents its own specific countries and ancestry.

Since Ann came from the PR space, she did all their media campaigns, so that they could get some nice press coverage. She probably emailed thousands of reporters and writers, and she got massive coverage by probably every women's magazine and beauty outlet in the media industry. All but one, that is–*Vogue*. No matter how much she pitched *Vogue*'s editors and writers, with many different kinds of stories, to this day they have never written about the Vamigas brand. Vamigas's Chilean rose hip oil was named an It Beauty Product by *Elle* magazine, and the brand has been highlighted by *Good Housekeeping*, *Town & Country*, *Oprah Daily*, and literally all the women's outlets out there. But for some reason, *Vogue* has never given the brand a shoutout. Ann and Christina think this says a lot about their identity and authenticity.

Ann thinks a lot of it comes down to this: "We were never really '*Vogue* material.' When we started out, a lot of beauty brands were trying to do this French, 'clean girl aesthetic' vibe, with beautiful photos that had all neutral colors and gorgeous (and expensive!) product photography. Since we have always been bootstrapped, we couldn't afford to hire a big fancy agency, and so we did it all in-house, eventually hiring a smart and very talented Latina social media professional named Camille, whose style was totally similar to ours.

"Our vibe was never 'French fashionista,' because that just wasn't us. If you look at *Vogue*'s pages, it's all a European high fashion aesthetic, 'it girls' from the Hamptons, old money, fashion week, and celebs. Our brand is what I like to call 'breezy Southern California Latina *ranchito* chic.' It's who we are, and we never tried to be anything other than that. Clearly, there aren't many brands out there like that. And, no joke, when we decided to embrace who we were on social media and show more of ourselves, people really responded, and that was the start of our beautiful close-knit community full of Latinas who were just like us. They also weren't into the French aesthetics thing. Had we tried to do that, they would have been like, 'WTF?' It would have failed.

"Our advice to you is never copy what's trending in your industry just because it's trending. We could have easily done similar content to what was popular at the time with general market brands, but we didn't bother. We want to see more of us and our cultures out in the world. Had we not been authentic and started posting pictures of twenty-year-old influencers who look like Hailey Bieber rubbing our rose hip oil all over themselves in their fancy bathrooms, our brand would have landed flat. When you go out into social media, be yourself, post things that you like, share details about your life, be vulnerable, and share your ups and your downs. Be funny. Be yourself. Never try to be someone else. It's a powerful and surprising strategy."

A Radical Señora never tries to copy a vibe that isn't her.

Radical Señora Boss Lesson #12: Never ignore yourself or your family

A few years back there was a viral story about a mother who adopted a baby who had been born prematurely and had to be cared for in the NICU. That mother was fired from her job because she needed time off to care for the baby. It seems the company didn't think she was "an actual mother," and so it fired her. The company CEO eventually apologized for what the team had done, but the brand damage was done. This is an example of a very old type of corporate thinking, where your family life comes second to your work life.

Ann is embarrassed that she forgot about her family for a few years. If she could turn back the clock, she would have made it a priority to come home and, while at home, to completely unplug from work. She will also never forgive herself for not going back to her homeland more often to be with her grandmothers before they passed. Instead, she wasted years when she could have been creating meaningful connections with them and making their last years more beautiful. She spent much of her twenties and thirties with her head buried in her work when she could have created guardrails around family time.

A Radical Señora doesn't try to choose between her job and her family. Family is always first.

Radical Señora Boss Lesson #13: Nothing is a life-or-death emergency

Sometimes you get stuck in an emergency loop, where you feel immediate panic if you don't hit a deadline or respond right away to an important email. The anxiety hits you hard, and you can think of nothing else than responding immediately or what will happen if you don't. What you're doing at work is important. We get it. But unless you're a surgeon, doctor, nurse, or physician's assistant, is the work that you're doing saving lives? No? Then that deadline is a made-up deadline in the bigger context of your life and the world. Fake work urgency is created by corporations to hit financial targets, which executives need to report financials in their quarterly reports. Investors in companies expect a return on their investment, so the founders are on the line to show growth somehow. This means that employees are stuck on a hamster wheel of having to perform at a rapid pace lest they get fired and replaced by someone who is younger and can run faster. This is all great for the company, but not for workers: It depletes your energy and is bad for your mental and physical health, because it puts company goals before your wellness. Then they fire you when you are older and aren't performing at the level you used to.

Don't ignore deadlines altogether, though—you've still got to grow your career, and we know many businesses require strict deadlines (media, publishing, and so on). This just means you have to learn to guard your energy and put up guardrails so that these deadlines don't seem like life-or-death situations and won't throw you off balance. Think ahead.

Radical Señoras know that work emergencies aren't life emergencies, and they don't stress over deadlines.

CHAPTER 4

A Señora
through the Ages

Crazy Old Ladies
of the Honey

THE MODERN-DAY Radical Señora wasn't born in a vacuum. She learned her rituals and habits from señoras of the past, such as her mother, older *tías*, her grandmother, her great-grandmother, and centuries of women before them. If you look hard enough, you'll likely find a magical connecting thread between your life today and the lives of these women in some of the smallest, most mundane things you do on an everyday basis.

I bet you did some sweeping this past weekend; maybe you tackled the kitchen floor or your dusty patio. Did you know that sweeping the temple was a critical ritual for Aztec women, which they carried out to honor the gods? Perhaps you made hot cocoa for yourself or your little ones this morning. Witchy señoras in parts of Guatemala were known to cook up chocolate with the objective of bewitching people's lovers and haters.

On a daily basis, Ann thinks about how her life and the lives of her *bisabuela* (great-grandmother) Maria, and her grandmothers, Mercedes and Margarita, who all lived in Chile, are similar. Maria was Mercedes's mother, and they lived in a small town in the valley of the Aconcagua River, in the Valparaíso region. Ann wishes she knew more about Margarita's mother, who is believed to have belonged to the Chilean Aymara tribe, which originated in the Andean highlands, but no records were kept during that time, given what little power Indigenous communities had. Ann wonders about their routines. How did they learn to sew? What was their favorite vegetable to harvest? She also ponders how they went through major tragedies and world events of their day, and what advice they might give her today—how much we could learn from them. At one time, our grandmothers were all just girls, and they made their way through life just as you and I do today. With little to no resources, they went through life's ups and downs, including times of peace and war, all while trying to keep everything together.

Christina doesn't know much about her paternal grandparents, but she knows they arrived from Oaxaca and eventually opened multiple Mexican restaurants in the Bay Area, long before Mexican food was trendy, bringing a little bit of that Oaxacan cuisine magic to California with them. Her maternal great-grandmother Matilda came from Madeira, a small island belonging to Portugal, and her grandmother Elsie was a first-generation Portuguese American kid and grew up in the Bay Area.

She often wonders what life as a new immigrant was like for her Mexican grandmother Virginia, what difficulties she had in this new country, and how hard her and her family worked to get ahead, especially as small business owners. And what Elsie's life was like trying to straddle two separate cultures and helping her immigrant parents navigate this different landscape. She feels lucky that she remembers some of her Mexican roots, like the many, many *asados* the family loved to have. She has been keeping this tradition alive through cooking, baking, and family barbecues, which add simple daily joys to her life.

The Señora Life isn't just aesthetic videos of cooking or sipping tea. It all comes from our heritage and rich cultural traditions and rituals. To be able to write a book about this, Christina and Ann knew that first they needed to understand the broader context of the women of the past, because they birthed the señora rituals of the present. Throughout hundreds of years, they held their *ranchitos, parcelas, fincas* and farms together; they cooked the food, swept their homes, mended and hemmed their family's clothing, washed the dishes (some with the help of other señoras), tended to the garden, took the kids to school, and helped the community. In our historical research, we found there were many different types of señoras.

A great deal of the preparation work to write this book involved poring over history books, old narratives penned by the señoras themselves, and records kept by the Spanish, who colonized part of the American continent. What is sad to Ann and Christina is there are many books about Latin American history, but there isn't much written about women's daily lives. In fact, many of the books they found about the women of Latin America are focused on their tragedies, and their stories are usually told from a man's point of view. In *Encarnacion's Kitchen*, one of the more magical books they found, which was recommended to them by a TikTok *amiga*, editor Dan Strehl talks about how, during California's early statehood, the voices of Mexican and Latina women writers who wrote from their own point of view were largely ignored.[1] During that era, editors "preferred images of beautiful señoritas as objects of description," and older women were never highlighted.

What they found was fascinating. Hispanic women's lives from the past era were rich and varied, influenced by ethnicity and economic status. They were truly the heart of their societies. Indigenous women wove baskets, which served an important purpose, and then sold them at the market. Colonial-era señoras organized church events, which helped strengthen their communities. Witchy señoras brewed magical elixirs made out of chocolate for carrying out incantations, and kept the *chisme* flowing. Señoras with chacras (farms) harvested delicious veggies and processed meats. Doñas, or elite city señoras, led posh lives that rivaled any stories of the women of the Gilded Age, and later were at the forefront of progressive movements, such as the fight for a woman's right to vote and own property. Their little rituals made their way down to you and still influence you in ways you've probably never thought about.

When Christina and Ann asked the women in their señora era online community what type of señora they were, some of the answers they received were similar to the identities of the women they found in books in the library stacks. Members of their community call themselves señora chefs, witchy señoras, "garden gnome" señoras, and fancy city doñas, and some even describe themselves as goth señoras. How they see themselves is really not that different than the identities of those señoras of the past.

To collect simple rituals, Christina and Ann had to time travel to various time periods, which took them to locations where some of the biggest events in world history happened. They studied the lives of Indigenous women before the Spanish invasion of the New World. (Please note that Christina and Ann don't call these Indigenous women señoras in this book because they think it could be seen as disrespectful to use a term that was invented in Europe and could be interpreted as another expression of colonialism.) Then they traveled to find the rituals of Spanish women who came to the New World alongside the soldiers during the colonial period. They also explored the lives of postcolonial-era mestiza women, women of mixed Indigenous and Spanish parentage. They got lost reading cookbooks written by women of the Californio era, who were Spanish-speaking residents of both Mexican California and Spanish California and lived in the area before the Treaty of Guadalupe Hidalgo, which ceded Mexican land to the United States. Ann and Christina then looked at the daily lives of señoras from the turn of the twentieth century and beyond, and this is where they get to your great-grandmother's generations.

To be respectful of their own cultural history, Christina handled the research having to do with Mexican culture, and Ann took over the exploration of the history of South American señoras. It was challenging to go through the lives of señoras of the past, for a few reasons. First, they are an incredibly mixed people, full of rich cultures, from a variety of countries, ethnicities, and more. Ann and Christina wanted to try as much as possible to include every region's cultural history, but it would be impossible to explore the cultures of eighteen different countries in a book that's under seventy thousand words. Some of us are *mestizo* or *castizo*, and this means not only understanding where our Spanish ancestors came from but also the cultures of our Indigenous grandparents or great-grandparents, which is especially challenging, because there is limited data.

Knowing that some of the readers of this book could very well be full Indigenous people, Christina and Ann tried to be as sensitive as possible to the horrors that your ancestors experienced during the Spanish invasion and beyond. Many of you reading this may be Black Latinos, from places like the Dominican Republic, Cuba, or Puerto Rico, and they wanted to try to include as much rich cultural history and routines as possible of the señoras in your regions. Some of us may have ancestors from many other countries and cultures. Our ethnicities are as richly multilayered as the beauty of our lands.

Second, the journey of exploring women's daily lives also took them close to some of the genocides in our cultural history, such as the Spanish invasion, slavery, and the massacre of Indigenous communities. Some of your own ancestors may have been driven out of their homes, killed in wars, tortured, enslaved, or forced to assimilate. Indigenous women were taken from their families, violated, and murdered. They were also cut down by powerful viruses that the soldiers brought. It's a brutal history we must never forget, because the ramifications of this period, the subjugation of Indigenous communities, are still felt today. It's also still happening today in many countries, with modern Indigenous communities among some of the most socially vulnerable in Latin America. Think about this: Between 75 and 90 percent of the Indigenous people of Latin America were wiped out when the Spanish arrived. Some of those may have been your extended family members: They were babies, moms, dads, grandparents, aunts, and uncles.

For this chapter, Ann and Christina pored over history books and peer-reviewed academic journals and first-person accounts. This book does not assign any value or opinions to historic events. There are many good books that focus on political and social injustices, and they encourage you to read further if you're interested.

Third, they focused more on the history of señoras from Mexico, where Christina's paternal family is from, and Chile, where Ann's family is from, because that's where their cultural memories lie. If you want to take a deep dive into your own country's señora habits, they encourage you to use tools like Ancestry.com, and your public library to learn more. It is guaranteed you will discover some insights about your forebears' daily lives. It's as simple as picking up a history book, which was the spark that created the idea for this book.

Finally, the term *señora* derives from the Latin word "senior," and so it isn't accurate to call pre-Columbian people who lived in the Americas señoras. Here, the term is used in a lighthearted way, though keep in mind it absolutely isn't historically accurate to call Aztec and Mayan women "señoras." The research for most of this chapter is based on the observational writings of Europeans, called "codices," and as they say, history is written by the victors. What's more, this info is skewed to Indigenous "elite" women, that is, noblewomen, priestesses, and the wives of rulers.

So, What's a Señora?

The history of the word *señora* goes back to sixteenth-century Spain, where it originally meant "lady" or "madam." Interestingly, the word comes from the masculine *señor*, which is derived from the Medieval Latin word "senior," or "lord," which is basically just a wise elder. So, you could say that being a señora is having a little bit of that "Wise Latina" knowledge that comes with experience. It's truly a representation of how much respect our cultures have toward older women.

The term *señora* is now a respectful way to refer to a woman over a certain age, usually forty, sometimes thirty, who is either married, widowed, or single and who keeps the house and kids in order. When young Latin Americans think of a señora, they usually think of their mothers and grandmothers. What things do you think about when you hear the word? It's probably shopping bags; flat, comfortable house shoes; aprons; vacuuming; gossiping with neighbors; and making sandwiches and soups. Essentially everything in the world that's cozy.

Try calling a young Latin American woman a señora and get ready for some stink eye, because the word has traditionally been associated with elderliness. That first time you get called a señora is almost a rite of passage for thirtysomethings, the equivalent of being called "ma'am" here in the States.

In this book, *señora* is defined as our *bisabuelas*, *tatarabuelas*, and *abuelas*, as well as their extended community. They didn't have many of the modern appliances that we do, and so everything was done slowly by hand. There was no such thing as instant oatmeal, no microwave or protein bars. All they had was maybe a stove or an outside oven. Nothing was single use; potatoes came in big sacks, and carrots and other root vegetables came straight from the ground. They washed the dirt off and made big pots of soup. They may have kept chickens. They shelled peas and deboned fish and made *pajaritos* (kefir) before it was trendy. They may have even made their own *casera* beauty line, a honey and oatmeal mask, or their own rose water. Sometimes they may have been entrepreneurial, hawking their wares at the *mercados*.

Your Aztec, Mayan, Taino, and Andean Ancestors

There were and are numerous Indigenous communities in Mexico, including the Zapotecs, Mixtecs, Purépechas, Otomis, and Totonacs. We wish we had more knowledge beyond the Aztec community in Mexico, but it is difficult to collect. The Spanish considered herbal knowledge heretical and thus forbade a lot of the recorded knowledge from being passed down to other generations. According to Armando Gonzales Stewart, PhD, an academic who has conducted research on medicinal plants used in Mexican traditional medicine, the Aztecs left a more robust record of their herbal uses, and so we have more information about their practices in particular, as compared to other Mexican Indigenous communities. Much of that knowledge was recorded in what's called the "Aztec Codices," which were a series of pre-Columbian manuscripts that described daily life and customs of Aztec culture. It is here where much of the knowledge we have today about them comes from.

The Aztec woman was a mother, midwife, or priest-herbalist—and once in a while possibly even a warrior. In his book *Daily Life of the Aztecs*, David Carrasco documents the typical lives of people in the Aztec community. Women's tasks focused on the home, and their primary job, besides tending the home and caring for the children, was weaving, which was an important part of their society. Tasks like sweeping were ways to purify a place and create a sense of good health, and so their homes were very clean. Sweeping was also an important ritual: Women actually had the responsibility of sweeping inside Aztec temples to honor their gods and deities.

The lives of Indigenous women were multifaceted, so it's difficult to generalize. However, in general, marriage was the focal point of society and of their lives. Around 95 percent of Aztec women were married, usually as teenagers, and the marriages were always of convenience, such as to keep a title or to create alliances between factions. This was true of both Aztec and Mayan cultures, where elite women were married off to military or political leaders.

In many Indigenous groups, women were viewed as hard workers, and the mother was tasked with caring for the babies, cleaning, managing religious routines, making food for the family, and performing other manual tasks, which were especially important. They were also in charge of agricultural work, pottery making and weaving. When girls were born, they received a gift of a spindle to get them "ready for housework." Aztec women also worked in the markets, often selling their handmade clothing. Elderly women were in charge of dyeing textiles with their common colors, like blue, yellow, red, and purple. Dyeing and textile production were very important to the culture.

Andean Indigenous women ran the household; they cleaned, cooked, and made chicha (a fermented alcoholic beverage used for every day enjoyment and for religious rituals). Women were also responsible for caring for the garden and harvesting and cooking their bounty. In some historical records, Spaniards who arrived in the New World observed that in this region, women did most of the work.

Indigenous cultures differed in terms of the degree to which women had a right to land and property ownership. In *The Women of Colonial Latin America*,[2] Susan Socolow describes how Mayan women could not hold or inherit land but were instead owners of personal property on the land; they were the keepers of home goods, ranch animals, beehives, and clothing. They could bequeath land but only to their daughters. Andean women could own land if their mothers had also been given similar rights. So, for example, you could own land if your mother had also owned her family's land, and so forth. On the other hand, Aztec women were allowed to have land, houses, and things like weaving equipment and furniture. To the Aztecs, most household goods were considered "women's property" (which they called *cinhuatlatquitl*).

Elderly women were very important to the Aztec culture. In the "Codex Mendoza," a sixteenth-century history of Aztec rulers, midwives are portrayed as significant keepers of childbearing. The codex, which should be taken with a grain of salt because it is a guidebook that was created by the Spaniards, depicts scenes with Aztec midwives, who organized a birth by preparing a mat using grass plants and drawing a tub of water, then bathing the baby. The midwife also provided herbal medicine and spiritual rituals. She would breathe on the water, let the child taste the water, let the water touch the baby, and would then chant: "My youngest one, my beloved youth, enter descent into the blue water, the yellow water. Approach thy mother Chalchiuhtlicue, Ahalchiuhtlatonac! May she receive thee... may she cleanse thy heart [, and] may she make it fine, good. May she give the fine, good conduct!" In this chant, Chalchiuhtlicue is the very revered mother deity of water, fertility, and baptism and is the patron saint of childbirth.

In the Andes, midwives were believed to be "blessed" because of their special powers of fertility. They were also healers and used medicinal herbs to cure illnesses and restore good health. Women were restricted from positions in warfare, politics, and religion.

Older women who had gone through menopause were thought to have magical powers and were often feared, because some thought they could speak to the devil. Some sources Ann and Christina read also noted that the Aztecs may have been afraid of older women's sexual appetites and called them *viejas locas de miel*, which literally means "crazy old ladies of the honey."

The Spanish invasion affected surviving Indigenous women's lives in various ways. After the colonization period, some Indigenous women transitioned into Spanish society, were married to Spanish men, had *mestizo* children, started businesses, and created new lives, given the situation. Others remained in their Indigenous communities, married Indigenous men, and continued to live their daily lives, albeit with new challenges brought on by the Spanish. Others languished in poverty or were enslaved by the Spanish. Others became the help for Spanish families' homes.

For example, Inés González was a Peruvian Indigenous servant of Rodrigo González Marmolejo, who went on to become first bishop of Santiago de Chile. After serving him for twenty-four years, he gave her a chacra (a farm) named Conchalí outside the city, two homes in Santiago, and various animals. On the other side, in Socolow's book, Ann and Christina read the account of an Indigenous woman servant who was hung from a roof beam and beaten by her "master" because she resisted his attempted assault.

When the Europeans arrived, they began to alter the gender roles in Indigenous communities. For example, in Brazil farming had been a task done by women of the Tupi culture, but the Europeans assigned the job to men. Indigenous people from Pueblo viewed construction work as women's work, but the Spanish announced it would be a male occupation moving forward. This created a lot of chaos.

Some of the Indigenous women who were able to escape harm used their talents and smarts to become masters of the marketplace and used Spanish commerce laws in brilliant ways. Women in parts of South America, for example, started selling items like chicha and Andean women's clothing (*anacos*) and making and selling food, beverages, and home goods. Some also acted as herbal healers, and others specialized in long-distance trade and created enough wealth to buy and sell real estate property and will it to their families. Some owned bars that catered to the "urban Indigenous" population, and others became pawnbrokers.

The Mapuche of Chile were the only tribe to resist the conquest by the Spanish for several centuries, and this is considered the most enduring and successful resistance on the American continent. This came to an end with a military occupation by the

Chilean government in the nineteenth century. The Mapuche venerated and celebrated feminine natural power through stories and songs and thought the world was created by a woman. In this culture, the man was the head of the household and assumed ranch tasks, like cattle and sheep care. Mapuche women, who first went to live with their in-laws after marriage, took care of the household and watched over kids, and they were also tasked with the safekeeping of cultural values. What's more, their female shamans (machi) played pivotal roles in the culture's rituals.

Women's fashion of the time was fascinating. Some wealthier Indigenous women may have worn pearls, silks, gold jewelry, shawls, skirts, and blouses from Europe. Others wished to create a new cultural mix of luxurious Indigenous clothing and jewelry from their own community, clothing from other communities, and pieces from Spanish and Asian cultures (which sounds like much of the fashion scene nowadays). Socolow suggests that these women used fashion to display their growing wealth and create a new identity. They did this simply to survive and try to keep a sense of dignity in a world that had almost completely stamped out their community and culture.

Señoras, Doñas, and Brujas in Latin America's "Middle Period"

In her book *Colonial Latin America (New Approaches to the Americas)*, writer Susan Migden Socolow outlines what it was like to be a señora at the turn of the eighteenth century. Marriage was particularly important during this period and was considered to be interconnected to ideas of race, social rank, and economic standing. Marriage actually protected women, be-

cause they had very few rights in society—especially those who
weren't part of the "elite" upper class. The upper classes in Mexico City society were made up of nobles and elite merchants.
They were merchants in Argentina, socialites in Chile, and land-
owners and bureaucrats in Peru.

Señoras in colonial Mexico City married anywhere between
the ages of seventeen and twenty-seven, with the average age
being around twenty. Women in colonial-era León married between the ages of sixteen and eighteen, with Indigenous women
marrying a bit younger. Courtship took place at church and religious events, and dating meant sneaking notes and gifts to each
other. It was not common for these señoras to marry for love, but
instead in favor of whatever was best for the family name, what
amounts to a business partnership of sorts. In general, for un-
wealthy women, marriage was not the norm, and they may have
had longer- or short-term partners, just as we do today. Free
women of African descent were more likely to be married.

In terms of the ships belonging to the Atlantic slave trade,
more revolts happened on ships with large numbers of women
on board, and researchers have pointed to a gendered pattern,
where more women fought back for their freedom, including
upon arrival in the Americas. Upon arrival, some women found
remote communities, back then called "Maroon Camps," where
they were able to be free, and others got jobs to become sub-
jects of the Spanish government.[3]

The first Black woman of African ancestry in Dominican society on La Española is remembered as "the Black Woman of
the hospital" due to the fact she was a healer who helped poor
people in need. Her name is unfortunately unknown nowadays,
but historical records show that she owned her own clinic and
so was likely a free person. She was so influential and helped
the community so much that in the first decade of the sixteenth

century, the island's first hospital was placed where her clinic had once stood by Governor Nicolás de Ovando, who, unfortunately, took all the credit.[4]

Records show that in 1575, Maria de Cota, a freed Black woman from Santo Domingo, requested a permit to travel to Peru after serving a Spanish family for eighteen years in Seville. She presented letters from acquaintances, who confirmed her status and history, and she was granted the permit and left Spain for Peru not long after that.[5]

Señoras loved to spruce themselves up. They may have worn religious jewelry, like a rosary made out of gold, silver, or even cotton. They also wore amulets, such as alligator teeth, magical amulets (*figas*), and beads. Wealthier doñas wore such items of adornment as gold combs, diamond pins for their hair, medallions, earrings, and necklaces, and they carried bracelets, fans, and silver snuffboxes.

The average wealthy colonial señora gave birth to an average of eight to ten children, and in general, only five or six survived childhood. Señoras in middle-income households had fewer kids and tended to marry later in life than their higher-income counterparts.

Day-to-day, higher-income señoras of this era managed the household, supervising their husbands, educating the children, and protecting their family fortunes and *terrenos* (land). They were considered almost the "junior partner" in the household, as they also sometimes managed the home's employees, collected debts, managed rental property, and even filed lawsuits. Husbands oftentimes granted their wives "power of attorney" privileges.

Though very busy, these señoras led a life of luxury. They often had servants and rarely had to do any type of hard labor. During their household "off days," they gossiped, drank tea while visiting friends, and participated in church activities. There were also many rules of etiquette for upper-class colonial señoras. The Mexican home was not just a home, Sonya Lipsett-Rivera writes in her book, *Gender and the Negotiation of Daily life in Mexico, 1750–1856*.[6] Etiquette set standards about "morality, honor, and hierarchy," and when entering someone's home, guests followed a set of rules based on each person's status. Honor was a running theme through the daily lives of Mexican señoras, and all Mexicans, for that matter. This mindset was influenced by both Indigenous and Spanish culture.

Wealthy Mexican señoras, for example, lived on the second floor of their buildings to telegraph their superior wealth and status. Mexicans with middle and lower incomes made sure that their homes were not gaudy and did not have too many decorations. What's more, the interiors of homes were designated the "female" portion, and when you left your home, you entered "male" territory. As a result, it was not proper for women in general to leave their homes, particularly at night.

The inside of the home of an upper-class Mexican señora was typically colonial in architecture, with rooms surrounding a patio. There was usually a *salón del dosel* (throne room), where family and nobility portraits were hung. The *estrado* and chapel were areas where señoras welcomed their friends for social hour. Some had music rooms in the front of the home, where they likely entertained their friends and family and where their children learned new talents.

Working-class señoras had a similar point of view when it came to their homes, which were often also colonial in design and included a center patio. It was not proper for women to leave the home, except for work, and never in the evening. It was proper only to have a minimalist aesthetic, with sparse furniture and decorations, and no sculptures or tapestries. The only art reflected stories from the Bible. In fact, one of the main critiques of the time of the homes of the wealthy was that they were overdone, overfurnished, and overdecorated, even with religious accessories.

Spanish, Indigenous, African, and mixed-race mestiza señoras of all other classes usually interacted in the kitchens and at the markets, where an interesting thing happened: They would share recipes for healing ailments and for general well-being, just as we might recommend a beauty brand today. Recipes containing things like herbs, roots, mushrooms, and chocolate were traded—and some were only whispered about, because some of these things were considered *brujería* (magic). For instance, chocolate was a very powerful elixir, and it was cooked and presented as magic by witchy señoras called *hechiceras* (sorceresses). These elixirs were put in drinks to make lovers come back. It was so common that Ann and Christina read of many complaints from men that they were in constant fear of women putting things in their drinks. If any señora got caught practicing *brujería*, that would mean a very harsh punishment, especially during the Inquisition.[7]

It was also the working-class señora's work to prepare cacaos, which were cooked, dried, roasted, and ground, then added to water, along with spices like vanilla and annatto. Ground cacao was also stored in blocks.

Encarnación Pinedo and the Californios (1800s)

Thanks to TikTok, Ann and Christina came across Encarnación Pinedo, a señora from one of the original Californio families who were in Mexican territory at the time of the Yankee invasion. Another one of their TikTok videos had gone viral, and an *amiga* in the comments suggested that they should pick up a book she had discovered, consisting of California women's recipes. They dug a little bit deeper and were stunned by some of the details of Encarnación's life. She was an "it girl" before the term was invented. She was from an elite Mexican family who lived in what is present-day Santa Clara County, in California (on Tamien Nation land). She had a very nice life until her family's lands were taken by Yankee invaders, who also murdered her grandfather and uncle.

She later became a cookbook author, and her book, *El cocinero español* [The Spanish kitchen], published in 1898, has become a cult classic because it was the first cookbook in Spanish to feature Mexican, Spanish, Indigenous, and European recipes.[8] She included recipes for jellies and jams, and recipes like *chiles rellenos, chilaquiles con camarones secos, salsa bechamel con setas para ostras, tamales de harina de maíz blanco, carne de ternera seca en tasajos* and, of course, *albondiguillas de merluza*. She also made it known how she felt about the Yankees who had taken her family's lives and lands by turning her nose up at their cooking, saying, "There is not a single Englishman who can cook, as their foods and style of seasoning are the most insipid and tasteless that one can imagine." What a señora burn indeed.

Your Great-Grandmothers and Grandmothers

Let's go back in time to a year when it was common to have chickens, bake your own bread from scratch, grow your own food, and listen to the evening news on the radio. Ann's *bisabuela* (great-grandmother) Maria lived in a tiny town called

Quillota, in the Aconcagua River valley area of Chile. Quillota is in the *zona central*, called the "Quinta Region," which also includes Valparaíso and the town where Ann was born, Viña del Mar. The great Joaquín Murrieta, who was the inspiration for El Zorro, is said to have been born here. (Although I know Mexico claims him, too, so who knows? Don't cancel me, please.) To this day, the area of Quillota remains an important agricultural region but is also very suburban and within just a few hours of major cities.

Ann can't promise that the scenes she's about to describe are 100 percent accurate, or that the timeline of her family's history is correct because her family left Chile many years ago, and most of the last generation has passed, so they lost touch with a lot of their family traditions. Ann can tell you what her *bisabuela*'s señora life *probably* looked like. It's a semi-fictionalized reflection of our modern lives now, and more of a romanticized version of the era rather than a historical slice of life.

If you don't know much about your own ancestral señora's routine, this will give you an idea of her day-to-day life, whether in Chile, Mexico, Peru, Puerto Rico, El Salvador, or Venezuela.

Maria's Daily Schedule, Quillota, Chile (1935)

After waking up at 5:30 a.m., Maria walks into the kitchen, where a young lady from a nearby town who helps her with household chores has already arrived and is putting on her apron. Maria's husband has already left to go to his job. Her first task is to plan the family's daily meals. With responsibility for nine kids ranging in age from nine to fifteen, she needs to be well prepared for the onslaught of the day.

Maria's home is a two-hundred-year-old Latin American colonial-style rectangular home, with side-by-side bedrooms and doors that face a covered outdoor walkway that leads to a courtyard shaded by ancient lucuma trees. It's sort of similar in structure to Frida Kahlo's Blue House, except it's gray and brown. The sun shining on the wood-planked courtyard floods the entire house with light. You need to be careful walking along the courtyard walkway barefoot, because you'll easily get a splinter from the wood.

Heading out to the *huerto* (orchard) behind the house, Maria or her helper collects eggs from the hens in her chicken coop for the day. Avocado, lucuma, and chirimoya trees are waiting to bear creamy fruit. Back in the kitchen, which faces the dirt path to the orchard, Maria grabs loaves of the *pan amasado* that she baked in her clay oven over the weekend, and alongside her helper, she begins to prepare breakfast. Avocado, ham or mortadella, freshly baked bread (sometimes from the store down the street), butter that melts just right, jam, and two types of cheese: *queso fresco* and *quesillo*, a special type of spongy Chilean fresh cheese made with cow's or goat milk, rennet, and salt. Keep in mind Mexican quesos differ a bit from South American quesos. Your great-grandmother may have had something completely different.

After breakfast, Maria's eldest child, Mercedes (Ann's *abuelita*), takes charge of the kids and ushers them out of the house. Maria begins tidying up, alongside her young lady helper, before prepping the meals for the rest of the week. She makes big pots of *porotos con rienda* (bean and spaghetti soup), *charquicán* (a stew with potato and squash, meat, onion, and garlic), and *cazuela* (yet another stew), as well as some *pan de rescoldo* (bread made directly over the fire) or chicharrónes.

In the afternoon, before the children return from their schools, Maria may pour herself a cup of black tea or may opt for herbal tea, using ingredients like mint, lemon balm, *paico* (an Indigenous Mapuche herb), or rue, which make great teas for sore stomachs or insomnia. She may decide to play her harp or guitar in the living room or spend time lounging while knitting a sweater. After her husband returns from his job, Maria and her helper will proceed to heat and serve dinner for everyone, including some uncles or aunts who have stopped by, as well as some cousins.

Perhaps later in life, as she grows older, she will do much less. She will invite her grown daughters and grandkids over in the afternoon to sit in the living room and play instruments alongside her harp or sing traditional songs. She always has guests. Sometimes they might listen to classical music, tango, or a classic bolero (an old romantic song type that originated in Cuba) on the radio. Some weekends she may also sit down and knit long blankets or create projects to hand out as little gifts to her kids, grandkids, and great-grandkids.

Through her life, you'll notice some señora moments, little corners of *tranquilidad* (calm), where you carry out an activity that makes you feel good. These rituals have nothing to do with productivity and are not goal driven. In fact, their purpose is just to force the señora to rest. Certain moments of peace and quiet in the señora's day are soothing, helpful self-care rituals that help her feel calm and joyful, despite her daily workload. These moments of what we now call "self-care," or "slow living" helped Maria and other señoras break the monotony of the day, even though back then, these activities may not have been purposely meant for this goal. They also served as an excellent transition into a señora's later years, when she may have created simple rituals, such as baking for the great-grandchildren, listening to the radio, knitting, and playing the harp. Sometimes baking or cooking one's favorite meal might even feel soothing.

Ann's great-grandmother continued to practice these rituals to the end of her life at nearly one hundred. In the 1940s her grandmother Mercedes was a wartime working mom. She was a doctor's assistant during her single years and a kindergarten teacher after marriage and kids. During her spare time, she helped the city's poor families and did her part to establish the city's first YWCA chapter, a women's club that met weekly for social hours and enriched the community with classes for building life skills and encouraging hobbies.

Mercedes's señora rituals were very eclectic. She loved knitting; crocheting; playing the guitar; preparing cakes, bread, sopaipillas (a type of fry bread), and empanadas; inhaling fiction novels and history books; recording herself and her kids on her record player, just as we do today with our cell phones; listening to local talk radio, Argentine tango, and Gene Krupa or the Benny Goodman orchestra; and drinking tea while in her kitchen.

Later in life she also napped in the afternoons to recharge for the evening routine, as many in Latin America still do. She ate light and generally stuck to healthy meals, with foods that weren't overly processed. Hers were rituals full of natural, slow living, and self-care that nourished her and likely gave her the strength to get her family through the uncertainties created by world wars, the country's economic downturn, and the very dark years in Chile during the 1960s, 1970s and 1980s.

These portraits from two generations of South American women are intended to give you a deeper understanding of where our modern-day señora era comes from and the rituals that defined them. Every culture's señoras were just as eclectic and different.

The Twenty-First-Century Señora

According to Google, the term *señora life* started trending as early as 2004. The exact origin of this meme is unclear, but it was most likely created online and ultimately shared worldwide, including among Latinos living in the US. With the introduction of Facebook, Instagram, Twitter, and TikTok, the popularity of the term exploded. Getting the urge to do things that the women of our recent past did may have signaled an important shift in our cultures. Essentially, the term was used to refer to a time in your life when you shifted to home-centered lifestyles and cozier hobbies. Articles at the time suggested it may signal an urge to slow down in our daily lives, and we were using the routines of our *tías* and grandmothers to do so. Other cultures had a similar concept called "Granny hobbies."

The simple routines look and sound an awful lot like some of the señora routines Ann and Christina have gone over in this chapter, like drinking tea or sitting on the porch with a *cafecito* or *tecito* (a little cup of coffee or tea), cleaning the house while you listen to iconic Spanish-speaking crooners Juan Gabriel, Julio Iglesias, or Luis Miguel on the radio (the equivalents of Frank Sinatra or Michael Bublé), or starting a garden. These are all signs you may have entered your señora era. If you break it down, it essentially describes a moment in your life when you begin to slow down and practice more moments of self-care, usually rooted in natural living; set up and take pride in your cozy home life; and create everyday routines that popular culture doesn't really highlight right now, because they seem boring.

There are many different reasons today's Latinas may want to be in their señora eras. Slowing down is a normal shift that might happen when you start to near your 30s, when you stop getting

FOMO (Fear of Missing Out), and no longer enjoy going out to attend parties or socializing every weekend. You start to see how lovely it is to make your home comfortable, tidy, and cozy, to craft and bake things, and to stay indoors more. It's in this era where you start to cement the routines that you will carry for the rest of your life. For example, you may remember that your grandmother loved to garden, but she likely started picking up this hobby in her thirties or forties because it was a relaxing routine for her, and so she continued it through her senior years.

However, the trend going viral on TikTok meant now that younger Latinas were being exposed to this fun phenomenon, and many started to talk about wanting to be in their own señora eras. They were sick of hustle culture, too, and wanted a way to balance their lives as they built their careers. They were just sick of being exhausted.

Here's how the phenomenon reached peak status. During the 2020 pandemic, the hashtag "Señora Era" started being used by millions of people on #hispanictok and #latinatok—a powerful TikTok ecosystem made up of millions of Spanish speakers. The meme was first used by TikTok user @adribecc, an actress and therapist from Mexico. In a hilarious Spanish-speaking video, she talks to a therapist about her señora symptoms, like keeping plants and asking people to wear sweaters because it's cold. The therapist ultimately tells her that she has entered her señora era and there is no hope.

The first viral señora era video on English-speaking TikTok, which was unearthed by *Bustle* magazine, belongs to TikTok user @pourintosoul. She documents her señora era by filming herself sipping coffee, washing dishes, and living a slow life. It received millions of views.

This prompted thousands of Latinas to document little moments of their own señora eras: drinking tea, resting, washing dishes, folding clothes—and their videos received hundreds of millions of views. The videos were positive and uplifting, set to songs from the 1950s, like Eydie Gormé and Los Panchos' "Sabor a mí," and featuring various forms of self-care. Even now, post-pandemic, the number of videos is still growing, possibly signaling a longing, a generational wish, to return to a slower life, given the harrowing, sad, and anxious last few years.

Our modern lives could not be more different than the lives of the señoras of the past. We have opportunities that women of the past could not have ever dreamt about. We have more rights and the ability to select our own path in life, as opposed to having it picked for us. We have a voice, and we no longer have to be restricted in how we dress or even sit on our balcony and in terms of whether we can leave our house safely. We can also leave the house, get a good job, and make money ourselves, so that we don't have to depend on our partner.

The modern señora era movement has borrowed a lot of the better elements from our ancestral past to help us deal with the modern stresses we have today. To Ann and Christina, being a Radical Señora is a way to mindfully cultivate the daily habits of the women of our family tree and leave out the dark side of the past, to help us feel more grounded, calm and, hopefully, a little bit happier in our lives.

CHAPTER 5

For Señoras in Their Wellness Era

Live the Slow Life

STOP WHAT YOU'RE doing and look around you. If you're somewhere in the US, everyone you see will probably die at an earlier age than their parents did.

Today US citizens are losing life expectancy years and living shorter lives. The United States has lost life expectancy two years in a row, with the average expectancy of seventy-nine in 2019 falling to seventy-six in 2021.[1] Younger people in America are dying now at faster rates than their counterparts in high-income countries, and we have the highest maternal and infant mortality rates in the economically developed world. Yet the life expectancy rate in Puerto Rico, a US territory with a Hispanic culture and ancestry, is actually improving.

Chances are you've had many great-grandparents and earlier forebears live to one hundred or close to it. Now think about older folks living today. You can probably count the number of seniors you know who lived past their eighties on one hand. As people in the US are losing years off their life, there is something interesting happening to US-based Latinos. Over the last few decades, we have been living longer than our non-Hispanic counterparts. This phenomenon is so significant that it has been studied and even given a scientific name.

In 1986, researcher Kyriakos S. Markides at the University of Texas, San Antonio, found that Hispanic people in his studies lived longer than non-Hispanic people. He created the term "Hispanic Paradox" (or "Hispanic Epidemiological Paradox" to be exact) to explain that our communities, regardless of having higher rates of diseases like diabetes and having lower incomes and less access to health care, live several years longer than our non-Hispanic counterparts. The medical community at first didn't believe him, nor did they think that his results were accurate, because–*gasp*–Latinos couldn't be healthy, right? According to media stereotypes, we eat only cultural foods that are fatty and full of unhealthy things, and our seniors don't know how to keep themselves healthy. Markides's colleagues even warned him not to publish his research.

Surprise! It's been forty years, and his findings are still correct, and this is still a phenomenon. In fact, in 2010 a National Center for Health Statistics report showed that we had a life expectancy that was more than two years longer than non-Hispanic White Americans, and in 2013 a CDC study found that we had lower death rates for the most common causes of mortality compared to our non-Hispanic White counterparts.[2] In 2014, the life expectancy for non-Hispanic White Americans was 78.8 years, compared to 81.8 years for Hispanics.

Then, researcher John Ruiz did an analysis of multiple studies (called a meta-analysis) and confirmed the "Hispanic Paradox," and he also found that our community has a 17.5 percent lower risk of dying from anything versus other ethnic groups in this country. This may mean that somewhere in the past, some ancestors at some point came to this country and brought traditions with them that they passed down through the generations. Ones that possibly made them healthier.[3]

According to family lore, Christina's great-grandmother left Mexico for California sometime in the 1900s. When she got there, she brought delicious Oaxacan cuisine to the corridors of the Bay Area, where she kept the food traditions of her region alive. Oh, how beautiful it must have been to sit in the chilly, bustling streets in turn-of-the-century San Francisco as you munched on a delicious *tlayuda* or drank some refreshing Oaxacan horchata. For her dad's side of the family, it meant having a distinct treasure trove of recipes to use in their kitchen for generations.

Now, before we anger half of TikTok again, I am not saying that we are better than everyone else. There is simply a possibility that we were given habits that keep us healthier as we age, ones that other cultures may even want to learn from and borrow.

A conversation about well-being shouldn't be only about food. Happiness and good health are interconnected. Being more positive, for example, may be correlated with a decreased risk of things like heart attacks and could even mean a longer lifespan.[4] What's more, there are differences between health span and lifespan. Lifespan means how long people live in old age, while health span means how long you remain in good health over your lifespan. You could have a long lifespan but a horrible health span if you succumb to diseases and have a bad quality of life. The ideal scenario is to improve both the lifespan and the health span, so that you lead not only a long but also a healthier life.

So, what can ancestral señoras—especially those who lived to nearly a hundred—teach us about increasing our lifespan *and* health span?

Coming to America

It was the day after Thanksgiving. Ann was forty-four years old, and she thought she was having a heart attack. She was having pain on the left side of her chest, and it seemed to be getting worse by the minute. Her entire family was visiting, and she didn't want to make anyone worried, so she didn't say anything. When a few hours passed and Ann was still in pain, her husband begged her to get in the car so that he could take her to the emergency room. Ann thought to herself, *OMG. Am I having a heart attack?* She was still young! Her anxiety went through the roof.

After the emergency room did an EKG test and gave her the green light to go home, Ann booked an appointment with her doctor, who then sent her to the cardiologist. Fortunately, her heart was fine, but Ann was told that her GERD had gotten worse. To make matters worse, her cholesterol was creeping up, and she was almost prediabetic. This meant she wasn't prediabetic but was bordering on it. Her grandmother had passed due to long-term complications of diabetes, so this put everything into perspective.

"You need to work out more. It's all about lifestyle changes," her doctor told her.

This came as a surprise to Ann, because she thought she was in good shape. She'd eaten pretty well during her twenties, an era that was accented by alcohol-fueled nights out and some pretty toxic diet habits (such as the maple syrup cleanse). Then she moved to San Francisco, the decadent restaurant and wine capital of the world. There she spent an entire decade drinking wine and eating out all the time. Ann was hyper-focused on work, which made it hard to fit healthy grocery shopping and workouts into her work schedule. She started drinking coffee excessively to keep up with the work demands, and she stayed at the office way too late, so take-out food was her love language. To relax, she would go grab whiskey or spend all weekend in Sonoma, drinking wine and wasting too much money.

When she had a baby at age forty, things just went off the rails. Her baby girl rushed into this world at the start of the pandemic, so she and her husband spent the next couple of years ordering takeout, not going to the gym, and not going anywhere, for that matter. They liked to joke that they were in a triple disaster: They were first-time parents entering their forties during a global pandemic. However, they managed to be even more unhealthy than everyone else. When everybody was stuck at home making sourdough bread, they were ordering DIY churro kits and joining mail-order wine clubs (a delicious mix but not very good for the cholesterol).

The reality hit Ann like a slap to the face. She had to figure out how to improve her lifestyle. She had never learned how to cook, and all she knew about being healthy was the trendy and toxic diets she'd picked up. This time, she needed something easy, intuitive, and nutritious.

One diet that she had always enjoyed wasn't a diet at all. Many years back, she had read the book *The Blue Zones*, which talks about a way of eating that's based on the Mediterranean diet. The book is based on data that researchers collected in countries that had the healthiest and longest-living people in the world. It turned out that such people lived in places like Sardinia (Italy), Okinawa (Japan), Icaria (Greece), and the Nicoya Peninsula (Costa Rica).[5] These researchers went around to each country on this list, observed and collected data on the lifestyle and eating habits of centenarians in each area, and created a game plan for everyone else.

In Costa Rica they found that a man of sixty had two times the chance of living until ninety as did someone living in the

There is nothing more delicious than eating fresh eggs or more grounding than collecting them each morning. *(Photo Credit: Alejandra Sone)*

Do you remember your abuela's lemon trees or your great-grandmother's *huerto*? It felt magical, didn't it? *(Photo Credit: Alejandra Sone)*

One of the most satisfying and healing routines you can create is going out in your garden every morning or evening, going out on your balcony, or just going for a walk at your local community garden. *(Photo Credit: Alejandra Sone)*

Little by little, your own *huerto* will begin to take shape. One day you may have your own strawberries *(Photo Credit: Alejandra Sone)*

Every family has had their own "secret" homemade multipurpose soap recipe for the home. This is the closest style you'll find: Ancient Aleppo style soap. *(Photo Credit: Alejandra Sone)*

When you make your own soap, you'll be tapping into soothing señora routines of the past — and you'll be creating less waste. *(Photo Credit: Alejandra Sone)*

In South America, our Mapuche indigenous ancestors used the quillay tree as shampoo, soap, and even detergent for clothing. The quillay cuttings would be boiled overnight and were even turned into shampoo. *(Photo Credit: Alejandra Sone)*

One thing many of our countries and cultures have in common is the avocado, aguacate, or palta. *(Photo Credit: Alejandra Sone)*

Chickens have their own personalities, and some can be divas.
(Photo Credit: Alejandra Sone)

A fire to gather around is a very important part of a Latin American señora's household. It is a special social time. Create your own Friday night fire routine at home, the park, or the beach.
(Photo credit: Alejandra Sone)

Tecito time can mean many things to different cultures. Create your own traditions and share them with your family and friends.
(Photo Credit: Alejandra Sone)

Señoras take notes throughout the day. My beautiful abuela filled pages of notebooks through the years with her thoughts and recetas that I can read and learn from today to keep the cultural traditions going. *(Photo Credit: Alejandra Sone)*

You'll be surprised just as how many types of *tecitos* are available to drink. The flavors are endless, and you can even start to blend your own. *(Photo Credit: Alejandra Sone)*

Yerba maté is a very specific type
of herb used in Argentina,
Paraguay, Chile, etc.
It's also very trendy right now
in wellness spaces.
(Photo Credit: Alejandra Sone)

The ingredients señoras have available
for homemade beauty recipes are endless.
Select versatile ingredients like beeswax.
More complex projects are lotions.
(Photo Credit: Alejandra Sone)

Lavender is a señora's best friend.
(Photo Credit: Alejandra Sone)

Learning the herbalism of your ancestors is good for your mood and your soul.
(Photo Credit: Alejandra Sone)

Being around animalitos will remind you that there's a bigger world outside of your problems.
(Photo Credit: Alejandra Sone)

Nothing can bring you more joy than caring for chickens and having delicious huevitos every morning. You can have a coop sometimes even if you're in an HOA. There's always a way.
(Photo Credit: Alejandra Sone)

Sometimes having chickens
is stressful, but hens
make wonderful friends.
(Photo Credit: Alejandra Sone)

Garden beds are great for you
if you have bad soil or
just want an easier start.
You'll have to buy soil though.
(Photo Credit: Alejandra Sone)

Imagine picking veggies for your dinner, just like your abuelas did at the rancho, at the parcela, or in her backyard. *(Photo Credit: Alejandra Sone)*

If you don't have the space for a garden, the next best thing is a vertical garden that you can put on your balcony or kitchen. *(Photo Credit: Alejandra Sone)*

Go outside and sit for a bit or go out for a señora walk every day.
(Photo Credit: Alejandra Sone)

Carve out some time in your day just to sit outside and breathe.
Some *tecito* is nice too, sometimes with a good book.
(Photo Credit: Alejandra Sone)

Making beautiful things with your hands will make you feel good.
(Photo Credit: Alejandra Sone)

A rosemary or romero bush is a great first herb to plant in your garden because you can make so many things with it — in the kitchen or for personal care. It also just smells good.
(Photo Credit: Alejandra Sone)

Ranchito life.
Photo Credit: Alejandra Sone)

There is nothing more delicious
than loose leaf tecitos..
(Photo Credit: Alejandra Sone)

United States, France, and Japan and had an overall life expectancy that was much higher than in most developed countries.

Centenarians from the Nicoya Peninsula eat a Mesoamerican-style diet, which includes the three sisters: squash, corn, and beans ("the three sisters" is an Indigenous concept where you plant these three crops together so that they can support each other). Typical Mesoamerican foods include corn, which is turned into tortillas, flat cakes, and tamales. They eat simple foods from the earth, which many of our ancestors were used to, and consume more plants than meat and dairy.

Specifically, the daily meal breakdown of centenarians from the Nicoyan Peninsula is 26 percent whole grains, 24 percent dairy, 14 percent veggies, 11 percent sugar, 9 percent fruit, followed by small amounts of legumes, meats, fats, and eggs. Most also drink a moderate amount of alcohol, though only socially. The centenarians in one of the Blue Zones areas completely abstain for religious reasons.

Researchers also found elements of these long-living cultures that don't have to do with food. For instance, the Nicoya Peninsula people have strong family networks: Many of the elders still live with their grown children and grandchildren. They visit their neighbors often, perform daily chores around the house and garden, and they walk a lot. The book talks about how the centenarians' Indigenous Chorotega traditions also help them avoid too much stress, and these include their interconnectedness to nature and how they honor the natural world, and their emphasis on craftsmanship.

The more Ann read about the Blue Zones, the more she realized that these habits were familiar. Our own Latin American ancestors also had strong group connections, ate nutritious, wholesome dinners, and only occasionally had treats like alcohol or pastries. Our great-grandmothers may have had fresh eggs and fresh cow's or goat milk every morning. They forged deep connections with their extended family and their friends. In fact, not a day went by without them seeing or talking to a person outside their family unit. During a typical day our great-grandmothers left their homes at least once a day—either to go to the *mercado* (farmers' market), to go out for bread, to pick up the daily newspaper, or simply to take a nice afternoon stroll. Community was everything to them.

In our modern lives, we have become accustomed to a very different lifestyle. We scarf down the Standard American Diet, which is full of ultra-processed food. Our default is now set to being inside the home all the time and having everything delivered. Ann remembers one mind-blowing conversation she had with a woman who was a recent immigrant from Colombia. When she asked her what she saw as the biggest differences between how we live here and how Colombians live, she said point-blank, "*Todos se quedan encerrados en sus casas*," which means "Everyone stays jailed inside their homes." Ann had honestly never thought that the fact we no longer left our houses was a problem. In fact, she had considered this a *benefit*. Like, we no longer have to go anywhere! Everything just comes to us! How perfect! Now we can just rewatch back-to-back *Bridgerton* seasons.

The fact that the suburbs are so spread out and you need a car for everything doesn't make things easier. We are now sitting around basically all the time. We sit as we work from home, or we sit in our cars to get to the office, where we sit for another eight hours a day. We come home and sit on the couch to watch the news. This means everything is easier, faster, lower in quality, and the complete opposite of the slow-living ways of our great-grandmothers.

We should never have normalized this. It's not normal.

Sometime over the past fifty years, a massive shift took place in the United States: the death of the community. Most of us now have never had a real conversation with the neighbors. In fact, many of us try to avoid them at all costs—we just look at them through the window suspiciously. When someone comes to our door, we panic. Gen Xers and millennials go straight to the floor like they're in a combat zone. We don't trust anyone. It's much harder right now to meet new people and make friends, creating deep connections. Too many people grow apart from their family members. Elders move away from grand-kids, and adult children move to cities where they can get good jobs. It's a sad, tangible reality. Two out of three people in the US think that they don't belong in their community. A surprising 64 percent don't feel like they belong in their workplace, and 68 percent in their nation.[6]

What's more, the foods we grew up eating or our ancestors cooked have been unconsciously demonized by modern culture, so over the past decades, we have relegated our great-grand-mother's foods to the "unhealthy" pile. Do a little thought experiment right now. Close your eyes and think about healthy food. Now open your eyes. I can almost guarantee you that cultural food from your ancestral homeland was not what came to mind. (If it did, congratulations!)

Modern trends have also worked to dismantle the love of our heritage. Brands through the history of marketing have made people believe that real well-being means things like green juice, maple syrup cleanses, detoxes, and eating only liver (yes, that's an actual diet). Trends like keto, paleo, clean, and even organic are all anybody talks about at the gym, and many of these trends have changed the way we eat in this country. Many of these wellness trends were created by smart people behind brands or by brilliant food marketers. There's nothing inherently bad about this, but it's like they've turned "being well" into something that just a small percentage of the population can afford.

The rise of wellness culture seems to be a signal that our modern culture is now making health and longevity a focus, and that's not necessarily a bad thing. Searching for tips and routines around wellness and wanting your body to be healthier became a lot easier to do after the 2020 pandemic, when staying healthy was important for everyone. But this isn't a new thing. People have been inventing wellness crazes for centuries. There was the radioactive water trend of the 1930s, when some people thought drinking radioactive water could cure you of many different illnesses. Cigarettes were once marketed as being excellent for throat health and a secret trick for women to get trim. Tapeworm pills were used as a fitness solution in the 1950s. Since then, people have even gone gaga over placenta juice, vinegar diets, and drinking untreated water. See how silly these all sound now? Wellness has been around for a long time. Unfortunately, about half of it has been a complete sham.

As Ann and Christina wrote this book, wellness was all about cold plunges, saunas, steam rooms, LED masks, cryotherapy, red light therapy, hyperbaric chambers, and paying thousands of dollars for a gym membership. Now, they are not saying these things don't work. Some of these tools and gadgets and trends may help—particularly those backed by science—but others are merely trendy things that in twenty years may go the way of eating tapeworms.

Well-being practices were carried out by our ancestral señoras for centuries. It's fine to do a cold plunge or get expensive facials. We all enjoy some of these at one time or another. The problem begins when we start to think that these practices are *required* for us to feel good.

Ann's Señora Zone

When faced with the health challenges of impending middle age, Ann knew she needed to make a big change. So, she decided she was going back to basics and would lean on what was familiar to her and what she remembered from growing up in Chile. That is how, in her forties, she actually learned how to cook for the first time in her life. First, she got herself a pressure cooker and focused on learning easy things for meal prepping for her family, incorporating chicken, beans, squash, fish, tortillas, and lots and lots of veggies. She also added things like nuts to their diet and started making her own easy dressings. They started eating dairy products like yogurt, goat milk, and feta cheese, instead of ultra-processed American cheese. This was more time she had spent in the kitchen in her entire life combined.

Ann adhered to the usual healthy eating habits pounded into our heads by doctors: She cut back on wine and coffee and started drinking tea. She also cut out fried foods and started eating more protein. Delicious things like empanadas were treats once in a while. All of these are things one does when you hit forty and you want to get healthier. Boring!

Not long after Ann started her wellness era, her husband started to complain that he felt unusually fatigued and had a hard time keeping up with their toddler. A doctor found that one of his carotid arteries—the vessels that provide blood and oxygen to the brain—was 30 percent blocked with cholesterol, which means that he had heart disease and was headed for a stroke within ten years. He started working with a nutritionist, and his new lifestyle meal plan ended up being a Mediterranean-style diet, in many ways similar to the Blue Zone diets, including an emphasis on eating little ultra-processed food. Lots of beans, veggies, and lean protein, like chicken and fish. Everything had come together full circle.

Once she got the hang of the kitchen, Ann started cooking some of the recipes she remembered from growing up in Chile. Nothing made her feel cozier than making her grandmother's zucchini with egg scramble, cooked with just a little olive oil and pepper, and sharing it with her toddler on a cold winter night. She also made her own bread. She had learned to bake bread during the pandemic, but this time she went on an all-out rampage. She relished feeding her little sourdough starter baby each day and making sure it was happy and healthy. This was completely foreign to her. Not too long ago, she had been living in San Francisco and eating takeout in her living room or rushing out to a restaurant every night. She had always hated cooking—and actually barely knew how to cook.

Then she got seriously señora and began trying out more advanced recipes. She had picked up a copy of Pilar Hernandez and Eileen Smith's *The Chilean Kitchen: 75 Seasonal Recipes for Stews, Breads, Salads, Cocktails, Desserts, and More* years before, but she'd never cracked open the book, because she'd always been just too busy with work. Ann began to dive deep into the recipes in the book. She tried what she thought was the easiest thing first, *pan amasado*, which is a South American kneaded bread made out of only flour, sugar, yeast, milk, melted butter, and water. In the book, Pilar and Eileen explain that bread is such an important part of Chilean culture that the country's most recognized poet, Gabriela Mistral (winner of two Nobel Prizes), wrote a poem called "Pan" to honor it. Pilar and Eileen were nice enough to share the recipe from the book with Ann and Christina. You'll find it at the end of this chapter.

Ann's initial experiments with the recipes were no Nobel Prize-winning creations, and she burned herself and nearly set fire to the kitchen (thankfully, the cookbook was fine). She was also so afraid of adding too much salt that she ended up not adding enough, and so her cooking became well known for being *desabrido*. But she tried again and again until she got it just right. Brushing each ball of dough with a little milk and piercing it with a fork was the coziest, most calming feeling in the world.

Nothing beats that baked-at-home smell, which takes you back to when you were a child, walking the street hand in hand with your *abuelita*, the scent of warm bread wafting from the little outdoor baskets of the *panadería*. It's the kind of memory that you'll see probably right after you die, if you believe all those descriptions of the afterlife. Some nights when she was overwhelmed with the thought of cooking because she had so much work to do, Ann learned just to throw a bunch of beans into her Ninja Foodi and add some squash, corn, veggie stock, and sweet potato. She would leave it cooking by itself, and thirty minutes later her house would smell incredible, and she would have a deliciously cozy *sopita* to serve to the entire family.

Beans became her favorite life hack, especially when she ran out of stuff to cook. When she needed to add more protein to a meal, she just looked for the beans in the pantry. Nothing made her feel more like the Head Señora than cooking a big pot of stew for the whole family, just like her great-grandmother and grandmother had done. Ann even started devising her own creations—Franken-*cocina* if you will. Dishes that were created when she started out cooking something traditional and halfway through got lazy and added her own ingredients to cut down on cooking time. She would start cooking a *cazuela* and would end up with kale and bean *sopita*. Whatever! It tasted just as good to her family. She even learned how to make cheese similar to the *quesillo* and the *queso de campo* from her great-grandmother's table.

Ann had become so disconnected from the culinary customs of her childhood in Chile, she didn't even know how to cook before entering her señora era at 40, which was embarrassing. She basically knew only how to boil an egg, and in her 20s had gotten lost in the shuffle of the trendy "wellness" diets of Los Angeles. So, there was nothing more radical for her than to say no to the toxic diet and detox culture for good and learn to cook wholesome, nourishing food just like the señoras of her family tree had done nearly a century ago.

Then something happened as she learned her way around the kitchen and created new cooking routines. She began to crave exploring more customs from her homeland. She became thoughtful about creating a new routine that got her moving. Ann planned out daily movement routines. She started walking more, sometimes after school drop-off and on other days, and found hidden trails throughout her neighborhood. She started having at least one meal outside, in her garden or on the patio, no matter what the weather was like. She created a new routine where she would go outside first thing in the morning and either sit down to drink her coffee or water her plants while sipping her *tecito*. Ann phoned friends more, texted to see how they were. She asked them how their families were doing, which was something she realized she missed from her culture. She never remembered people here asking each other how their families were.

The señora routines Ann added to her life started stacking up, and she began to feel the effects. She felt energized, and had more energy than ever before, and so that allowed her to be motivated to exercise more. She was also sleeping better. All this walking actually led to her having fewer aches and joint pains. She was even able to move easier or pick up the toddler with less effort. She lost some of the extra weight from her pregnancy.

These little changes she implemented, each inspired by the women from her ancestral past, were clearly helping her feel better, no matter how small and boring they were. Not surprisingly, her blood panel started looking better and better as she began to undo the damage that she had done over the past twenty years. Her husband's own blood analysis showed an incredible turnaround, and he is probably healthier now than he was in his thirties. Both even lost the extra fat, and worked hard to replace it with muscle, which is so important as you begin to age. From now on, there were no crazy detox diets—it was all about aging better, and helping to extend their health span.

Michael Norton, author of *The Ritual Effect: From Habit to Ritual, Harness the Surprising Power of Everyday Actions*, writes about the importance of having rituals—which are more powerful than mere habits—in your life.[7] He writes that rituals add special elements that enchant our lives, invigorate our spirit, add special meaning to the monotony of life, and help us get over challenges. By emulating the routines of their great-grandmothers, Christina and Ann were actually creating new routines, which they repeated daily or in moments when they needed them the most.

What's so radical about cooking or drinking tea at the same time every day? By mindfully and thoughtfully learning new skills or expanding on old ones, you're forcing new routines into your life. Routines keep you organized and lower your stress and anxiety, because you feel like you have more control in your life. They also free up cognitive resources by creating a template you use daily, building healthy habits, and promoting self-discipline. Following routines has even been found to help you sleep better![8] [9] It also just feels good to look forward to doing something you know you love. For example, you might have chamomile tea every evening right before bead, while reading a book. It's a special treat—especially after a hard day's work.

These señora habits that translate to our modern life increase our quality of life and help us age well.

Radical Señora Wellness Habit #1: Avoid trendy diets and junk food

While doing research for this book, Christina and Ann found that ancestral señoras ate a range of colorful whole foods. They walked to the *mercado*. They visited friends. They worked in their garden or in their rancho. They made big pots of soup and rich stews when the entire family came over on weekends. They made many things from scratch. This was a very ancestral way of eating, one that many other cultures share.

There were no "detox diets," and no one was gulping down green drinks to have the abs of some celebrity (although some girlies did covet the bodices of hot opera singers of the time). Food came from their garden, the corner store, the *mercado*, or a nearby farm. Their staples may have been the three sisters: corn, beans, and squash. Your señoras may have made delicious warm tortillas with homemade masa or warm *sancocho* if you're from the Caribbean or Ecuador or Cuba, or arroz con pollo if you're South American. These are all meals that historically were made to seem like they were bad for you or were bland and boring, and they are just now starting to get some of their shine back. So how did our cultural foods get such a bad rap?

According to dieticians who focus on Latina populations, seeing our cultural foods as "bad" may date back to colonial times, when the Spanish arrived in the Americas. They introduced things that were not available in the Americas, like wheat, pork, oil, and dairy products. Essentially, the foods of original Indigenous people were made less common and nearly extinguished with the introduction of these new foods and culturally with the idea that Indigenous foods were bad.

There are echoes of this to this day in how we talk about nutritional guidelines and examples of mainstream diets. For example, when modern nutritionists say, "Eat like this," and they show you brown rice, veggies, and unseasoned chicken, they are unintentionally telling Latino clients that this is the only correct and healthy way of eating. Latino families don't see their diverse foods represented in this visualization. That's where Latino nutritionists or books like *The Latin Anti-Diet* by Dalina Soto come in.

In many of our homelands, global trends also made our home cuisine uncool. This happened thanks to the globalization of mass media, consumerism, urbanization, and the expansion of industry and manufacturing. For example, in the early 1900s, elite Mexican señoras started viewing foods like maize, beans, and chilies, which underprivileged Mexican people ate, as inferior. They considered customs like buying produce and other foods from the street—think a street vendor or a *mercado*—uncivilized. To them, European cuisine denoted wealth and status, and suddenly no one in the upper class wanted to make their grandmother's recipes anymore.

In 1901, sociologist Julio Guerrero talked about how the underprivileged in Mexico ate "tortillas, beans, cactus leaves, quelites, zucchinis, unripe fruit, chile, little meat and no eggs." He was among the first to promote Spanish and French cuisine, instead of what they called "uncivilized" food, in order to improve Mexican citizens' diets. Private and public cooking schools, like the Escuela de Artes y Oficios para Mujeres (the School of Arts and Crafts for Women in Mexico City), began teaching European culinary arts, which have influenced generations of Mexican chefs up until this day.[10]

Doctors of the era recognized that traditional Mexican food was nutritious, but they started promoting a heavier intake of protein for the general public because they figured that "poor people's food" wasn't nutritious enough. A series of chain reactions led to the Mexican government attempting to change Mexican citizens' daily eating habits to reflect more European standards. This trickled down to señoras, who completely changed how their families ate. This ultimately created an entirely new type of "Mexican food" that would be unrecognizable to many of your ancestors.

This story repeats itself in many other Latin American countries, and as a result, some of our ancestral foods were lost to history. For example, in Chile, British tea habits began to influence the local culture when a group of fifty thousand British immigrants arrived in Valparaíso during the 1800s, creating what came to be called the Colonia Británica. This led to some transfer of food culture, giving rise, for instance, to the routine of *la once*, a practice of drinking tea with bread, and various other finger foods, which is very similar to the British "elevenses" teatime in the afternoon. In the south of Chile, there was some German influence, and this made foods like *Kuchen* (small cakes) very trendy. It also meant that during this time some of Chileans' traditional dishes, as well as Indigenous foods, started to become uncool to eat, because everyone wanted to be like those stylish European influencers! *Once* and German foods are great, but it's sad to think that their popularity at the time devalued some of Chile's Indigenous food staples, like quinoa, beans, and maize.

Little by little, señoras' traditional ways started disappearing. Later, when our families moved to the United States, many of those leftover food traditions were extinguished when our ancestors—or parents—began to assimilate. Only recently have new crops of Latin American chefs tried to reconnect with the history of Indigenous people's food culture.

Ann even remembers when certain foods arrived in the supermarkets of Chile sometime in the 1980s. Foods like sugary cereal, store-bought mayonnaise, and ultra-processed cheese and bread weren't really popular when Ann was growing up in Viña del Mar, but these things slowly became the norm there, too. Before then, you made your own mayo with eggs, lemon, and oil, you bought cheese and bread from the corner deli where it was made fresh, cereal was unheard of, and junk food—or what we called *comida chatarra*—was too expensive or hadn't even launched in Latin America. Ultra-processed food was in grocery stores, but it hadn't yet caught on. Ann even remembers when the first donut shop came to town—older folks were suspicious of this new desert from the US, but the kids were ecstatic to try them.

We can't blame the United States for all of this (maybe just the marketers). For every US resident who eats the ultra-processed SAD diet, there's a pioneer-era ancestor who harvested her own veggies. For everyone with Italian ancestry whose entire week consists of restaurant takeout, there was an Italian *nonna* a hundred years ago who made authentic dishes using fresh veggies and pasta and so on. So, what happened culturally to put us in this mess?

In *Food Politics: How the Food Industry Influences Nutrition and Health*, Marion Nestle, a pioneering professor of food studies and public health at New York University, argues that the massive shift in food habits in the United States is due to the gigantic food industry's extensive lobbying efforts, marketing strategies, and financial incentives to influence food and nutrition policies so that companies could make as much money as possible.[11] This likely began in the 1970s, when the US government answered the call to produce more food for the world, causing American farmers to increase their supply. This set off a chain of reactions that started with the government's need to sell a surplus harvest, which, in turn, shot the number of daily calories consumed by Americans from thirty-two hundred a day up to four thousand, with portion sizes getting bigger both at the grocery store and in restaurants. More notably, synthetic ingredients were added to make food more attractive to us, such as additives that made things more crunchy, colorful, and "fun," so you ended up taking in more calories than you actually needed to (in other words, the SAD diet).

This is a major contrast to other parts of the world, where portion sizes are smaller and people eat more nutritious foods with fewer calories. You remember those big plates your grandmother used to make? They likely had fewer calories and had more vitamins and minerals than any big plate at a modern take-out place.

Doesn't this make you angry? That your señora ancestors had the answers all along, but these traditions were erased? You never should have had to get mixed up with toxic diet culture or follow influencer trends or be ashamed about bringing your cultural food to school for lunch.

The research shows that the Blue Zone señora diet is truly your best bet—more whole food; less ultra-junky, ultra-processed food; less added sugars; less unhealthy fats; food more often cooked at home; and staples from our homelands, like beans, corn, squash, mangoes, and papaya, which are all full of nutrients, fiber, and antioxidants.

Beans in particular are a big part of Nicoyan centenarians' diet; they eat beans at almost every meal. They're an excellent source of protein, micronutrients, and fiber and help you stay full longer and stabilize blood sugar levels. Corn, another staple in the señoras' diet, was eaten as tortillas and in traditional dishes. This is a great complex carbohydrate and also a big source of vitamins and minerals. All this is to say that the stuff you've been eating all along is just as nutritious, vitamin packed, and essential as any of those health foods and detoxes.

You don't need to have a garden like your great-grandmother (but if you're into this, you'll read all about it in Chapter 6). Just go to the farmers' market, or at the grocery store, shop in the outer aisles to avoid junk food. Eat mostly real food that doesn't include additives, colorings, or other fake stuff that is just used to make food tastier. You could go the extra mile and talk to a nutritionist who is culturally competent, meaning they will understand your culture and country. You can create a plethora of señora era rituals just by learning about your country's cooking habits and native ingredients.

An easy way to remember what foods to avoid is to equate unprocessed food with the corn on the cob you might get at the market. Processed food would be corn from a can (still nutritious!). Ultra-processed food means the Doritos made from that corn. See the difference? Unprocessed and processed food are your friend. Ultra-processed foods like frozen pizza, packaged cookies and cakes, and powdered drink mixes should be a treat once in a while.

It's a radical idea to say you do not accept this concept that your cultural food is bad for you, and you want to use our ancestral knowledge and habits to make your life a little better.

Radical Señora Wellness Habit #2: Find your *comadres*

In 2023, Surgeon General Vivek Murthy gave a warning in the form of a report that the US was experiencing a crisis of loneliness, isolation, and connection. His team found that even before the pandemic, half of US American adults experienced loneliness and disconnection, which deeply affect mental and physical health. The risk of loneliness causing premature death was similar to the risk of dying due to smoking daily. In fact, they noted a 29 percent increased risk of heart issues, a 32 percent heightened risk of stroke, a 50 percent risk of dementia, and a 60 percent rise in the risk of premature death in those experiencing loneliness and disconnection. The report laid out a pioneering National Strategy to Advance Social Connection, which is meant to increase people's sense of community and belonging. Having social ties has been shown to lower levels of stress hormones, like cortisol, and this has a beneficial effect on health.[12, 13]

They say that when people are on their deathbed, they don't talk about their appearance or wish they were richer, or had looked younger. Instead, they wish they had had more time with their loved ones. People like us and our families who have immigrated here are intimately aware of how important social connections are. When you arrive in a new country, your connections to your homeland are cut off, and you're left without the "village" that once provided you with emotional and physical support. That's the moment when you realize just how much worse life can be without your people.

Some of us found ourselves in a world where people weren't as friendly as they were back home or eager to create a friendship. If you try to make friends, sometimes people will think that you want something from them. Here you have to pay to join a community, you have more superficial friends but no close ones, or you don't know anyone outside your smartphone. Maybe you have a few friends from work, but you don't tell them everything, and they don't come over to your house. You pay to be part of your HOA community and have access to the clubhouse. You pay for the gym or for CrossFit or Pilates to get access to a community that might share similar fitness interests. We have very few close friends but a lot of acquaintances or "party friends." We spend so much time online that a term started to trend during the 2020s where you called some people "extremely online" because they spent so much time in online communities.

In their (ironically) online community, Ann and Christina have heard so many of their *amigas* talk about how lonely life is right now. It's an isolating time right now, and we Latinos might be particularly sensitive to this, because we are literally built for community. In his article "Why Americans Suddenly Stopped Hanging Out," writer Derek Thompson analyzed government polling data and found that socializing face-to-face began to decline even before the pandemic for all genders, ages, ethnicities, and income levels, but particularly for young people and the poor.[14] In fact, from 2003 to 2022, unmarried Americans hung out 35 percent less, and for American teens, the decline in face-to-face social time was over 45 percent. He notes that several researchers and authors have speculated that this is because of three things: more screen time, less leisure time, and the fact that the country's costly housing market has forced US Americans to move away from their families.

This eventually led to the disappearance of community centers, which are what's called "third places," where people in a town gather for activities, public discussions, and information; for social services, such as childcare and advocacy; and for classes, cultural heritage celebrations, or community connection. An example of this is Hull House—founded in Chicago in 1889 by Jane Addams and Ellen Gates Starr—which became one of the most famous community houses and a model for future ones in the country. Their mission was to provide services for working-class families, particularly immigrants in the city and surrounding areas.

Even the most influential and oldest longitudinal study on happiness, the Harvard Study of Adult Development, came to the conclusion that the ticket to happiness is fostering and enjoying good social relationships. This means that all of us should be practicing "social fitness" just as much as we talk about the importance of physical fitness.[15]

The Blue Zones research uncovered how Okinawan centenarians embrace the concept of moais. In Okinawan culture, the "moai" concept means community support and social networks. It came from the Ryukyu Islands, which include Okinawa, and it manifests as a group of people who come together for a common purpose, giving each other mutual aid and overall help and support. Groups can be made up of friends, neighbors, or colleagues and serve various purposes, such as providing financial support and childcare or fostering emotional well-being. How fitting that moais are also the statues created on Chile's Rapa Nui (Easter Island) to represent ancestors, chiefs, and other very important figures—a community of ancestors.

Ask any of the *tías* in your family what it was like growing up in their homelands or in certain neighborhoods of Miami, Los Angeles, Nueva York, or Texas. They'll tell you that their family was their community, but they also had the entire community to lean on. They likely had dozens of cousins, who were also their friends, and they knew the personal life of every single family on the block. The *chisme* flowed like wine and was more like a hobby. The barbecues have likely been lit for centuries in your family tree, and everyone probably has some fun *carne asada* memories. If you still visit your homeland, you'll likely be invited to many of these wonderful *asados*.

Our grandmothers had an easier time making and keeping friends. They had a big network to get support from. When something happened and a family member was in trouble, the entire family would show up at the door. Through good times and bad, the *tías*, *tíos*, and *primos* were all there for each other. Outside the home, there were social clubs, like the Rotary Club and the YWCA and Casa de Cultura, and even resorts like those you might see in the Catskills, where families could go stay for the summer or just a weekend. It was also very common for them to gather on Sundays in churches of every denomination and follow it up with a delicious lunch surrounded by friends and family.

If they didn't feel like hanging out with the family, our grand-mothers, tías, and great-grandmothers had many organizations to choose from where they could socialize. These included women's clubs, like the YWCA, charitable organizations where you could volunteer your time to help others in need or just play a round of ping-pong or a board game.

Going back even further to your great-grandmother's and her grandmother's time, our ancestors had a wide array of places where they could connect with each other. Community gather-ing places were the focal point for socializing throughout Latin American history. In Mexico there were central plazas, called zo-calos, where the townspeople gathered for political rallies, town festivals, markets, and more. After the Mexican Revolution, Ejido systems, agricultural community centers where land was collec-tively owned by workers, met in houses for organizational meetings and social gatherings. Throughout Latin America there were Casas de la Cultura, where people could explore art, en-gage in cultural activities, and pursue education, and each city may have had a community hall for the same purpose.

In Blue Zones research, Costa Rican centenarians were shown to have very strong social connections to their families and a sense of purpose. Like our own señora ancestors, their networks consist of friends, neighbors, and family members. The elders of the Nicoya Peninsula understand the importance of having a friend group and belonging to the community, and this is tied to overall life satisfaction for them. Little did they know that this common routine is a practice that would help keep them alive and healthy to the age of one hundred.

You may be reading this and trying to get out of going outside your house more and making new friends. You're probably thinking, *Well, my husband (or partner) is my BFF. I don't need anyone else*, but according to author Rhaina Cohen, this isn't necessarily the best strategy. In her book *The Other Significant Others: Reimagining Life with Friendship at the Center*, the author argues that we can create more meaningful lives by prioritizing friendships with others over friendships with our partners. She explains that in the past, it was more common for women to focus on friendships with their girls instead of with their husbands or partners. Today you may attend a wedding and hear that the bride and grooms are also "best friends," but this is a modern phenomenon, one that wasn't common for our ancestors.[16]

In Latin America non-romantic friendships are more important than in the United States. A quick review of the research shows that networks—or what Latin American scientists call *capital social*—have been found to be important when it comes to improving economic situations, moving up at work, improving health behavior, and even creating better living conditions for older folks.[17]

When Ann goes to visit family back in her homeland, one of the weirdest things to get used to is how close everyone is to their neighbors. Much like in a sitcom, people know their entire neighborhood's cast of characters and full family history. Neighbors are often invited over for tea, dinner, or cocktails, just for fun.

Isolation and a lack of connection on this side of the world have been problematic for a few years, and they got particularly bad during the pandemic. In fact, one of the pillars in US Surgeon General Vivek Murthy's 2023 report involves "creating a culture of connection." A lot of this has to do with how we're constantly on our phones, checking the latest trending Instagram reels, or stuck on YouTube spirals. The futurist Faith Popcorn predicted this phenomenon way back in the 1980s. There would come a time, she says in grainy videos that are now on YouTube, when the digital world would overwhelm our physical life, and things would get so overwhelming for us that we would start to retreat into our little houses. She called this *cocooning*.[18] A lot of this seemed to worsen right after the pandemic, when no one was quite sure when to start socializing again, and so the default became to stay home.

A multitude of studies have closely tracked the awful mental health consequences of social isolation and loneliness. These have been linked to an increase in cognitive decline as you age, as well as depression and anxiety. Furthermore, they can affect your cardiovascular health and immune system, cause sleep problems, and even have been tied to an increase in mortality. If you feel isolated, you're also more likely to experience debilitating degenerative disorders, like dementia, later in life.

In his book *Bowling Alone: The Collapse and Revival of American Community*, author Robert D. Putnam explores the decline in social capital in the US and concludes that this decline has terrible consequences for individuals and our communities, with far-reaching implications that impact everything from democracy to public health, our mental health, and even economic inequality.[19] He argues that institutions are responsible for a revival of the community togetherness of the past, and toward this end, they must institute policies that support families more, as well as work policies that encourage work/life balance within the workplace.

We don't see this happening any time soon, so while we wait, the onus is on us to take matters into our own hands. What better way than by using your culture to create a new social framework for yourself?

Enter the *comadre*, which literally means "midwife" or "godmother," but she is more like a close friend that you talk to about everything. She was and still is an important cultural symbol of social support for women in Latin America. Even her name is powerful; *comadre* literally means "co-mother." Traditionally, the *comadre* was the godmother of your kids, but it's now come to mean a close friend beyond family, religious, or spiritual bonds. In a rite of passage called the *compadrazgo*, the godparents of a baptized child are selected as almost a third parent and enter into a kin-like connection with the family so as to always be there for help and support no matter what—especially in times of stress. *Comadres* are often the *tías* and the best friends of the family, the ones who are always there for you.

When she lived in San Francisco, the only thing that made Ann feel less lonely was a small community of professional women who got together to raise money for the LLS: Leukemia and Lymphoma Society. Through that organization, she found her own comadres whom she will likely be friends with for the rest of her life, like Anjou, Sara, Lauren, Jen, and many others. These were friends who she knew she could count on for help when anything went south, or for some simple *tecito* and gossip. Back in LA her comadres were Maggie, Liz and Desiree, who she had a long history with, and a very special bond with.

In her book *The Women of Colonial Latin America*, writer Susan Migden Socolow explores *compadrazgo*, where women visited friends to play cards and drink tea, attended church events, and attended *tertulias*, which are almost like literary coffee hours, where they talked about literature, politics, and more.

Social visits happened between five and eight o'clock in the evening, and women usually went without their husbands. During weekends, these doñas went to their country homes, where they invited friends over, cooked, and drank wine.[20] Those sound like lovely hangouts.

You may know that you're feeling isolated, or perhaps you have symptoms of feeling alone, like irritability. Use your ancestral señoras' habits to fight your feelings of isolation. The first step is to lean on your family. Invite them over. Go to their house. Bug them over text or blow up their WhatsApp. Express gratitude for the little things they do for you, and do little things for them in return, because they make a big difference.

When Ann started using her great grandmother and grandmother's routines as a model for hosting people at her home, her family's lives changed for the better. She did little things that made her guests happy. That might look like serving cookies or English tea sandwiches and tea or preparing old-time recipes. Find out what your family matriarch used to do long ago and incorporate that into your routine.

If you don't get along with your family, because they have toxic tendencies or don't accept you for who you are, find yourself some *comadres* who do. Think about the person that you love talking to. Schedule time every week to check in through text messages or even a phone call. You might schedule weekly shopping trips, followed by a *cafecito* or *tecito* at a café. Or you can go fully old school and host them for tea—or a full dinner—at your house. Ann bought herself a complete traditional tea set, and it's always a huge hit with guests. It's also helped her create her own cozy teatime routine to wind down in the evening.

You can also call on the power of your neighbors. In the United States, it was once common to know your neighbors, but that tendency was slowly lost because of mobility, digital technology, increased commuting times, the more hectic pace of modern life, and a cultural shift toward wanting more privacy. In 2016 only 20 percent of Americans spent any amount of time with their neighbors, and a third had never interacted with them.[21] Knowing your neighbors is excellent for your health. In fact, a research study in Switzerland found that a strong connection with your neighbors during COVID buffered some people from the negative effects of the pandemic on well-being and trust.[22]

We dare you to go outside right now and offer your neighbors some *empanadas* or lemons from your tree. Honestly, you'll be surprised. Sometimes people seem like they want to keep to themselves, but when you make that first connection, they will be surprised but thrilled. Simple things like this will improve your quality of life and theirs too.

Are your neighbors not your cup of tea? Start your own señora gang. Search for fun local Facebook groups that interest you or look for them on TikTok or Instagram. If you're a mom, maybe you want to join a mom group. Ann always seems to find Latina groups everywhere she goes (because we really are everywhere!). The local Latinas group in her town is a really fun group of *amigas* who go to restaurants and wineries together. Not finding any group you like? Start your own! How about a Latina mom group that goes out with their strollers or gets coffee and scones and talks smack about their teenagers? Or one that goes out with strollers and works out together? Christina and Ann didn't think they needed that type of stuff until they tried it. Being around more people, instead of being holed up in your own house, will make you a little bit happier.

The casual socializing that our ancestors did long ago served an amazing purpose—to foster wellness and mental well-being for everyone involved.

Radical Señora Wellness Habit #3:
Let's get spiritual

On the Nicoya Peninsula, centenarians also have a strong sense of spirituality. Attending church or participating in traditional rituals strengthens the señoras' social connections. They also draw on their faith to find comfort and build resilience during tough times, which helps them cope with stress. Engaging in rituals, prayers, or acts of service has also given their lives a sense of significance and direction, which helps promote well-being and resilience, especially as they have got older and have faced health issues.

Many Latinas, like Christina, are part of a church. Churches provide a sense of belonging, contribute to a sense of identity and self-esteem, and encourage you to practice acts of charity or volunteering to help others who are in need. Going to church helps you create a nice routine, where you get ready every Sunday morning, and you see your friends, learn a few new things, maybe volunteer to help people in need. It satisfies a very basic need for closeness. This is probably how her great-grandmother spent her Sundays back in Oaxaca many years ago.

If you are worried about religion's track record with LGBTQ+ issues, there are several churches that are allies and are open and in tune with the needs of the community. You might search for local LGBTQ+ churches online. According to Pew Research, those that are Presbyterian, Episcopal, traditional Jewish, Evangelical Lutheran, Quaker, Unitarian, and United Church of Christ are said to be more inclusive.[23] Catholic churches are also becoming more and more inclusive and progressive. You just have to do your research and ask around.

If you are like Ann (a "nonpracticing Catholic"), create something that speaks to you. Maybe you enjoy spiritual practices on the mat. Yoga is said to strengthen your connection to the self through mindfulness and meditation, which can encourage more inner harmony and calmness. The word *yoga* actually means integration, because the practice seeks to connect the mind, body, and spirit through postures (asanas), breathing exercises (pranayamas), and meditation, which have been shown to promote well-being overall. Ann isn't an expert in yoga principles but knows that when she's on the mat or doing some breathing exercise, she feels calmer, softer, more in tune with her inner thoughts, and ready to take on another day or week of work and chores.

In his book, *Together*, Dr. Vivek Murthy explains that another great way to connect with spirituality is through acts of service. He also emphasizes that helping others—in your community or your inner circle—is one of the most effective ways to combat loneliness and isolation. Volunteering could very well fulfill this need too.

Being a Radical Señora means selecting a practice that makes you feel like you belong, that gives you spiritual guidance, and that is (hopefully) inclusive of all people.

Radical Señora Wellness Habit #4:
Get into wellness
but don't take it too seriously

When you hit the magical age of forty, everything starts to hurt, especially if you are chasing kids around the house. If you're in your thirties, and you haven't started thinking about your health, you need to start listening to your doctor's advice now. The research is out: The earlier you begin to prepare your body and mind for the aging process, the better your aging experience will be. You'll be less likely to develop things like heart disease and diabetes, or even a degenerative disease like Alzheimer's. These little healthy habits that you stack up will add up over time.

In the 1980s it was all about "getting physical" with Olivia Newton-John. Nowadays, everyone's about their wellness eras, and there are hundreds of "antiaging" influencers on YouTube and beyond who are talking about the importance of preventive testing, working out, avoiding the SAD diet, living longer, and really making the second half of your life count.

There are some basic things that are known to help slow down or support aging. It does mostly come down to genetics, but the longest-living and healthiest señoras in your family probably walked a lot instead of sitting on the couch and watching TV; ate nutritious whole foods, like veggies, fruits, beans, tortillas, rice, corn, and other cultural foods; and dined mostly at home.

Common knowledge and your doctor—and even your holistic practitioner—will tell you that healthy aging comes down to these things:

- Regular exercise
- Healthy diet
- Adequate sleep, since when your sleep is healthy, your hormones and cells are better off
- Stress management, because chronic stress is really bad for your health
- Maintaining social connections, which create emotional well-being
- Developing a meditation or calming practice, which helps you bust stress
- Routine and early health screenings for things like cancer, high blood pressure, and diabetes
- Protecting yourself from the sun

- Drinking enough water throughout the day, which helps your entire body, including your digestive system and skin
- Continued learning as you age and pursuing hobbies and the things you love to keep your mind sharp

These are time-tested habits that were the keys to good health and better aging for the señoras of the past. Truly, this list reads like the daily life of a typical señora. It's the way our great-grandmothers, grandmothers, and many women in our ancestral line lived; rooted and grounded in family and community life and healthy living. It's likely why embracing our inner señora helps us feel better overall. It's a way of life that encourages health and wellness, because these are time-tested, free habits promoted by cultures and doctors all over the world. It really is as simple as that.

The trend right now is for extreme antiaging online content, and you're seeing things like how to optimize your daily life, so that you age better and feel better, with things like injections, drugs, cold plunges, genetic tests, cryotherapy, and many supplements and protocols.

However, beware if you get some of your health knowledge online about these topics. You should primarily be listening to doctors with legitimate medical degrees, dietitians and nutritionists, physical therapists, and others who don't really have much to sell you, especially when it comes to something like supplements. That means more likely taking the word of your own doctor, maybe getting a second or third opinion if you're unsure about something you're feeling. Just don't go down the rabbit hole of "YouTube MD."

So, how do you know you're getting wellness information from a good source? Always ask yourself, "What are this person's credentials? Are they fake or legitimate degrees? Are they from real schools? And is this person trying to sell me something?" Look at the "About Me" section, and then look at what products they are selling or what brands they push. Type their medical claims into Google and see what you find. Sometimes wellness content is more entertainment and fun to watch, and it can be soothing, but make sure you're digesting it carefully.

Radical Señora Wellness Habit #5: Just nap

Señoras all have one thing in common, and that is that they take naps regularly. One of the things Ann misses the most about her homeland is the short, delicious catnaps, which leave you more refreshed and energized than if you had just had a *cafecito*. Naps aren't as standard in the United States as they are in your family's homelands, but a good 80 percent of US residents nap right now.

In Latin America entire towns nap together. Travel to any city and you'll find that shops close at 3:00 p.m. for a few hours, and that's usually because everyone goes home to nap or grab lunch. In some Spanish towns, as in many of your homelands, businesses shut down at around 1:00 p.m. and stay shut down until 3:00 p.m or 4:00 p.m., and it's a ghost town until everyone comes back to open up for dinner or an evening coffee. That sounds lovely, doesn't it?

What's so special about naps, and why should you consider adding one to your routine? Many research studies have highlighted the benefits of napping to cognitive function, mood, and overall health. One study conducted by Catherine E. Milner and Kimberly A. Cote and published in the *Journal of Sleep Research* in 2009 found that short naps (around ten to thirty minutes) can improve alertness, enhance cognitive performance, and mitigate the negative effects of sleep deprivation.[24] A study by Brooks and Lack that was published in the journal *Sleep* in 2006 showed that naps can improve memory consolidation, leading to better learning and retention of information.

However, there are caveats to consider when it comes to napping. Research suggests that naps longer than thirty minutes can increase the likelihood of experiencing sleep inertia, which can impair performance immediately after waking. Another concern is the potential impact of napping on nighttime sleep quality, especially if naps are taken too late in the day or if they disrupt the regular sleep-wake schedule. To avoid this, either avoid napping or sleep longer at might. Experts say twenty- to thirty-minute naps are ideal.

If you work from home, that's the ideal situation for napping. If you work outside the home, take a quick catnap when you get home. Otherwise, weekend naps should help out a lot.

Radical Señora Wellness Habit #6: Keep your socks on and don't open a window

A señora's folk tales are legendary. The moment you felt an uncomfortable tickle in your throat, your *abuela* or *tía* would suggest you put your socks on and never go outside with wet hair. You would roll your eyes so hard that you could see behind you.

Modern science is actually now confirming that some of these señora "old wives' tales" are partially right! Here are just some of the *remedios caseros de señoras* (natural remedies of señoras) that turned out to be true.

1. Swallowing a teaspoon of honey for your sore throat: Some research has found that giving kids a spoonful of honey before going to bed helps symptoms and diminishes discomfort.[25]

2. Gargling with salt for a cough or sore throat: Yes, gargling with salt water has been shown to ease symptoms of a cold by getting rid of excess fluid in your throat and also loosening mucus.[26]

3. Eating soup for your cold: Eating soup will hydrate you, the salt in the soup will help your sore throat, and the soup's heat will help your sinuses.

4. Keeping your socks on: As much as we hated to hear, "*Ponte los soquetes*," there is something to this. Studies have found that people whose feet were chilled for twenty minutes were more likely to get sick, possibly because cold constricts the blood vessels in your nose, and dries out your nasal passages, providing an optimal pathway for bacteria and viruses to enter your body.[27] What's more, noroviruses have been shown to replicate more in colder temperatures. So put on those socks, and your jacket, or you may literally catch a cold.

5. Using Vicks VapoRub (aka Vaporu): This has been in señoras' medicine cabinets for more than 125 years. There is something to this goopy medicine that's the favorite of abuelas everywhere. Vicks has been found to work by cooling your air passages and tricking your brain into thinking your throat is clear and you're breathing better, which helps you sleep.

Radical Señora Wellness Habit #7: Get that smartphone out of your face

Señoras of the past didn't have a personal computer inside the pockets of their aprons, with an entertainment portal made up

of millions of articles and podcast episodes. We are really addicted to our smartphones. It's bad. We're basically a very scary
social experiment, the first generation to always to carry this
thing and have it in our faces all day and night long.

When the first smartphones launched, we were all excited
to be connected to our friends. But one evening, while at a bar
in Hollywood, Ann remembers looking around, and everyone
was staring down at their phones (back then it was a T-Mobile
Sidekick), the glare of social media staring back at them. At first,
she thought it was exhilarating and cool, and it would usher us
into a whole new era of an optimized, tech-enabled lifestyle.
Here we are twenty years later, and adults are more depressed
and isolated than ever before, and kids and teens are having a
mental health crisis. Members of Gen Z are more likely to be depressed, and the risk of suicide doubled for kids between the
ages of ten and seventeen between the years 2007 and 2017. Researchers think this may be due to screen time.[28]

Many studies since then have found that using social media
too much, constantly scrolling, watching short video content,
and receiving lots of phone notifications have contributed to
worsened attention spans and a harder time concentrating on
tasks. There is even research that shows the higher your social
media usage is, the more depressed you're likely to be.[29] Today
we are spending three to four hours per day on our phones,
which adds up.

In his book *The Anxious Generation: How the Great Rewiring
of Childhood Is Causing an Epidemic of Mental Illness*, author Jonathan Haidt warns about the big problem of kids and
smartphone usage. Research is showing that too much smartphone use too early is having devastating effects on our kids'
brains and also increasing anxiety, depression, the risk of suicide,
and much more. Young boys are burying their noses in content

that's bad for them—pornography and gaming specifically—and girls are facing lower self-esteem and self-harming behaviors due to too much exposure to the unrealistic lenses of Instagram.[30]

We're simply on our phones way too much, and it's making us depressed, isolated, and weird. One researcher found that when we use our smartphones, neurological connections are created in the brain that are similar to those of opioid addiction and how drugs like Oxycontin work on pain.[31] Other studies have found that overuse of social media leads to more self-reported isolation, depression, and anxiety. Research published in the *Journal of Social and Clinical Psychology* in 2018 found that the less participants used social media, the less depressed and lonely they were.

How do you break the dependence? In her book *How to Break Up with Your Phone*, author Catherine Price outlines fifteen questions to ask yourself to find out if you're overusing your phone and if it's affecting your quality of life. For example, do you have a hard time going anywhere without your phone? Is your phone always with you—including at the dinner table?

We can almost guarantee you that our ancestral señoras were more grounded, more in the moment, and more focused than you are. Instead of having their faces on a cell phone all the time, they were reading magazines, listening to the radio, or reading a good book. They would have been horrified to see a group of people sitting around in a circle, looking at their phone; or parents focused on Instagram instead of on their toddler; or kids watching terrible content on YouTube all day long instead of playing outside.

You might start by setting limits on your phone use. We know it's hard for many of us to do this, because some of us check our emails constantly for work. Because of this, we can't give you a limit, so do what works for you, but we can recommend what helps us set limits. Start to subscribe to print magazines and weeklies with long-form articles, like *The Atlantic*, *National Geographic*, *Vogue México*, and more. Get lost in an audiobook instead or get sucked into the latest podcast series everyone's talking about. It's basically like the señoras' radio shows. Pick up a book again. It's refreshing to see people reading in a waiting room instead of on their phone.

In her book, Price talks about the profound impact that adding playfulness and fun can have on your well-being, after you put your phone down. She recommends embracing hobbies, connecting with loved ones, or seeking new adventures–things you may have never tried before. She reminds us that joy is not a luxury but a fundamental aspect of leading a fulfilling life. This is a powerful thing.

It's radical to go against the grain and pull out a book or a podcast instead of a smartphone and give your attention span a break, just like the señoras of the past.

Radical Señora Wellness Habit #8: Balance your news

Ann gets irrationally angry when someone tells her to turn off the news. There is a lot happening right now, especially things that are affecting our communities, and we need to remain informed and fight things like misinformation and people trying to sell you wacky things or get you to join all kinds of cults. However, there is such a thing as too much news. To increase your quality of life, you need to avoid doomscrolling and getting sucked into constant tragedy porn. Consume news carefully, try not to spiral too much, and don't get your news only from TikTok. To be a knowledgeable, intelligent consumer of media, limit your intake of news, make sure your news is from a variety of sources, and don't spend your entire day sitting on the couch.

Look, in some regards, we are much better off right now than the señoras of the past. For instance, it's safer in the street for children. Right now, crime levels in the United States are as low as they were in the 1960s, and only 2 percent of US residents are victims of violent crime, and 15 percent of some type of misconduct. During the time when our ancestral señoras lived, there were violent government overthrows, revolutions, tanks in the streets, economic crises, overall instability, world wars, civil wars, and more. The difference is that we're now seeing *all* the crime on our TV screens, social media, the Apple News app and, of course, on Nextdoor. The more we see bad things happening, the more it feels like it's everywhere around us. Instead, tune out the clickbait and balance real news with positive content, which can be anything that makes you feel good. For example, when Ann is overwhelmed with the news, she turns on her favorite health and wellness podcasts and YouTube channels, because that makes her feel grounded and motivated.[32]

Radical Señoras stay aware of world events, but don't go overboard and don't let it run their lives.

Radical Señora Wellness Habit #9: Start an *asado* wellness tradition

A few months back, Ann's great-aunt visited her from Chile. Ann was just learning to light the firepit and asked her great-aunt if she wanted to join her outside to help. As she fumbled with the coals and the paper, Ann's great-aunt graciously took the materials from her and said, "Let me help." Ann thought, *Sure, why not?* But she hoped her great-aunt would be careful not to burn herself. The wise family señora then proceeded to expertly add the coal and the paper to the charcoal chimney, light the paper just so, and turn the pit into a perfect fire in about five minutes. Ann was flabbergasted. How did this señora know how to light a fire so well?

There is nothing more culturally *us* than the *asado*, and it's true for most Latin American countries. Barbecues are central to Latin American culture and are done often, usually with no special occasion needed. They provide a time for families to spend together and keep each other up to date on the happenings of family life. They are also good for helping to pass down recipes and special ingredients that are specific to your particular culture, they provide a symbol of the hosts' hospitality toward friends and neighbors, and they force you and everyone else to get outside.

Firing up your firepit out back is a great way for you to connect with your family, relax after a long week at work, or just listen to your podcast, while forcing yourself to get outside for some fresh air. Studies have even shown that *asados* can help lower blood pressure. Researchers believe this is because, for our prehistoric ancestors, fire symbolized *safety, nourishment, warmth, and light*, creating a sense of comfort and security.

If you don't have a backyard, find a park or a beach that allows barbecues, but be sure to bring a comfy chair and blanket and invite family or friends to join you. Create your very own personalized *asado* routine. Learn new ways to grill; ask family members or grab cookbooks. Buy new tools and try new meats to grill every week. Upgrade to grilling fish and veggies, or stick things like clams and mussels on the *parrilla*. Make it your own. Barbecue traditions vary across cultures, including everything from *asados* to *churrascos*, and from *carne asada, barbacoa,* and *lechón asado* to *puerco asado.* You'll find so many new techniques to level up your barbecue style. If you have kids, throw in some s'mores, too.

Radical Señora Wellness Habit #10: Know your *sopitas*

Both of Ann's *abuelitas* used to make this bright green soup, which she hated. It was kind of a lazy soup, where they would just throw onions, zucchini, potatoes, greens, and squash into a pot, cover them with water, add olive oil and salt, cook, and then blend. She hated the soup because it was a gross color. Ann knew it was all veggies, and all she wanted was *jamón con queso* sandwiches.

However, it's been four decades, and she has come to the realization that this goopy green señora soup was perhaps the most wholesome, healthy, and nutritious dish her family ever ever made. Ann has seen detox programs at posh restaurants and wellness clinics, as well as meal plans, that offer these types of green soups for health, wellness, and rejuvenation, and they cost one hundred dollars more than the soups our grandmothers made. The other day she saw soups being sold at an LA farmers' market, where people were lined up to get their batch of green soup.

Now when Ann finds herself with a big batch of greens and zucchini, she throws everything into a pot, adds onions and seasoning (not too much salt), and blends it all together. Then she tops it off with olive oil. It's among the easiest ways to get five to seven servings of antioxidant- and vitamin-rich vegetables into your diet each day, and it's an excellent way to give more nutritious food to your little one, as a substitute for more ultra-processed meals.

Our cultures are absolutely full of gorgeous, nutritious, hearty, and delicious soups. In your culture, it may be *caldo de pollo* (chicken soup), *pozole rojo o verde, sancocho, sopa de lentejas, sopa de arroz con albondigas, mondongo, aguadito de pollo,* and so much more. Some of these soups may hold a special place in your heart because the señoras you knew and loved very likely used to cook them for you with love. Learning to cook these soups and making them for yourself as self-care or for your family to enjoy is a radical act, because you're keeping this significant, healing tradition going through the ages, long after your loved ones have passed.

Radical Señora Wellness Habit #11: Cut back on booze

Some of y'all are gonna hate me, but what doctors are saying right now is that no amount of alcohol is healthy. Remember those research studies in the 1990s and the aughts that said that red wine was good for your health? It turns out that later studies questioned whether the amounts of resveratrol in red wine was sufficient to produce any health benefits. Worse yet, a reevaluation of the data shows that any benefit of red wine may not outweigh the risk that's associated with drinking alcohol. Alcohol is a carcinogen, which means it's been correlated with increased cancer risk. Some of those "studies" from the 1990s and the aughts were actually funded by the alcohol industry.

Moderation was once the recommendation, but that's now shifted to light drinking—meaning one to two drinks per week. Small drinks (not slushie sized).[33] Both Ann and Christina nearly cut out drinking during their wellness eras and saw drastic improvement in their health and how they felt each day.

They also credit that with improving things like their cardiovascular health and fat loss. They tend to stick to either one glass per week or drinking only during special events. Excellent alternatives include really getting into mocktail culture, selecting alt drinks like kombucha, and upping your tea game.

Pan Amasado (Kneaded Bread)

Photo of Pan Amasado from the book The Chilean Kitchen. PHOTO CREDIT: ARACELI PAZ. THE CHILEAN KITCHEN. SKYHORSE, 2020.

Makes 12 small loaves

Pan amasado *is generally a small production, made by individuals who sell it baked fresh, and it is entirely handmade.*

Along the highway from approximately the fourth through the eighth region of Chile, you will see people shaking a white cloth at arm's distance, and that means that somewhere nearby, there is an horno de barro *(wood-fired clay oven) where someone is bak-ing the next batch of empanadas or* pan amasado. *If you happen to be driving by and you see the white cloth, you'd be a fool not to stop and pick up a dozen loaves.*

The milk wash gives this bread a crisp crust, and the single rise yields uniform holes and a crumb that makes the bread re-sistant and springy. When it's hot, tear off pieces and spread them with butter or top with salsa verde/*parsley-onion salsa. Larger loaves of* pan amasado *are used for sandwiches, like the* chacarero/*farmer's steak sandwich. Bread is such an elemental food and so important in Chile that Gabriela Mistral, one of Chile's two Nobel Prize-winning poets, wrote the poem "Pan" in homage to it.*

INGREDIENTS:

1 teaspoon granulated sugar
1 cup warm water
1 packet dry active yeast
4 cups all-purpose flour
1½ teaspoon salt
2 tablespoons melted butter
¼ cup milk, for brushing

INSTRUCTIONS:

Dissolve the sugar in the warm water in a small bowl and then add the yeast. Mix and let rest for 10 minutes. The yeast mixture should be foamy.

Meanwhile, add the flour and salt to the bowl of a stand mixer set with the paddle attachment and combine. Next, add the melted butter and mix.

With the mixer running on slow, add the reserved yeast mix-ture to the flour-butter mixture. Work until a soft dough forms.

If required, add more water 1 tablespoon at a time. Switch to the dough hook and knead for 5 minutes.

Divide the dough into 12 equal portions and roll each one into a ball and place it on a baking sheet. Cover the baking sheet with a kitchen towel and let the dough balls rise for 1 hour.

Preheat the oven to 350°F.

Brush each ball with milk and pierce the surface three times with a fork.

Bake for 30 minutes, or until golden.

Enjoy warm.

Oaxacan *Tlayudas*

CREDIT RECIPE: ART RODRIGUEZ-CHAVEZ

Tlayudas hold a special place in Oaxacan cuisine and are often referred to as the "Mexican pizza" due to their size and the layering of ingredients. They are a staple in local markets and street food stalls, and are commonly enjoyed during social gatherings and festivities. The dish showcases the rich agricultural heritage of Oaxaca, emphasizing the importance of corn, beans, and locally sourced produce in the regional diet.

The preparation and consumption of tlayudas also highlight the communal aspects of Oaxacan culture. Vendors often engage with customers in lively exchanges, reinforcing social bonds and community ties. This tradition has been preserved over generations, with recipes and techniques passed down within families, underscoring the dish's role in cultural continuity.

We selected this dish—made by our good friend Art Rodriguez-Chavez from Latino Foodie (latinofoodie.com)—because it's likely one that *Christina's ancestors brought from Oaxaca to San Francisco.*

Tlayudas *refers to the dish as well as to the large corn tortillas used to prepare the dish. Store-bought* tlayudas *are precooked, but they can lose some of their crispness. Reheating them in the oven or on the grill brings back that crispness.*

If you can't find tlayudas *at your local Mexican market, you can roll your own using prepared masa. Divide the masa into balls and then flatten each ball into a disk with your hands. Next, roll out the disks between two pieces of parchment paper to a diameter of twelve to fourteen inches. Carefully place a disk in a large skillet or on a hot comal over medium heat and cook it until it is crispy on both sides, about five to eight minutes.*

Asiento *(sometimes spelled* aciento*) is a traditional Oaxacan paste made from leftover cooked meat (usually pork) and rendered fat. It is used sparingly, the way some smear butter on a warm tortilla.* Asiento *is a more flavorful spread than butter. If you substitute two ounces of coconut oil or olive oil for the lard or shortening in the recipe, the resulting asiento will have the aroma of coconut or olive oil. Use chicharrónes with meat attached (*chicharrónes con carne*) for the best results. You may also substitute crispy pork belly.*

Whole pieces of grilled meat, such as cecina *and* tasajo*, are often placed on top of the* tlayudas*, but you can slice the grilled meat before serving.*

Makes 2 *tlayudas*, 2 to 4 servings

Asiento

INGREDIENTS:

> 1 cup chopped *chicharrónes de carne*
> ¼ cup vegetable shortening or lard

INSTRUCTIONS:

Combine the ingredients in a food processor and process until smooth. Spoon the *asiento* into a container and store it in the refrigerator until needed. *Asiento* may be refrigerated for up to one month.

Tlayudas

INGREDIENTS:

2 cooked *tlayudas*

2 heaping tablespoons *asiento*

1 cup refried black beans

1 cup shredded green cabbage

1 cup shredded Oaxacan cheese

1 medium Hass avocado, peeled and sliced

1 medium tomato, sliced

OPTIONAL TOPPINGS:

2 tablespoons minced cilantro

2 radishes, sliced

¼ cup crumbled cooked chorizo or Soyrizo

¼ pound grilled meats, such as *cesina* and/or *tasajo*

Salsa, to taste

INSTRUCTIONS:

Preheat the oven to 375°F.

Spread 1 tablespoon asiento and ½ cup beans on each *tlayuda*. Sprinkle half the cabbage and half the cheese over each *tlayuda*. Top each with the avocado and tomato slices and add the optional toppings of your choice. Place the *tlayudas* on baking sheets and bake until the cheese has melted, about 5 to 8 minutes.

Serve the *tlayudas* at once with salsa, if desired.

Oaxacan Horchata
CREDIT RECIPE: ART RODRIGUEZ-CHAVEZ

Makes 8 servings

INGREDIENTS:
1 cup uncooked long-grain white rice
½ cup raw almonds
2 cinnamon sticks
12 cups water
1 cup granulated sugar (or ½ cup monk fruit sweet-
    ener or ⅔ cup agave syrup, or to taste)
1 teaspoon vanilla extract
Ice, to serve
Prickly Pear Syrup, to serve (see recipe below)

INSTRUCTIONS:
Combine the rice, almonds, and cinnamon sticks in a large
bowl and cover with 4 cups of the water. Stir briskly with a
spoon, cover with a clean kitchen towel, and allow the mixture
to soak for at least 4 hours and as long as overnight. Meanwhile,
make the Prickly Pear Syrup (see recipe below).

Strain the rice mixture through a fine sieve and discard the
soaking water. Add the rice mixture and 3 cups of the water to
a blender and puree on high for 3 minutes.

Strain the rice liquid through a fine sieve into a pitcher and
discard the solids. (If you wish, strain the liquid a second time
through a nut milk bag for a smoother horchata.)

Add the remaining 5 cups water, the sugar, and the vanilla
to the rice liquid in the pitcher and stir until the sugar has dis-

solved. Pour the horchata into glasses filled with ice. Drizzle 2 tablespoons Prickly Pear Syrup on top and enjoy.

Store horchata in your refrigerator for up to five days.

If the horchata separates while in your refrigerator, gently stir it before serving.

Prickly Pear Syrup for Oaxacan Horchata
CREDIT RECIPE: ART RODRIGUEZ-CHAVEZ

This aromatic Prickly Pear Syrup is delicious, but if you prefer the flavor of strawberries, you may substitute fresh strawberries (12 ounces) for the prickly pears in this recipe to make Strawberry Syrup.

Makes approximately 1 cup

INGREDIENTS:

6 red prickly pears, peeled

1 cup water

⅓ cup granulated sugar, or to taste (or use 3 table-spoons monk fruit sweetener or 3 to 4 tablespoons agave syrup, or to taste)

1 tablespoon freshly squeezed lime juice

Pinch of salt

INSTRUCTIONS:

Place all the syrup ingredients in a blender and puree on high for 30 seconds.

Strain the puree through a fine sieve directly into a medium saucepan and discard the solids. Cook the prickly pear liquid over medium-high heat, stirring occasionally, until it thickens slightly, about 10 to 12 minutes.

Transfer the syrup to a bowl and allow it to cool. Cover and refrigerate until needed. Prickly Pear Syrup may be refrigerated for up to 5 days.

It's easy to focus on the sweet and beautiful side of our great-grandmothers' lives in the homeland, but we must not overlook the fact that there was a lot of bad stuff happening back then. There was asbestos in the walls of many homes. There was lead in the pipes and in many foods. It was common for children to get run over or die from a sickness as common as the flu or as horrible as the bubonic plague, which raged through South America in the 1930s. Things like domestic abuse often went unchecked and were just seen as "normal things married people do." Men smoked cigars pretty regularly (some still do!), and they drank a whole lot. Some *tío abuelos*'s adventures in town were probably legendary. Yes, maybe sometimes it resembled the Wild West from *Back to the Future Part III*. I don't want to take away from the fact that the past was not, in fact, very health and wellness oriented. But being a Radical Señora means understanding this fact while learning from how the señoras of the past dealt with those difficult times. It means taking the best of their coping habits and making them your own.

CHAPTER 6

For Señoras in
Their Clean Beauty Era

Casera *Beauty Rituals*

A FEW YEARS AGO, Ann decided to undergo IVF after she received some difficult news. She was in her late thirties, about to
get married, and curiously decided to get her eggs checked.
She had no reason to worry, because she felt healthy, and results from her physicals were always good enough. But when
she got her test results back, she was mortified. One doctor told
her she had the egg count of a woman 10 years older than her,
meaning her egg supply was quickly shrinking and she didn't
have much time left to have a baby.

The IVF procedure is long and painful. First, your eggs are
retrieved with this very long needle. Then sperm and the eggs
are mixed in a petri dish. Then one or more fertilized eggs are
placed back into the womb. It's a tough process: You have to
take countless meds and daily injections, all of which turn you
into a weepy, bloated mess for a few months.

Ann had only one shot for this to work, because each round
is very expensive, and her insurance covered only one round

of treatment. Like any diligent, goal-oriented Latina, she leaned in and tried to learn everything she could about how to increase their chances of it working. In one of the most popular books about conceiving, *It Starts with the Egg*,[1] author Rebecca Fett gives a science-backed overview of the research around environmental factors that might influence egg quality and IVF success. Ann was shocked to learn that it's not just genetics that plays a role in the success of a treatment, and the quality of the eggs and embryo, but the environment, too. For example, research has found that antioxidants, a balanced diet, vitamins, good sleep, and the avoidance of BPA and phthalates all play some role in egg development and quality. How much is still up for debate.

All these healthy habits seemed in line with what some clinics ask you to do before you undergo the procedure. For example, doctors ask you not to wear deodorant, perfumes, or any strong scents, because some of the chemicals in these products could harm the embryo, which is particularly sensitive to environmental conditions.

You might be asking yourself, "What does this have to do with beauty?"

In beauty and personal care products, the term *fragrance* can be used by companies as a catchall term for thousands of chemicals. There are some chemicals that have been shown to suppress the growth of ovarian follicles, which are responsible for releasing the egg. There is actually a connection between having high concentrations of phthalates in your bloodstream and suffering from fibroids or endometriosis and even possibly cancer. These chemicals are linked to BPA, which is in things like Tupperware and other food containers, usually made from plastic. In fact, BPA has been linked to chromosomal abnormalities and miscarriage.[2] [3]

Many of these and other synthetic chemicals are in things that you use every day, so they're hard to avoid. The problem, however, is when you put them on your body every day for many decades. This increases what's called your toxic load, which is repeated and prolonged exposure to these chemicals, which can contribute to their accumulation in the body. This may overwhelm the body's natural detoxification mechanisms and lead to bad health effects over time.[4]

Well, you better believe Ann went through her bathroom cabinet, shower caddy, and makeup bag and got rid of any tube, powder, or bottle that had some of these problematic ingredients in it and that had a fragrance. Ann may have gone a little overboard, but she wanted to do as much as possible to make this work. After all, she and her husband had only one chance for IVF to work (because of health insurance), and so she wanted to give this round of treatment everything she had.

Something happened after her skin-care detox, however. Her skin cleared up, and her hair became luxuriant. Her mood also improved, she stopped having weird hot flashes and her periods improved, becoming more regular and less heavy. It was likely that Ann had started to have perimenopause symptoms, and this helped her with these symptoms too. Everything she'd done leading up to her IVF procedure—generally getting healthier—had considerably improved her everyday life.

Ultimately, her IVF procedure didn't work; but immediately after, she got pregnant without the technology, which was remarkable given she had such a diminished ovarian reserve. Ann would like to think it was because of all the changes she had made. She came out of that IVF era with a new skin-care routine. She became hyperaware of the ingredients in her personal care products. Her philosophy today is to try to buy things that have minimal, high-quality ingredients or to use brands she trusts. Ann always looks at the ingredient list, and if there is any ingredient she doesn't know, she'll take the time to look it up.

Christina's Health Scares

If you're thinking about getting breast implants, Christina will be the first to tell you that you need to do some deep digging into the potential risks of the procedure. In her late thirties, she began to have strange symptoms, like extreme fatigue, joint pain, brain fog, weird rashes, and autoimmune issues. She even had a breast cancer scare. Her symptoms were suspiciously similar to those of something called breast implant illness, which is a series of symptoms that women with breast implants began talking about over the past decade.[5] Researchers think this illness could be due to things like silicone toxicity, where one's biology reacts negatively to the silicone in the implants; immune system reactions leading to inflammation; or bacterial or fungal contamination of the implants.[6]

Christina was introduced to a Facebook group with hundreds of thousands of women who all felt just like she did. They shared their symptoms and resources for getting healthy again. Like many of the women ended up doing, Christina went through the long process of getting the implants removed. This inspired her to do a personal care routine overhaul and she got rid of most of the makeup that she had used throughout her life, because she had read about the possible links between some beauty product ingredients and bad long term health outcomes. She learned how to read the ingredient labels on beauty products and, like Ann, avoided anything that had a potentially problematic reputation.

Ann and Christina's two experiences, which they shared with so many women, were the backdrop for how their beauty line was created, which landed at major beauty retailers.

Some Background on the Beauty and Personal Care Industry

Just a few weeks before the writing of this chapter, the FDA found concerning levels of mercury in skin-lightening creams, and in 2022 it was discovered that when used, some hair-straightening products released formaldehyde, which is a hazardous material and classified carcinogen associated with neurological effects.[7] In 2016 the FDA had pushed a major mall "children's beauty" store to recall its products for kids that contained asbestos. And in 2024, a woman in Boston lost part of her vision due to high mercury levels in the skin-lightening beauty creams she had in her home.[8]

A study conducted in 2021 at the University of Notre Dame, Indiana University, and the University of Toronto found that over 50 percent of cosmetic products sampled contained high levels of PFAS ingredients. These per- and polyfluoroalkyl substances are a harmful class of chemicals widely used in consumer and industrial products, including Teflon, nonstick coatings, and water-resistant packaging. However, these compounds have been linked to a host of adverse human health effects and may be toxic even at extremely low doses.[9]

What's even more concerning is that many of these are products that our communities use a lot, like hair-straightening chemicals. Latinas spend 30 percent more on beauty products than the general population, which means that we are taking more of these chemicals into our bodies over the course of our lifetimes. There are racial disparities in reproductive health, and some researchers have been studying ethnic differences in endocrine-disrupting chemicals.[10] There also seems to be a connection between endocrine disruptors in hair products—especially those for curly hair, which women of color tend to use more often.[11]

This all sounds scary, but there is no need to panic. Everything is made up of chemicals, including food and beauty products. To assess the safety of chemicals in food and personal care products, the FDA (Food and Drug Administration) tests how we use these chemicals in our daily lives. They measure the safe "daily intake" of a chemical that humans might consume each day. Anything beyond that they consider dangerous. The research that's been done is also correlational in nature, and causation (meaning proof that one thing causes another) is always very hard to prove. *Pero uno nunca sabe.* One never knows.

Unfortunately, at the time of this writing, the beauty industry is not regulated and lacks transparency, and the FDA has very little of the oversight needed to act quickly when an ingredient shows adverse health reactions. The FDA basically have their hands tied. There are many organizations that are tracking these problems in the personal care industry and trying to create change, such as the Environmental Working Group and Think Dirty, and there are even regulatory bills that are trying to fight this. Many retailers, including Credo Beauty, Whole Foods, the Detox Market, and others, have made it a mission to sell only products that meet certain safety standards and quality.

Researchers Ami R. Zota, a population health specialist at Columbia University, and Bhavna Shamasunder, assistant professor of Urban and Environmental Policy at Occidental College, wrote an opinion piece for the *American Journal of Obstetrics and Gynecology* in 2017 in which they discuss how much companies have failed to disclose ingredients that may be problematic to re-productive health, and have also historically targeted certain beauty products to Black, Latina, and Asian women.[12]

This means that some products that are being marketed to Latinas and other women of color tend to have more question-able ingredients. Oftentimes, these ingredients are cheaper, which means companies can charge us less for beauty items but still make a huge profit. Some of the makeup products that you find in very inexpensive brackets, usually sold in large online marketplaces, are made overseas, in countries that have even less regulatory oversight than we do.

This doesn't mean that all cheaper beauty products are prob-lematic, however. When you're dealing with high-end brands or others that you trust, you're simply less likely to encounter questionable ingredients. The FDA can do only so much to pro-tect consumers from exposure to these problem ingredients. That seems kind of anxiety-producing, doesn't it? Wouldn't we want a more prudent approach to our family's safety? If this all sounds crazy, that's because it is. How has so little been done about this? What's clear is that the FDA needs more power to regulate and monitor chemicals in beauty products *and* the power to pull products off the shelf.

The Personal Care Products Safety Act from 2021 is promis-ing new legislation that grants the FDA more power around ingredient regulation. Cosmetic brands and manufacturers now have to manually register where they develop their products and note information like ingredient lists and any serious ad-verse health effects that have been shown with specific products. The FDA now can ask for a recall of a product with problem ing-redients, inspect the brand's premises, and even require warnings if something has caused a person harm. It seems like it would be problematic for brands to be saddled with more regulations, but honestly, this is a very good thing for the consumer since it keeps them safe.

This problem with potentially problematic ingredients is magnified because only a select group of people can afford to experiment with healthier beauty options. This makes healthier beauty less accessible to many people: usually working-class folks, immigrants, and Black and Latino communities. This means that many people have no way of being protected against ingredients that could potentially be hurting them long term. Unless they avoid them completely. How fun would it be to completely avoid beauty items?

We also want to add a few disclaimers here. First, we are not against chemicals. We love science, and man-made chemicals have helped usher us into the modern world. Second, we're not saying that the beauty industry is doing all of this on purpose. We're in the beauty industry ourselves and we know this isn't the case. What's simply happening is that it's much cheaper sometimes to use certain ingredients. Most companies nowadays no longer use parabens or phthalates, and there is a big movement in beauty to get rid of these ingredients once and for all. What's called "clean beauty" is now the mission of pretty much every company in the market.

If you want to dig deeper into this problem, we recommend one of the books that inspired our own healthy beauty journey, *No More Dirty Looks: The Truth About Your Beauty Products and the Ultimate Guide to Safe and Clean Cosmetics*, by Siobhan O'Connor, or the HBO Max documentary series *Not So Pretty*, which goes into detail about the ugly truth behind the beauty and skin-care industry. Also, look into Dr. Shamasunder's research projects, like Taking Stock, which looks at the impacts of beauty products on Latina, Black, and Asian women's health.

Here's what inspired our Señora Clean Beauty Era.

Radical Señora Beauty Secret #1: Watch what you put on your skin

So, what should we do, considering the fact there isn't any consensus or concrete solution around the problem of beauty product health and safety? Food writer Michael Pollan says, "Eat food. Not too much. Mostly plants." Our philosophy is pretty similar to this but with makeup. We love using beauty products—just not too much, and mostly with minimalist ingredients. Why? You can never go wrong with beauty ingredients when there are just a few of them.

You can also start by always reading the ingredient list of any product you're considering. Ann does this now out of habit. Use apps like ThinkDirty and Environmental Working Group's Skin Deep Cosmetics Database to find out more about ingredients in your personal care and beauty products.. If you're not sure about an ingredient, simply look at the list to check for its score. The score takes into account potential health risks, like cancer risk, reproductive toxicity, allergies, and more. Personally, Christina and Ann also prefer more naturally derived ingredients, because those are usually some of the simplest ingredients out there, and time-tested for generations.

Radical Señora Beauty Secret #2: *Casera* beauty

Look at the routines of the señoras of the past for inspiration for your own beauty routine. To them, it was all about multipurpose, homemade, and simple ingredients, sometimes with things collected from their garden. These will give you the same, if not more, peace of mind than buying any expensive products on shelves.

People with skin issues like eczema or sensitive skin will see a huge benefit from finding products that have minimal ingredients or from making their own simple beauty products with gentler ingredients, like beeswax or shea butter. Knowing exactly what's in your products and knowing you're using safe ingredients will simply give you more peace of mind.

There are so many benefits to making your own beauty products. Re-creating recipes from the past will help you connect with your roots. Working with your hands is good for you and is an easy way to enjoy a new mindfulness practice. Studies show that engaging in hands-on activities, like arts and crafts, may lead to reduced levels of stress and anxiety[13] and that engaging in creative activities is associated with better cognitive function and a reduced risk of cognitive decline in older adults.[14]

We're not saying you have to cook your entire skin-care routine! No one has time for that, and if you don't want to do this, by all means don't. But if you can devote an hour on Sundays to making a new recipe, alongside your meal prepping for the week, we can almost guarantee that you'll get lost in the process and want to do it again. The key to making your own skin-care products is to have the ingredients ready to go beforehand by knowing what to buy and where to get them. Then incorporate a recipe that you know your ancestral señoras loved—maybe it's a family recipe passed down for generations—into your beauty routine, or try one of the recipes below.

To learn how to make her own beauty products just for fun, Ann turned to the online school called Herbal Academy, which kick-started her love of herbalism, natural beauty, and tea recipes. If you're looking to learn more advanced formulation techniques to become a beauty founder, they also recommend Formula Botanica's online school. If you want easy ingredients and ready-to-make kits, try Bramble Berry. If you want free classes, hit up YouTube, where you'll find thousands of easy and beautiful recipes for any beauty product you want to make.

A note of caution: Any formulations that you don't add preservatives to won't have a long shelf life, so be sure to follow the instructions in the recipe to either refrigerate the product or use it only for a few days.

Radical Señora Beauty Secret #3: Know the history of beauty in your culture

It brings Ann and Christina a lot of joy to think about the daily beauty routines of the señoras of their family trees, particularly in what ways the old routines are similar to theirs. One of the most fulfilling things they did tied to their beauty line was research the cultural beauty and hygiene habits of their ancestors.

To your Aztec ancestors, hygiene was very important. So much so, in fact, that the plundering Spanish soldiers were taken aback. Certainly, the Aztecs were cleaner and had better hygiene habits than Europeans, whose cities at the time were filthy, with city streets full of garbage, rats, and human waste, and for whom baths were rare. According to Francisco Javier Clavijero, an eighteen-century Franciscan Jesuit and historian, the Aztec people bathed a lot, sometimes twice a day, and usually in the rivers and lakes.[15]

For our ancestors, hair and body care rituals were elaborate. Much of it was focused and centered on herbal work. Right now, there are more than fifty Indigenous languages spoken in Mexico, and each community has very specific herbal practices, passed down the generations, and many of these practices are alive and well today. For the Aztec people, hair also had some emotional elements. Hair was a big part of funeral rituals—they made their hair look unkempt when someone they loved died. They boiled the leaves of the chaca tree to make baths; they used *estropajo* (loofah) leaves to make bath infusions, and *estropajo* fruit to make a lice shampoo. They took aromatic baths not only to heal ailments but to keep clean and smelling good. The fruit of the copalxocotl tree and roots from the amole plant were also used to make soap.

For Peruvian and Chilean Araucanos, hair was considered atrocious, and it was a tradition to shave or pluck all hair from the face. After the colonial invasion, long hair–and particularly braids–was considered Indigenous, and so mestizas avoided this hairstyle so as to not show their Indigenous heritage.[16]

Aztec ancestors bathed their bodies using the fruit of copalxocotl, the "soap tree," and the root of the xiuhamolli plant, which was a lathering plant. They may have also used flowers to wash their hair and make their breath fresher. In South America our Mapuche Indigenous ancestors and *mestizo* people used the bark of the quillai tree as shampoo, soap, and even detergent for washing clothing. This is because there is a natural chemical in the tree bark (saponin) that acts as a detergent and creates foam. The quillai bark would be boiled overnight and turned into a shampoo.

Later in history, methods of shampooing your hair included using herbs, in the form of either herbal decoctions or infusions. Decoctions are when things like roots and dried flowers are boiled for long enough to extract nutrients from them. Infusions happen when the softer parts of plants–like petals, seeds, and more–are covered in boiling water and steeped for a few minutes. Think of how you make tea. That's an infusion. *Maceration* means grinding up the parts of a plant, submerging the ground plant material in alcohol, and leaving it to steep for a few hours. Then the mixture is strained to remove the plant material, leaving just the liquid. A great way to learn more about this is in an Introductory Herbal course over at the Herbal Academy. Your Mexican señora ancestors may have made flaxseed water to detangle hair.

Rose water was a señora's favorite concoction made with rose petals. It became widely known in our homelands during the colonial period, when Spanish people brought this recipe, which originated in the Middle East, to the New World. It was used in religious ceremonies, food recipes, and beauty routines. It didn't hurt that the tonic had a delicious scent. In fact, Ann connected with a distant US American cousin with whom she shared a long-ago family connection. She learned that the new relative's great-grandmother, who was from Chile, made her own rose water because it reminded her of her homeland.

Your ancestors likely had gardens—or pots—full of herbs for healing and also personal care. Shampoo herbs may have included rosemary or specific flowers based on your ancestors' geographic location, like calendula, or they may have made almond oil for rubbing on the skin. In general, your family likely did not wash their hair every day—instead just once or twice a week.

There was a clear moment in time when ancestral beauty rituals began to fade from everyday life. If your grandmother was in her teenage years during the 1950s, chances are she used the brands that were also popular in the United States—brands like Estée Lauder, Revlon, and so on, which all launched in Latin America at some point in the 1950s and 1960s. This was the moment when many of our ancestral beauty traditions started to become lost to history.

When times were tough, señoras of that era made beauty products from food staples in their pantry or the market, like honey, aguacate/palta (avocado), oats, coffee, and all kinds of herbs that they also used for *te* (teas). Many who couldn't afford North American beauty products perfected their own hydrating masks and whipped face creams and made their own super simple soaps. Some of them may have also created recipes based on wild plants or weeds that grew around them, like rosa mosqueta, a rosebush that grows completely wild in certain areas of the Andes, unbothered by humans and fed by natural mountain run-off. A beauty serum, Chilean rose hip oil is made from these rose hips. Rose hip oil is big business now, but in the past, it was simply an oil that you used to get rid of skin imperfections.

Our ancestral señoras even dabbled in beauty supplements that are so on trend right now. Nowadays you'll find "beauty powders" and supplements at your local beauty retailer. Back then, there were tonics and pills that were supposed to keep your face and body beautiful. For example, for a moment in the nineteenth century, it was all the rage in Chile to buy *pilules orientales*, which were tonics that were supposed to give your boobs a glow. There was also a huge push toward creams and waxes that got rid of the hair on your face. Other supplements included herbs and botanicals that we now call superfoods, and that go back to the days of the original Indigenous people of these areas. These included edible things like cacao, maca, and the superfood berries maqui and acai.

Relying on señora beauty secrets is the simplest way to make sure you're protected from potentially harmful ingredients. It's simply a matter of being practical and not making things overly complicated. Some people might say that merely talking about potentially toxic ingredients in beauty products is fearmonger-ing, but we call it being careful. *Porque uno nunca sabe*, as our ancestral señoras used to say.

There are other benefits to channeling your inner señora for your beauty routines. Simply put, you'll feel better. This has everything to do with the fact that when you're whipping up these beauty products, you're using your hands and giving yourself a mindful practice that might bring a little more joy to your life.

Beauty Recipes as Creators of Joy

It feels really satisfying when you create something using your own two hands and then add it to your bath or lather it on your face. There is an element of focus, and what author Catherine Price calls "flow" in her book *The Power of Fun: How to Feel Alive Again.* What Price calls flow is when you get into a state of mind where you're so engaged in your activity that you lose track of time. She thinks that to feel true joy in your life (not fake, Netflix-binging joy), you need three things: flow, playfulness, and connection. When your *abuelas* were carefully and diligently making rose water for themselves, they were also probably offering some to their sisters. This process gave them flow (careful and focused ingredient stirring), connection (making some for their sisters), and playfulness (the fun of making the recipe).

Ana and Christina think this is why there's a big push right now around powder face masks, which you have to mix with water. They mimic what your *abuelitas* used to do—mash herbs into powders, add water, and turn them into a beauty mask. It's deeply satisfying to enjoy something that you have made yourself and to know the exact ingredients you're applying to your face and body.

There are a few key simple recipes that ancestral señoras relied on for centuries to feel beautiful, age gracefully, and keep joyful during their daily lives. In this chapter, they are organized according to specific ingredients, followed by their various uses. What's great is that they won't take you hours and hours to whip up. It often comes down to just boiling water.

Radical Señora Beauty Secret #4:
Age gracefully like a proud señora

Aging nowadays is such a difficult thing for women, but it hasn't always been this way.

Anecdotally, we think you'll agree that our grandmothers and great-grandmothers aged powerfully. They had other things to think about besides obsessing over their lips and butts or how toned they were. Sure, we remember them mentioning their wrinkles, but they never really took that anxiety as far as we do nowadays.

Research shows that elderly folks in Latin America, most specifically in Mexico, feel happier about their lives and themselves as they get older.[17] They also have different views about body image. Researchers think that Latinas may be protected from some of the negative body image effects because of our collective culture and emphasis on interconnectedness, which means that emphasis on a Latina's worth isn't primarily tied to her weight and looks.[18] [19]

What's behind this change in how Generation X and millennials feel about themselves and their bodies? Probably entertainment and reality TV stars, who oftentimes aren't famous for any other reason than being famous. Social media is also likely having an impact on aging. Things like scrolling too much on Instagram is messing up teenaged girls' self-esteem, encouraging eating disorders and disrupting their mental health, because of unrealistic beauty standards. This absolutely extends to older women, who see women their age looking younger due to Instagram and TikTok filters or great lighting or surgery.

To age like a señora means to not look outside yourself for acceptance and to look at the successful aging routines of your past for a model that you can emulate as you start to grow older.

Señoras focus on a positive outlook, living in the present, and enjoying their family and community.

Señora Beauty Era Recipes

Chamomile

Ann's *abuelita* on her father's side was big on chamomile. She was Indigenous, from a line of people who came from a part of the Andes. There was nothing she couldn't do with chamomile. She grew it in her garden, made tea with it, and boiled it in water or used the petals to create various skin-care solutions.

Chamomile is a native plant in Europe, Africa, and Asia and was used by ancient Roman, Egyptian, and Greek civilizations. In Greece the word used for it means "ground apple" because of its similarity in flavor to the fruit. This is why it's known as *manzanilla*, which means "little apple," in Latin America, where it was popularized thanks to Saint Martin de Porres, the region's first Afro-Latino saint and the patron saint of multicultural public health workers, barbers, innkeepers, and everyone seeking racial harmony. The legend says that the saint would collect chamomile in the forest to treat sick and indigent people in the community.

Chamomile has always been a staple in a señora's botanical garden and medicine pantry and cabinet, because it's well known to be a soothing, calming tea for *"nervios." Nervios* is a catchall term in Latin American culture and literally means "nerves," but it actually means many different things to people, including that you're nervous or anxious, or you just don't feel good mentally. In fact, it's the afternoon or evening tea for many señoras worldwide. For Ann and Christina, it's a stand-in for a glass of wine after dinner, because it helps calm them down without the wine crash, anxiety, and stomach issues.

In the life of a señora, chamomile has a very special place in her beauty cabinet. It does everything from healing dry, itchy skin to helping open up your pores and creating a calming bath, and the señoras of the past used this wonder herb religiously.

On the skin, chamomile is used to treat conditions like post-partum cracked nipples, chicken pox irritation, diaper rash, eye and ear infections, and poison ivy. It's also commonly used as an ingredient in DIY creams, perfumes, soaps. and detergents and is dropped into the bath to help with—you guessed it—*nervios.*

DO THIS TO HIGHLIGHT YOUR HAIR:

- Chop 1 cup of dried chamomile petals (or 3-5 chamomile tea bags) and boil in 2-4 cups water for 15 minutes
- Strain the chamomile water and discard the petals
- Rinse your hair with chamomile water and wait for half an hour before rinsing with fresh water
- Do not go into the sun before rinsing the chamomile water out of your hair

DO THIS TO RELIEVE DRY, ITCHY SKIN FROM THE WINTER COLD:

- Bring 8 ounces of water to a boil
- As soon as it begins to boil, add 1 cup dried chamomile petals
- Add a few sprigs of fresh rosemary or 4 tablespoons dried rosemary
- Strain the concoction and add the chamomile-rosemary water to your bath

DO THIS TO ENJOY A CHAMOMILE STEAM FACIAL:
- Bring 12 ounces water to a boil in a saucepan
- Add 2 cups fresh chamomile petals (or multiple tea bags) and let soak for 5 minutes
- Pour the hot chamomile water in a large bowl
- Put your face over the bowl and a towel over your head and feel the healing effects of the chamomile steam on your pores

Quillai

This botanical is so useful that it's still used in modern, industrial shampoos. What you're doing is going back to basics, using it like some of your ancestors may have. The quillai is a tree from South America and was first described by the famous Chilean-Spanish Jesuit priest and botanist Juan Ignacio Molina in the 1700s, when he was kicked out of Chile by the Spanish (and who, by the way, started writing about evolution forty years before Darwin).

First, make sure you know where you're buying your quillai bark from, because it's illegal to export tree bark from Chile given that this tree is close to being extinct there. The Mapuche Indigenous folks would boil this tree bark and use the water on their hair as shampoo or use it as detergent. Ann struggled with putting the quillai shampoo recipe in the book, given that it's so hard to find non-Chilean quillai, but she knows her community of readers are scrappy gardening besties, and so she's confident you can find alternatives. For example, Ann found quillai extract at an online store.

Quillai Shampoo (Champu)–also called Quillaja

The quillai is a pretty rare tree in the United States, though it's endemic to Chile, and so quillai bark likely won't be available to you locally. You can find quillai trees in some areas of the country, such as in Santa Barbara, San Francisco, and Silicon Valley.

In the event you are able to get access to a quillai tree or purchase the bark, and you are more advanced with your skin-care product-making skills, give quillai shampoo a try. This is a very informal recipe, so it is recommended that you make it just for fun and to try it out.

If from the tree:

- Soak quillai leaves in water for at least 24 hours
- Rinse the quillai leaves
- Boil the leaves in a pot
- Let them rest in the pot for a few minutes
- Pour the liquid, minus the leaves, into a shampoo-friendly bottle and let rest.
- The shampoo is ready to use when you see it getting foamy. Use as you would any normal shampoo
- We have seen others use it as a hair spray while they are combing their hair

Avocado

Called aguacate in Central America and palta in some South American countries, the avocado is Latin America's most popular and important fruit. Researchers have traced its origins to Puebla, in Central Mexico, about ten thousand years ago, with Mesoamerican tribes (like the Olmec, Maya, Zapotec, Teotihuacan, Mixtec, and Mexica [or Aztec] tribes) domesticating the fruit five thousand years ago. The Aztecs even used it to give their warriors strength and energy. The Spaniards took the avocado back to Europe, where it boomeranged its way back to Latin America. It was slathered on toast during teatime by our señora ancestors but was also used by them as a luxurious—and very green—skin-care staple.

As a skin-care ingredient, avocado is high in vitamin A, D, and E and contains essential minerals, like potassium. Its fatty acids help protect your skin from UV rays, help with moisture retention and fine lines, and help with collagen metabolic processes, and the fact that the avocado is high in antioxidants means it protects you from free-radical damage.

The chunky green avocado mask is the epitome of the señora nighttime wellness routine.

HYDRATING AVOCADO AND OAT MASK/*MASCARILLA DE PALTA Y AVENA*

- Soak 1 tablespoon rolled oats in water for 24 hours
- Mash half of an avocado and mix in 1 teaspoon lemon juice in a medium bowl
- Drain the water from the oatmeal and add the oatmeal mush to the avocado-lemon mixture
- Next, add 2 tablespoons almond oil and 2 tablespoons chamomile tea to the oatmeal-avocado mixture.
- Mix well and spoon into a glass jar
- Apply the mask, leave it on for 25 minutes, and then wash it off with tepid water

Rosa Mosqueta Oil (Chilean Rose-Hip Seed Oil)

Chilean señoras have been using rose-hip seed oil for centuries to heal their skin. Rosa Mosqueta oil comes from the seeds of a wild rose that grows in the Andes and was also used by Araucanian Indigenous people. It is rich in vitamins A, C, and E and has been found to contain regenerative properties.

As their children were growing up, señoras like Ann's grandmothers and *tías* (aunts) swore by Rosa Mosqueta oil to treat skin wounds, like small burns, and chicken pox, but its greatest use was said to be on *manchas*, or what we currently call hyperpigmentation.

This oil is not only great for hair and nails, and helps things like stretch marks and fine lines, but it also fights infections, stomach issues, and inflammatory diseases. So this wild rose is truly a genius botanical. It has even been studied by universities to treat eczema, neurodermatitis, and cheilitis, and the results have been extremely promising.

What's the magic behind rose-hip oil? Multiple studies show that its vitamins and fatty acids seem to regenerate cells, help with collagen production, and help regulate moisture.

The history of this plant is also kind of hilarious and involves a pig. One of the likeliest origin stories behind this plant is that in 1974 a Chilean engineer, Carlos Amin, "discovered" rose-hip oil through his work with pigs. Pigs have surprisingly soft and healthy skin, but he noticed his pigs had particularly luscious skin. Through analysis Amin and his team discovered that the pigs were chomping on the fruit of Rosa Mosqueta bushes! They researched the properties of this plant and found that the oil regenerated skin tissue. Ann used the term "discovered" in quotes because Mapuche people may have already been using this for generations. Modern-day research has consistently backed up centuries-old findings, suggesting that this oil is effective.

Rose hip is the ultimate señora self-care product because it gives you an incredibly soothing, nourishing feeling on your skin before you go to bed and will put you right to sleep.

Application:

Apply Rosa Mosqueta oil liberally to your face. Your skin will feel soothed and hydrated; it's a wonderful way to create a self-care routine to close out your day.

Rose Water

Rose water is the ultimate *belleza casera* for your señora era. It's been popular in Latin America for hundreds of years and is still popular today. It was likely brought over to Latin America by the Spanish, who were introduced to it during the Moorish conquest of Spain. In fact, you will see rose-water mists are as popular as ever before and are actually still trendy in the US Beauty industry. Even Vamigas had a rose-water mist. Rose water is really easy to make. It's very easy to infuse hot water with rose petals (below), or you can cook it over a double boiler.

Rose Petal Recipe from the Herbal Academy

BASED ON A TUTORIAL IN THE HERBAL ACADEMY'S BOTANICAL SKIN CARE COURSE AND USED WITH PERMISSION.

Beautiful rose for our Herbal Academy's rosewater recipe.
The recipe for Rosewater was developed by one of our favorite
spots online to learn about herbalism, The Herbal Academy
(herbalacademy.com). PHOTO CREDIT: HERBAL ACADEMY.

Rose water is an herbal preparation known as a hydrosol, a delightfully aromatic liquid produced by steam distillation of plant material—in this case, rose petals. This process uses heat to volatilize aromatic compounds, which separate into an essential oil portion and a water-based hydrosol. The hydrosol portion can be captured through condensation.

One thing to point out here is that a hydrosol is quite different from essential oils, which you may be more familiar with. Essential oils are highly concentrated products composed of a plant's volatile aromatic constituents and need to be diluted prior to topical application. Hydrosols are dilute blends of the water-soluble and aromatic components of the plant and can be applied directly to the skin without dilution. Hydrosols provide a very sustainable alternative to essential oils, particularly because they can be produced at home by the canny herbalist, using simple kitchen equipment and plant material from their own garden!

SUPPLIES NEEDED:

Clean, flat brick

Sanitized large enamel or stainless-steel pot with a
    domed lid*

Several large handfuls of fresh, aromatic rose petals
    (Pick plenty!)**

Filtered or distilled water

---

* Before beginning, make sure that the pot, the bowl or the measuring cup, which you'll use to collect the rose water, and the glass jar are clean and sanitized. (The rose water itself will be sterilized through the distillation process but can be contaminated by microbes on hands or equipment during packaging or storage, which will result in a much shorter shelf life.)

** While some herbalists use only the freshest plant material to produce hydrosols, others leave the plant material to wilt slightly before distilling. Wilting allows for a small amount of water loss, concentrating the aromatic oils. It also means you can pack more plant material into your "still" to get a better yield. Experiment with rose petals to see which method you prefer!

Sanitized glass or metal bowl or large heat-safe glass
measuring cup (the bowl or measuring cup must
fit inside your pot)

Ice bucket filled with ice cubes or 1 large ice brick
(made by freezing water in a quart-size plastic
container)

Sanitized glass bottle or other container (for storing
the rose water)

Turkey baster (optional)

INSTRUCTIONS:

Prepare a stovetop still: Place the pot on the stove. Set the
brick in the bottom of the pot. Heap rose petals in the bottom
of the pot, up to the top of the brick. Add fresh water to cover
the petals. Place the bowl or measuring cup on top of the brick.

Put the pot lid on upside down. You want the handle to face
down into the bowl, so that as steam forms on the inside of the
lid, it will condense upon contact with the cold lid and drip off
the handle and collect in the bowl or measuring cup.

Heat the pot until the water just comes to a boil, and then reduce the heat to a simmer. Leave the lid on the pot but listen to
the sound the water makes to get a sense of what's going on in
there. The water should simmer and produce steam, but not
come to a full boil.

Next, fill the center of the lid with ice. This will help the steam
condense more quickly on the lid. After 20 minutes or so, use a
turkey baster to siphon up any water left in the lid from the melt-
ing ice. That way it won't spill into the pot when you lift the lid!

Moving quickly and carefully, take off the lid and remove
the inner bowl or measuring cup, which contains the rose water,
so you can empty it. Then replace the lid as quickly as possible,
so you don't lose too much steam, but be very careful. Everything is very hot!

Next, pour the rose water into the glass bottle. If you wish, place the bowl or measuring cup back inside the pot for another round of distillation. If the rose petals you used still have a strong fragrance, you can reuse them.

The length of the whole process depends on a few factors, such as how many petals you have in your pot and how fresh they are. You can rely on your senses to guide you here. With each successive cycle, you may notice that the distillate is a little less potent: The liquid may be clearer, and it won't smell as fragrant. At a certain point, there won't be much aroma left in the rose petals, and you'll want to stop distilling before you dilute your rose water too much.

Using and Storing Rose Water and Other Hydrosols

Once you've finished the distillation process and your rose water has cooled, you can bottle and label it for storage. Most hydrosols will keep for at least six months. You can extend their stability by storing them in the refrigerator and by using sanitized storage bottles.

How will you know if your rose water or other hydrosol is past its prime? Watch for the development of bloom, a misty, cloudy, or jellylike swirl that develops near the bottom of the bottle. It's recommended to use clear bottles for storage so you can keep an eye out for bloom. It's also a good idea to store your rose water or other hydrosol in glass, especially for extended storage. Over time, the volatile oil content, and consequently the aroma, will be absorbed by plastic.

Your rose water or other hydrosol can be used as a room or body spray, or as an aromatic additive to almost any skin or hair recipe you can dream up! Add hydrosols to lotion, toner, bath blends, shampoo, hair rinse, and more.

(Note: The authors are affiliates of Herbal Academy.)

CHAPTER 7

For Señoras in Their Garden Era

Get More Veggies and Other Beautiful Things into Your Life

IT WAS A lovely, sunny Saturday afternoon, and while most families in Southern California were out at the beach, making beautiful memories, Ann was inside her garage, with her hand up a chicken's butt.

One of her chickens had become sick, and the local animal vet had suggested she "check" for an impacted egg, which means you put your hand up there and feel around. Just two years earlier, Ann was living the fast start-up life of coffee and cocktail outings. To say this era caught her off guard was an understatement.

It wasn't an easy transition for her. Instagram, TikTok, and YouTube have you thinking that life in the *campo* is easy. You see women in crisp white aprons and flowery milkmaid dresses, harvesting bountiful veggie garden beds, braiding their horse's hair, and these big, beautiful houses filled with antique-looking farm furniture that's the perfect level of worn out.

In reality, it's really hard, time consuming, and expensive to live in the country. Actual farmers have been struggling financially for a long time. Those YouTubers' aprons are likely some luxury label brand, the big garden boxes cost them thousands, and the antique-looking furniture is brand new. Some of these influencers don't do any work. A lot of this is just for entertainment and monetizing—plus, it's expensive to keep up a homestead. Remember that the next time you get the urge to buy some *terreno* and have fresh eggs every morning.

For many of us in our señora eras, the *huerto en casa*, or the home garden, is what we aspire to have. Before the time of food retailers, families all over the world have always had vegetable gardens, because they provided them with a consistent and secure source of food. Your Indigenous ancestors were often masters of the land, and because of this, they had many of their agriculture secrets brutally stolen from them by the Spanish. Some of your *mestizo* ancestors may have lived on ranchos, where they grew things like corn, beans, avocado, chiles, nopales, and more.[1] My great grandmother had a *huerto*, an orchard, chickens, and a bread oven out back.

Your señora ancestor's garden was the most important part of her home. Farming and cooking what was harvested was central to her life since it sustained her family during the good times and the bad. Both the garden and the chicken coop were primarily the señora's territory, whereas the men dealt with things like cattle or horses.[2]

The types of gardens señoras cultivated varied based on country or culture. A *huerto* (home garden, dooryard garden, or roof garden) meant you had a small to mid-sized crop system close to the house. A *milpa* meant you had a large crop system away from the main home, one that sometimes sustained the family because it functioned as a small food business. The *ekuaro*, an agroforestry system created by the Purépechas in Michoacán, Mexico, included a farm and also cattle. In South America your ancestors may have had a *chacra*, with large planting fields or a home *huerto*, like Ann's great-grandmother Maria in Quillota; or *fincas*, ranch estates run by a señora's entire family.[3]

What did your ancestral señoras plant? This also varied based on country of origin. The señora garden may have had corn, zucchini, potatoes, artichokes, chamomile (*camomila*), rosemary (*romero*), and avocado trees grew in the orchard. Mexican señoras may have planted these and also things like *verdolaga* (purslane), *quelite* (lamb's-quarter), *papalo* (*papaloquelite*), and other unique staples, alongside some *nopales* somewhere in the property. Chileans and other South American people may have also planted things like *matico, chilco, chaucas*, and *murta* and may have had *lucuma* and *chirimoya* trees.

The Beauty and Function of Having Your Own Garden

The era of the pandemic collapsed health care systems. Lockdowns and curfews brought out the worst in people and uncovered some concerning gaps in modern society. While millions of people were dying and hospitals reached capacity, we also saw how quickly the supply chain collapsed. Soon the entire world was left to scramble and stand in line at the market for groceries. For many of our families, they had seen these lines before, during government collapses in their homelands.

Ann had her baby one week before San Francisco saw a sharp rise in COVID cases and hospitalizations. The city was deadly quiet after lockdown, except for the constant wailing of ambulances. If you were a new mom during this time, things were particularly stressful, because you had to make sure that you always had a surplus of baby formula and diapers, and that you didn't bring the virus home to infect your tiny baby with a not yet fully developed immune system. The greatest anxiety was the breastfeeding, mom's worst enemy, because you can't breastfeed well if you're experiencing much stress, which we all were at that time.

This was the first time in Ann's life when she saw restaurants shut down, curfews, and food lines that snaked around the block. Watching the news made her so anxious that her attempt at breastfeeding was a nightmare. She was still recovering from a pregnancy-related injury, which made even walking very painful. Ann was a moody, bloody, irritable postpartum mess. Her mom stayed with them, and so it was the three of them, plus a newborn and a dog, in a small San Francisco apartment.

To pass the time, Ann started watching garden-themed YouTube videos, which led her down a rabbit hole of modern "homesteaders." She started dreaming of having her *terreno* someday, where the baby could run wild with the family dog, not be stuck indoors all the time. Ann wanted to feel the earth underneath her feet, and to find out what it was like to grow your own food, like they did on those *parcelas*. At night, she would dream about the family *asados* she remembered at her grandmother's beach cottage, some *pollo asado* cooking on the grill, accompanied by some refreshing *chelas* with the *primos*. *Aire puro*, *asado*, and her own *verduras*, she thought, sounded like three of the most incredible things on earth during those tenuous days. She wanted wide-open spaces, a garden, and a little oasis for her entire family. But she was far from her family, really far from her homeland, and she and her husband were parents stuck in the city with a newborn during a global health crisis. That would soon change.

Gardening and Self-Sufficiency

There's a reason why so many of us are skipping over our parents' generation and sliding right into our grandmothers' eras, with a newfound love of "granny hobbies." The world's been feeling really scary over the last few years. Things like global economic unrest, war, poverty, and weather chaos mean we're experiencing some rough air right now. Our home is one of the only things we have control over, so it's only natural to want to build a more self-sufficient way to live.

Your ancestral señoras—and maybe even your parents—may have been through similar times of unrest. They had to get very resourceful with household goods and groceries during the tough times. In our homelands, tough times meant revolutions, economic depression and extreme inflation and stagnation, and natural disasters. The food distribution pipeline was often the first supply chain to collapse, so grocery store aisles became empty, and you had to contend with lines around the block to get basic things like bread, milk and pasta or rice. There was no Amazon or Instacart to deliver groceries.

Some of our parents who grew up in Latin America still remember tanks in the streets, the military shooting student protestors, systematic kidnappings and mass murders, and the country's near economic collapse. Ann used to listen to the stories of her family about the rough periods in Chile starting in the 1970s, when Chile's economy tanked and groceries were hard to find, followed by a government coup when many innocent people lost their lives. Her great-grandpa Salvador sprang into action and organized a trade for goods and would procure large boxes of groceries. Every branch of the extended family tree would then stop by and pick up what they needed. That's how resourceful your family likely was, too, during their own periods of disaster.

Maybe you go a little farther and get a chicken coop to have delicious fresh eggs every morning, or you get bees for the pounds of free honey. These activities are also part of your cultural heritage. It's great to be prepared for any type of emergency, from earthquakes to floods to power grid disruptions. Shipping disruptions are still happening and will happen again. In 2025, tariffs disrupted the economy. These have the capacity to increase prices for consumers, create more supply chain disruptions, economic slowdown and inflation, and much more. There have also been major corporate recalls happening of the most common things, like apple juice and lettuce. Even before the pandemic there was a shortage of refrigerated trucks to transport food. Some of us just want to have a little bit more control over our food supply due to this instability.

When something called the avian flu, a disease detected in the US in 2022 that affects chickens, disrupted chicken production plants, eggs were suddenly 70 percent more expensive. This disrupts the entire industry because when there's an outbreak, a commercial poultry plant has to cull all its chickens. The prices continue to climb as of this writing.

Ann and her husband had purchased a little coop from a family business nearby, and at the time they were collecting as many as twenty-four eggs each week. They had so many eggs to spare, Ann started giving them away to her family and the neighbors. It felt so good to have their own chickens as backup. Local homesteading groups in every city got really creative. They started trading things from their farms with each other, such as beeswax for eggs, homemade candles for firewood. One of Ann's local friends had chickens in her backyard—in an HOA! Once, someone who had just moved into the community posted an offer to build a community garden on his property, and he got dozens of volunteers, all ready to help prep the land.

Gardening also has some major benefits. Sometimes you just need a good excuse to push yourself to go outdoors more. As you'll see in the next section, just being outside will completely improve your mood. Even talking about being outdoors or planning a garden has a calming and soothing effect on your *nervios*. When Ann is having a bad day, going out to the garden is something that has never failed to improve her mood.

Gardening Feels Good

We know it seems like the most obvious advice. *Of course* going outside improves your mood. But why do so many of us ignore that simple fact? Ann spent some of the best years of her life in San Francisco, a city in the most beautiful natural setting, but she was largely holed up at home, at the office, or inside restaurants. What was she thinking? Now when she wakes up, the first place she goes is to the garden to water her plants. It doesn't matter how cranky or sleep deprived she becomes because of the little one; the power of her garden to improve her mood is unmatched.

Research has found that gardening can boost mood as much as biking, other forms of exercise, walking, and even eating a delicious meal at a restaurant.[4] There's a reason why so many people took up gardening during the pandemic—if we couldn't get that dopamine boost from hanging out with our friends or traveling, the next best thing was talking to the plants out back.

Being outside more has been shown to have major mental health benefits. For the past twenty years, something called "horticulture therapy" has become popular. It's a form of garden-based mental health care launched in parts of Europe in the mid-aughts. In the Netherlands something called "green care," which entails learning to work with animals, was created to help people with drug dependency issues, impaired mental health, or learning disabilities.

The US has a long history of linking gardening to well-being. In the States during the 1800s, a University of Pennsylvania professor found a link between working in a garden and recovering from "mania." In the 1970s, programs and alliances like UNC Chapel Hill's Horticultural Therapy Program and the American Horticultural Therapy Association studied the power of plants to promote health and well-being and, using this knowledge, devised a holistic therapy for the public. A project in Pittsburgh by the Phipps Conservatory and Botanical Gardens gave regular people tools to garden, and 70 percent of recipients continued to garden three years after the project ended. Many hospitals, rehabilitation centers, and homes for people with dementia now have gardening programs as part of their services to support patients.[5] [6]

Unfortunately, this is one of our ancestral wellness secrets that was lost as your relatives left their hometowns or when your own families moved to the cities.

Gardening Is Good Food

Do you remember your great-grandmother's or grandmother's backyard garden or rancho? How delicious and vibrant those veggies were that she grew! That garden was sustainable and organic without even trying (no certifications needed!). The eggs she collected in the morning and the lettuce and snap peas she grew in her garden not only tasted better but were more nutritious, too.

Is this a real thing or only some imagined effect? Some researchers think it's the real deal. A team at the University of

Texas at Austin, for example, used historical data and modern measurement for forty-three different veggies and fruits and found that over the past fifty years, there has been a sharp decline in the nutrients protein, calcium, iron, vitamin A, vitamin C, and more in this produce. They deduced that this may be due to overfarming, some modern intensive farming techniques, and soil depletion, but it's very hard to say definitively.[7]

In his book *Mini Farming: Self-Sufficiency on ¼ Acre*, Brett L. Markham observes that fresh veggies and fruit from the farmers' market are more nutritious than the ones you buy at the grocery store because selling products to hundreds of thousands of people can only be done at the expense of the nutritional value of a crop. Crops are selected for their ability to stay looking good after days of shipping and cold storage.[8]

Even the tea that your grandmother or *tías* grow in their herb gardens tastes better than the tea in tea bags. Señoras have always known there is nothing more beautiful than pinching off a few leaves of your favorite herb on your windowsill and making yourself a delicious cup of hot tea to wind down for the evening.

Garden Era Launched from Pandemic Mom Era

During the pandemic, Ann and her husband were, like other parents, isolated, lonely, and at the stage of newborn parenting where you're just a sleepless shell of a person. So, they started planning their move to be closer to her family in Southern California. They picked a beautiful little place with rolling hills, Mediterranean weather, and vineyards that was closer to her parents. Because it was outside of major cities, they were able to get *terrenos*—a few acres and a cute little house right in the center—for the same price as an average home in the city.

Thanks to her husband's job, Ann was lucky enough to be able to take a temporary break from her job to care for the baby and focus on breastfeeding, diapers, and teething. She started taking the baby out on walks in the orchard, which already had a few orange, lemon, grapefruit, and apricot trees. It also had one avocado tree, which still hasn't managed to give them any avocados. But it inspired her. Each time Ann went outside, she started to add something new. Maybe a little cactus or a cute little statue. Her mom brought over a fairy village, one by one, which they placed around the yard for the baby to find,

You know how you're supposed to plan your garden carefully—maybe sketch it out on a special app, assiduously measure the square footage of your area, understand what type of shade you need, what kinds of crops you want—and then get to work?

Yeah, Ann did none of that. She just did the bare minimum. She ordered raised garden beds online, which were way too expensive, because there had been a run on them locally and so there was nothing left at the stores. She went to a local nursery chain and got a bunch of seedlings and some big bags of dirt.

Both she and her husband had lived in suburbs and cities all of their lives, so they basically had no idea what they were doing. The first garden bed they planted was the easiest because they just added a bunch of herbs. They added spearmint, chamomile, basil, thyme, and oregano seedlings. Adding mint to the garden bed was a huge mistake, because it took over all the other herbs, and soon the bed was just a giant messy blob. They also hadn't yet learned how to deal with predators, which started eating their harvest. At one point, they were feeding half of Southern California's gopher, mole, squirrel, and rabbit population. They knew to come to their house because it was an all-you-can-eat buffet.

Once Ann and her husband had finished the herb bed, they delighted in the fact that for all that work, they had a few little branches with tiny herbs, which they used... enough for one cup of tea and maybe half a plate of pasta. But the tea garden helped teach them how to actually garden, and Ann soon wanted to learn more.

Ann discovered the Herbal Academy, an online herbalism school that offers courses on blending teas, making perfumes, creating children's activities, working with mushrooms, and developing herbalism skills from beginner to advanced levels. After everyone else fell asleep, she would power up her laptop and learn things like how to make tinctures and teas; the differences between decoctions (extracts using the roots of herbs and plants) and infusions (extracts using the softer parts of herbs); how to wildcraft and forage for herbs in your own garden; and how to make things like salves, balms, and incredible body butters. She made chamomile and mint tea every night, and she concocted a full body balm from beeswax, along with some dandelion root that she collected from the back of the property and roasted (hoping to God the dog hadn't peed on it). She made sun tea in the one-hundred-degree heat of the summer.

Soon enough, she started picking up new skills from watching YouTube videos and reading gardening books, and she harvested and fermented red onions from the beds and black olives from their trees. According to Ann, it's the most incredible feeling in the world to be able to pick ingredients from your own backyard and actually do things with them. Like, make all this stuff she used to get at the store. It was a truly amazing feeling.

Then an interesting thing happened.

Gardening became Ann's automatic mood booster. No matter how chaotic the baby was that day or depressing the day was, spending a little time with her plants was instant medicine. This is exactly what she had craved when she was dreaming back in San Francisco. Even getting up very early to check on the chickens helped her get out of her head and start the day right. Ann started enjoying things that she wouldn't have had the patience for just three years ago: weeding, planting seedlings in the ground, growing her own seedlings from seeds, monitoring how well things were growing. These activities also provided her with little moments of alone time where she could just focus on the fresh air, the beautiful sky, and the earth under her feet. As a mom, it was really important to get some "me time," but that applies to everyone. Just the feeling of being among your *plantitas* is the most soothing feeling in the world.

When Ann is having a particularly stressful day at work, or a case of the Monday scaries, one trip to the garden to plan a new garden bed improves her mood and dissolves her anxiety.

Don't believe it? Do a little experiment with me. Over the next few mornings, go outside as soon as you wake up and before you start your morning prep for school or work, or both. Walk around your garden, maybe sit down for a moment. Walk the dog for a little longer. If you live in the city, walk around your block and take stock of the environment around you.

Do you live in what feels like an Arctic tundra? Open all of your blinds, and turn on a cozy farm or baking or garden themed YouTube channel, ideally one where the protagonist doesn't talk. Compare how you feel on these days, versus on days when you don't do these things, and go from bed to work or school drop off. Ann's favorite YouTube channel in the morning is Her 86m, but there are many others.

Little by little, the dream *huerto* started to take shape. What had started out as one herb garden has grown to multiple garden beds with automated irrigation, where Ann's family has grown tomatoes, zucchini, squash, corn, pumpkin, artichokes, chamomile, mint, thyme, carrots, peas, beans, potatoes, strawberries, blueberries, kale, lettuce, microgreens, calendula, olives, and much more. Her daughter loves to eat fruits from their trees, which include peaches, plums, oranges, and apples, and they never have to buy lemons for as long as they live because their lemon tree is always blooming. The little one loved asking Ann to lift her up and put her inside the strawberry garden bed so she could grab some snacks and sure enough, as she grew older, strawberries were her ultimate favorite snack. The couple's *huerto* has grown to include a path with a trellis, which creates structure in the garden; a seating area with a gazebo, where they serve dinner on sunny afternoons (or take a break from being cooped up indoors when it's been raining); and a solar panel system to keep the garden and the house off-grid for a few hours a day—and not spend so much money on electricity.

Ann's garden is similar to the one her great-grandmother had, except for one thing. She and her husband garden with the help of modern technology. They have access to new power sources, alternative energy, and advanced composting systems. It was much easier for them to get the garden up and running in a few days, because they could go buy what they needed at the Home Depot or Tractor Supply Co., or it arrived from Amazon overnight.

In this book Christina and Ann talk a lot about using a señora's ancestral wisdom to help us in the present day, but being a Radical Señora means also using modern technology methods, inventions, and innovations to improve and optimize the *huertos* of the past and still reap the benefits, like having more control over where your food comes from.

A Note on Señoras and Privilege

It's pretty hard to have a garden right now unless you own a home, and we know how much harder owning your own home has been getting with each passing generation. Many of us are bogged down with crushing student loan debt, houses got really expensive, and older folks aren't moving out of their homes as much, pushing up prices. Inflation doesn't help. So not only is it a privilege to have a veggie garden, but it's also a privilege to be a homeowner. Being a Radical Señora means those of us who can afford a garden with food have to remember that we have some privilege or we just got lucky. We should also remember to pass it forward and do things like finding a food bank to give to or a women's shelter to donate money to, or volunteering, or supporting other folks on their way up through mentorship or financial support. As we saw in Chapter 4, giving back was a big part of your ancestral señoras' lives.

Here are some simple things Ann learned throughout her own garden era journey.

Radical Señora Gardening Secret #1: Grow like a Señora

Before Ann set up her garden, she knew zero about mulch, hardiness zones, perennials, and tree fertilizer. She just threw stuff together, forgot to water it, and then complained when she got nothing. Her husband was much more organized, and thanks to his tweaks and garden purchases to optimize the whole process, they started having better harvests.

One of the first things you need to find out before starting is how good your soil is. If you have crappy soil, you'll never be able to grow anything in the ground, because your *plantitas* need good nutrients to survive. If your soil sucks, you'll have to use raised garden beds, which you can buy online or at your local home improvement retailer. These are an excellent choice because the soil inside is not as compacted. It drains better and water runs through it more easily, and the dirt gets warm earlier in the spring, which will allow you to start planting earlier in the season. You can start with basic rectangular or square garden beds, which you might find at Walmart or Amazon or anywhere online. They are usually made of wood or plastic. The cheapest options are generally on Amazon, and the most expensive ones are e-commerce brands, like Epic Gardening or the posh Birdies modular beds, which you just screw together. There are also smaller brands that are more affordable. For a no-cost option, use material you might have lying around the yard, like cinder blocks or wood, and get creative. Ann even saw photos of raised garden beds using planter wall blocks on a blog called Driven by Décor. The creator used cement blocks and long pieces of wood to make planter boxes.

Your deadline for having the garden beds installed is about three to four weeks before spring planting season starts. You'll want to start these a few weeks to months before you start planting. Ann and her husband threw the garden beds into their garden. It took them weeks to get them assembled, and both of them to make it happen, so it was a process.

If you want to get more advanced, you can do the "double dig" method, where you loosen two layers of the soil on the ground, dig each row, and then add compost. Or you could do the *cochinadas* Ann did and just dump soil into the raised garden bed itself and call it a day.

Start farming slowly–señora style. Experts recommend that you start with one, maybe two beds, get the planting started and then add more beds when you have more time or space. Ann's family just went to the store, and they dumped everything into the garden when they got home, like it was a big garden stew.

Your garden will be your life for the next twenty-plus years. Remember Don Corleone in his tomato patch at the end of *The Godfather*? That could be you. So, you'll want to make sure to allow space to sit among the garden beds, comfortably add your seedlings, and do other work on them. You'll also want to remember to weed anything that looks like it's sapping nutrients from your plants.

You should be ready to start planting seeds in the spring, but the exact time depends on what growing zone you're in. Google "What zone am I in?" and you'll understand when the "last frost" is in your area. You'll want to plant after that date. You'll find loads of calendars and recommendations for when to plant which items in your zone. You'll also be limited as to what types of items you can sow. So, first, you'll need to research growing conditions for whatever it is you want to plant.

This dang growing zones system will be your enemy, and you'll find that the system isn't incredibly accurate. Ann had always wanted to grow lucumas, which are native to her homeland and are able to be planted in zones 9–10, and one of those is her zone. Unfortunately, they grow well only when the temperature is between 50°F and 80°F, and excessive heat is a major problem for them. They drop dead like a fly. So there went Ann's dream to grow her great-grandmother's tree in California.

What if you have a tiny garden or none at all? Maybe you live in an apartment. You'll want to get something called a vertical garden, which is sold online and at retailers near you. This is a stackable-layer garden system, where you plant a different crop in each layer. Some of these are really easy to water because they have little built in plates so that you don't have to water each layer individually. You can place these inside your home or on your balcony. The price range is thirty dollars and up.

What if you absolutely have zero space or live with roomies or your parents? Ann remembers living with her parents during her twenties and not having anywhere to plant. She wishes she'd known about vertical gardening back then, because she would have added a vertical garden to her parents' backyard. You can also seek out community gardens. These are designated gardening areas that are shared by a group of people, each with their own little plot of land. Google or search on Yelp for "Community gardens near me" to find the garden nearest you. If there isn't a community garden near you, post on your local Facebook group or neighborhood app, such as Nextdoor, that you'd like to gather a group of people together and start an urban garden. You'll be surprised at how many people will jump on board and help. Then just start organizing.

You can get started with elaborate tools, or you can get started using the bare minimum. That's the beauty of gardening like a señora—because your great grandmother didn't need raised garden beds, an irrigation system or a greenhouse. Some affordable or free alternatives include making your own paper pots to make seedlings, or using tin cans, yogurt pots, or glass jars. You can also create seedlings the old fashioned way and press your seeds into any tray or wooden box. That's likely how your señoras did it.

Señoras also used kitchen scraps. Many veggies actually regrow, like lettuce, potatoes, green onions and celery. Soil is also very pricey, so use food scraps to make compost to create your own planting soil. Some cities may even have free soil programs.

If you want to get started quickly and affordably, Ann and Christina created simple guides and tips that you can download on their website (senoraera.com).

Radical Señora Gardening Secret #2: Go to the *mercado*

What if you're an introverted Latina who hates socializing (aren't we all?), or you don't have the *ganas* to build a community garden from scratch? There are other places where you can get fresh vegetables and save money, and going there is one of a señoras' favorite pastimes: the *mercados*. The señoras of the past went to *mercados*, farmers' markets or farm stands. You actually have the same option today: your local farmers' market.

When Ann's father goes to farmers' markets, he complains that they are so much more expensive than regular grocery stores, and too fancy. Farmers markets are actually notoriously misunderstood. They sure seem to be more expensive than natural food grocers, like Sprouts or Whole Foods, but that's only because of the cute specialty booths, with things like organic vegan macaroons, which usually cost more than a regular donut. Many of you first gens already know that farmers' markets have been staples in a señora's routine for many centuries, and some of you may remember going to them with your *abuelas* each week.

Latin America is famous for its *mercados*. In Chile, for example, there's the La Vega Central market (also known as the Feria Mapocho), which was created in the eighteen century as a loose grouping of farmers who started to sell their products in the Chimba area of Santiago. The actual market was developed in 1895, when warehouses were built and a market system was launched. Now elder Chilean señoras, posh señora moms, small business owners, tourists, and chefs alike shop there for delicious fresh ingredients and things like *pan amasado*, nuts, meat, and much more. It's always a treat for Ann when she visits Santiago.

Ann spent half her childhood mornings at Viña del Mar's Feria Estero Marga Marga with one of her *abuelitas*. It was always pretty boring for her to go food shopping, but knowing what she knows now about fresh food, Ann would have paid a lot more attention to how her grandmother and her friends selected their produce. Strolling among delicious, colorful produce with our little baskets, seeing all the colors of the fruits and vegetables, catching the scent of fresh lettuce mixed with the aroma of the ocean air coming from the beach—that's one of her favorite memories of growing up.

Christina didn't grow up in Mexico, but she remembers that visits to farmers' markets were indeed magical experiences, rich in culture and invigorating food scents that could make anyone hungry. In Mexico *mercados* are an important institution. These are called *mercados públicos* (public markets) or *mercados municipales*. The oldest farmers' market in Mexico is the Mercado San Lucas, in Mexico City, where you can grab food and check out the famous clown shop. There are also specialty markets, in Mexico City, likes the gorgeous Mercado de Jamaica, where you can find only Mexico's most popular flowers.

Mercados evolved from weekly open-air pop-up markets called *tianguis*, which are ancient establishments in Mexico. The word *tiangui* originates from the Aztec word *tiyānquiztli, or tianquiztli,* meaning marketplace. Markets have even been found in the ruins of places like El Tajín, in Veracruz, and entire towns were created around markets, like Santiago Tianguistenco and Chichicastenango in Guatemala. In Christina's ancestral city, Oaxaca, the most popular farmers' market is the Mercado de

Abastos, where hundreds of vendors sell crafts, home goods, and food. She often dreams of going back one day to Oaxaca, researching her family's local roots, retracing their steps through the same *mercado* aisles, maybe looking for the same delicious ingredients for their weekly meal prep for the family. One day.

You may think that your local farmers' market here in the States has always been there, but it hasn't. In fact, it's a North American ancestral establishment that fell out of favor for a long time. In the US, having a farmers' market in your town was pretty common until around the 1940s, when grocery stores, improved roads, and transportation systems became more developed, and the modern "food industry" was created, where the goal of food production was to make it easier for working families to cook, and to make the food tastier so they would eat more.

Farmers markets remained out of fashion until the 1990s, when they started popping up again in many areas of the country, helped by the US wellness craze of the 1980s. By 2019 there were around eighty-seven hundred farmers' markets in the US. The señoras of your ancestral homelands were going to farmers' markets long before you were trying to grab the latest smoothie recipe alongside Justin Bieber at the Calabasas Farmers Market.

There are so many benefits to going to your local farmers' markets like a true señora. They're mood boosters: You'll get an instant boost after a couple of hours at the *mercado*, getting fresh air, getting your steps in, checking the food scene, maybe grabbing some snacks or breakfast. You'll be able to explore delicious new ingredients and create a game plan for much more nutritious meals than if you were just relying on the deli counter at your local market. Ann feels so much better during the weeks when she has the time to cook fresh meals. She has more energy and feels less sluggish and bloated, and her mood is much better than on off days.

There's also the social element to farmers' markets: You can meet your local farmers or the founders of your favorite food brand. Strolling around like you're the main character, with a book and your tote bag in hand, is the coziest feeling. Farmers markets have all the elements of a trendy "wellness cure"–and they're free to visit. No wonder your ancestral señoras' favorite pastime was strolling around a good *mercado*.

A huge benefit of shopping at farmers' markets and farm stands is that you're more likely to eat locally sourced foods. Buying locally is good for your carbon footprint, because you're not forcing your apples to travel two thousand miles to your kitchen counter. Your food is more likely to be fresher, have more nutrients, and have fewer pesticides, and it will just taste better.

So, to get the benefit of having a garden without actually having one, you have many options. What about the idea that farmers' markets are more expensive than regular markets? Recent studies show that they're actually now up to 40 percent less pricey than grocery stores. Only eggs and potatoes are less expensive at stores. In addition, some farmers' markets, farm stands and farm box delivery services across the US are now fully SNAP/EBT operational.

What if you don't have a farmers' market near you? One of the benefits of living in the *campo* is living near farms and also having farm stands on the outskirts of town that sell fresh produce. Ann found a *mercadito* right outside of San Diego with not only veggies and fruits but also candies (*mazapan*, which she remembers from growing up in Chile), fresh fruit juice, fresh bread, ice cream, and even wood for your outdoor fireplace.

Thanks to farmers' markets around town, Ann has also met local farmers, gone to dinners and *asados* (barbecues) on their properties, and bought things like fresh turkeys from them for

Thanksgiving. She can honestly say that theirs are the most delicious, juiciest turkey she's ever had. There are farms and homesteads outside of town that sell fresh eggs from their coops and honey from their honeybees. Many small farmers also operate farm boxes, and they can even deliver the boxes of produce to your home. This is especially good for folks who might be disabled and homebound. There are national companies, like Farm Fresh to You, a delivery service founded in 1976, that are like customizable online farm stands.

How do you find these in your town? Dig around in your town's Facebook groups or on Nextdoor. Do a search for things like "[city] Homesteading Group," "[city] backyard gardening," and "[city] urban gardening." Look for areas that may have farms or ranchos and farming families selling produce. You'll be surprised at what you can find!

Radical Señora Gardening Secret #3: Expand to crops that would be familiar to your ancestral señoras

If you have some outdoor space, such as a balcony, the easiest way to start a garden is by creating an herb garden. You can do this by buying a basil plant from your local grocery store and making sure you keep that plant alive. Then why not launch right into chamomile? It's your ancestral señora's favorite plant and an easy herb that you can plant even in the wintertime—as long as it gets four hours of daylight each day in order to germinate. You'll need a pot that's at least twelve inches in diameter and seeds from your local home and garden center or online. The best online shops to buy seeds from at the time of this writing are Johnny's Selected Seeds, Botanical Interests (recently bought by the YouTuber Epic Gardening), Ferry-Morse,

Baker Creek, and Seed Savers Exchange. For cheaper options, go to Amazon and Etsy, where you'll find local homesteaders selling seed packets. Ann even found a free seed exchange program at one of her local libraries. If you search for it, you will find it...

The seedlings will need an environment that is at least around 70°F, so if you have a cold kitchen, place them near the oven (but don't forget about them there!). If your bedroom is nice and warm, take them into your bedroom overnight and place them by your television. To keep all your seedlings tidy, organized, and efficient, you can get your own "build your own" greenhouse made out of piping and plastic on Amazon, as well as a heating pad or grow light. This greenhouse is small enough to place in a corner somewhere in your home.

If you're an intermediate or advanced gardener, why not experiment with herbs that señoras from your homeland loved? This will be a lot harder and more time intensive, but the mental and physical health benefits can't be beat. There is nothing more soothing in the world than knowing that you're planting, caring for, and harvesting something that your ancestral señoras likely did, too.

For a great overview of the herbs from your home country, go to Google Scholar and find a research report outlining your country's herbs. Ann owes a big thanks to The OG Pickle Queen from her TikTok community, who sent her a PDF with a historic overview of plant life from Chile, focusing specifically on Mapuche herbs. An excellent and detailed guide to the home gardens of our ancestors is the 2022 article "Home Gardens in Latin America: Wild Foods in the Mesoamerican Ekuaro of P'urépechas, Mexico and the Andean Chacra of Kichwas, Ecuador." You'll find many books at Walmart, on Amazon, and at your local library for free.

If your ancestral señoras were from Mexico, you might try growing *epazote*, which the Aztecs used for flavoring beans and which is supposed to be great for your tummy. It can be grown in the hotter areas of the country. Or, you might want to try Mexican oregano, which has a citrus flavor as compared to Mediterranean oregano. If you live in zones 2a–12, you might try *huauzontle*, which is a cousin of quinoa. If you're in zones 4–9, how about the cilantro alternative, *papalo*, which will grow really nicely in your summer garden (because cilantro is a hard to grow plant). And if you're in zones 7b–10b, you might want to check out Mexican marigold, which the Aztecs also used to season foods and which is said to be a good substitute for French tarragon. You can also add the leaves to your salads.

If you're from Latin America and live in any of zones 4 and above, why not try planting quinoa, a highly nutritious whole grain that's gluten free? Unfortunately, it doesn't do super great in temperatures over 90°F. Once harvested, be ready to take some time out to process the seeds, which need to be removed from the heads. You might want to try achiote, or annatto (zones 10–11). Try your hand at the yuca plant (zones 4–11), which is really hardy. It's a root staple in many Latin American cuisines, and people boil, fry, and ferment it. If you're into fruits more, try passion fruit vines (zones 9–11), which yield a tiny fruit that's delicious and slimy and sweet-tart.

To cultivate these exotic plants a, you'll want to sit down and make a list of the ones that speak to you. Google their perfect growing conditions, find out how to start them from seeds and where to find good seeds. Then order the seeds online and get to work. Sometimes it will take some effort and trial and error.

Once Ann's family garden was more developed, she set out to "señorafy" it. She borrowed ideas from what she remembered from both her great-grandmothers' *huertos* and from her paternal grandmother, Margarita's tiny garden on her suburban patio, and she also selected herbs from her home country that she wanted to try.

Ann started by trying to plant Chilean rosebushes, where rose hips come from, and that play a huge role in Chilean beauty culture, and in her and Christina's beauty line, Vamigas. She specifically wanted to plant the rose species *Rosa rubiginosa* because of its particularly nutritious rose hips. This species is primarily grown in the Andes. However, the species she found online was the more common *Rosa canina*, which grows all over Europe as a weed. In her search, Ann even called plant nurseries that she knew were super knowledgeable, but all she got was a lot of confused questions. She eventually gave up and grabbed *Rosa canina* rosebushes from a nearby nursery and threw them into her garden.

Out of the ten that she planted, only one survived. Two died because she forgot to water them, three were accidentally murdered by her well-meaning gardener, and one just died randomly in the orchard because she had taken too long to plant it in the ground. But it just takes one! The one that took is now a big, beautiful bush at the front of her property, by the chickens, and it's an everyday reminder of her homeland and family back home. Try, fail, try again, and you'll eventually strike gold. Maybe in the form of beautiful rose hips, too.

Radical Señora Gardening Secret #4: Become an herbalist or just get "tea adventurous"

Ann's paternal grandmother, Margarita, had many herbs in her kitchen, one for every type of cough, sinus problem, or sore throat you could imagine. Some were to relax, while others were just to taste delicious. All served a purpose. One of your grandmothers was likely the same way. Ann's maternal great-grandmother's grandmother was an herbalist in her town, and so people likely came to her from far and wide to ask for her healing syrups and tonics.

If your ancestral señoras go back a few generations in Latin America, chances are that one of them was or knew of an herbalist or even a *curandera*. In our homelands, herbalism and *curanderismo* are deeply rooted in Indigenous cultures, and knowledge of the healing properties of herbs was passed down from generation to generation. When the Spanish invaded your Indigenous ancestors' lands and cultures, they took that knowledge home with them and introduced their own recipes using European healing herbs, leading to something that was a mix of both continents, with a major influence from Africa and Asia due to migrations and the horrific transatlantic slave trade.

Herbalism as we know it right now means using different types of plants and their various parts—leaves, roots, stems, flowers, petals, seeds, and so on—to create things like teas, tinctures, capsules, salves, extracts, and more that promote physical health and wellness. The benefits are influenced by which chemical compounds are in the herbs themselves—things like alkaloids, flavonoids, terpenes, phenols, and more. Herbalism may also include making things like skin-care and beauty products!

The herbs used depend on geographic location and culture, and maybe your family background is mixed and so you may notice a little bit of everything. For example, India has a strong Ayurvedic tradition, which focuses on the health of the whole person (diet, lifestyle, spiritual, and so on), while traditional Chinese medicine (TCM), which is thousands of years old, includes things you may have heard of or tried, like acupuncture. North and South American herbalism traditions incorporate herbs and seeds like sage, echinacea, ayahuasca, sacha inchi, and much more. If you'd like to go deep into herbalism, there are many books to get you started on your learning journey like Rosemary Gladstar's *Medicinal Herbs: A Beginner's Guide*. There are also organizations that provide courses that teach you about Latino and Indigenous herbalism traditions, such as the California School of Traditional Hispanic Herbalism, and Hood Herbalism, and you can access some of these online. Of course, more general schools like The Herbal Academy are great places to start your journey.

Many herbalist recipes are more straightforward than you think, though they do take some time. When Ann made dandelion root tea (*diente de leon*), she foraged for dandelion in her backyard, sliced off the roots, washed them really well, cut them into small equal-sized pieces, put them in the oven until they had dried (dehydrated), and then added them to her crockpot to roast them. She then blended the pieces and used the remaining powder as tea. Scientific research says that dandelion root tea may support the liver, aid in digestion, help reduce inflammation, and help with bloating, and that it has loads of antioxidants. Of course, when she doesn't have two hours free to prepare this herbal tea concoction, which is most of the time, Ann buys the dandelion tea bags at the market. But when she's feeling fancy and has some free time, she knows that going through this tea-making process will have all the added benefits of a calming, mindful routine.

Interestingly, what Ann found is that when she prepares any of the herbal recipes she finds in books and classes or any of the old family herbal recipes, it forces her to slow down and think clearly and feel more at ease. She believes it's a mix of being focused on an activity, using your hands to craft something, and enjoying the beauty or deliciousness of the end product.

During seasons when Ann has more time, usually wintertime, she likes to select her next herbalism project based on what her family is experiencing at the time and what family members need help with. For example, during cold season she learned to make easy lemon and honey cough drops to help soothe the throat. There was a learning curve to figuring out the gelatin situation (and yes, there are vegan alternatives), but it was so satisfying to see her toddler asking for her cough drops when her throat hurt. She didn't love the taste, and she tried to give many away to the dog, but it gave Ann a special sense of pride and accomplishment to have created something helpful with her own two hands. That's part of the beauty of herbalism—it helps us achieve mastery of something that helps other people, especially our loved ones.

Ann didn't always know that she had an herbalist in the family. About a year after she had started her herbalism projects, her *tía* Blanca came to visit from Chile and happened to tell Ann about her ancestral señora who was a town's herbalist. When her great-grandmother Maria was little, she would go into her kitchen to see all kinds of little jars with powders and teas in them. It was deeply joyful for Ann to think about that connection across time that she had with her great-great-great-grandmother, and to know that her kitchen perhaps looked a little bit like this ancestral señora's—except Ann's had a Ninja Foodi and a coffee machine, which she probably would have thought were positively alien.

Ask your *tías* or your grandmothers if they remember a señora herbalist in their family tree. We can almost guarantee that you'll find that a señora in your family tree had a tea for every type of cold, a syrup for every cough, and a tincture for every headache. You may have ancestors from different cultures, so you could even incorporate things from Ayurveda, traditional Chinese medicine, and Indigenous folk medicine or bush medicine from the Caribbean into your projects, too.

Why should you incorporate herbal work into your señora tool kit? For one, you'll be connecting with your culture, and you'll feel a sense of rootedness that you may never have felt before. You'll be connecting with plants and flowers, and we know how good it feels to dig into working with nature. Herbalism is also a creative pursuit and will help with creative expression, which you might be searching for, because you're following recipes, creating new ones, mixing herbs, figuring out what to grow, and learning new techniques and methods every week.

It's also a built-in mindfulness practice. For something to be a useful mindfulness practice, it has to hold your attention and force you to be present and in the moment. Creating a fun and easy herbalism practice checks off all those boxes. You'll likely be more relaxed after a session, and you'll be able to approach your day with more clarity. A side benefit: You'll have delicious concoctions and potions for your family to try or gifts for the holidays. To start, check out the class that started it all at the Herbal Academy (herbalacademy.com).

Radical Señora Gardening Secret #5: Expand your tea collection

Here we get to one of the señora's favorite pastimes—*tecito*, or tea. There is nothing more soothing for the señora than a cup of tea. Without a doubt, most of the señoras of your family tree loved to take their tea outside and have a moment of relaxation on the porch. It was a critical part of their daily routine because it made them feel good and lifted their spirits.

There's a reason why tea is such a big part of women's lives. Two to three cups of tea per day have been connected with a decreased risk of early death, heart disease, stroke, and even diabetes.[9] Tea contains polyphenols, or flavonoids, which have been found to make teas healthy by acting as antioxidants, which mitigate the free radicals in your body. These free radicals can alter DNA and be harmful to our health. Research shows that all types of teas—except for decaffeinated ones—have similar levels of these antioxidants.

Señoras have a special relationship with black tea and chamomile, but there are so many different types of teas from your homelands that you'll never get tired of discovering new flavors.

Here are a few flavors that will help you reconnect with the señoras of the past.

1. Yerba Maté: This ingredient originated in South America, in countries like Argentina, Paraguay, and Uruguay. It's a traditional herb made from the leaves of the maté shrub or tree (*Ilex paraguariensis* plant). The flavor profile is earthy and bitter—so it's not everyone's cup of tea. Locals drink yerba maté using a gourd with a bombilla, which is a metal straw. To improve the taste, you are welcome to add a little bit of honey, but be advised that doing so may get you canceled by the Argentinians, because they like their maté unsweetened.

2. Hibiscus Tea (*Agua de Jamaica*): This tea is made from dried hibiscus flowers, and it originated in parts of Central America, like Mexico, and the Caribbean, but can be ultimately traced back to Africa. The flavor profile is tart, floral, light, and even fruity. You may not even need to add sugar to it. Some folks love hibiscus tea cold and with lime juice.

3. *Guayusa* Tea: This one comes from the Amazon and is drunk by people in Ecuador, Peru, and Colombia.

It is made from the *Ilex guayusa*, a species of holly tree, has lightly sweet flavor, and has high caffeine.

4. Lemon Verbena Tea (*Cedrón*): This tea, made from the plant Aloysia citrodora, is made from a strong herb used in Latin America, native to Argentina, Peru and Chile, that has a citrus/lemon flavor. It's said to be great for helping the tummy and relaxing.

5. *Boldo* Tea: This tea is made from a Chilean medicinal tree (the *Peumus boldus* tree) that has a somewhat bitter flavor. People in Chile drink the tea after meals to help with digestion.

6. Anise Tea (*Té de Anís*): This tea is made from the anise plant, and it is very sweet and has a flavor akin to licorice. Anise tea has digestive properties and also can offer some respiratory relief during cold season.

7. Cinnamon Tea (*Té de Canela*): Made from ground cinnamon or cinnamon sticks, this tea is spicy and has warm flavors. It is common in Mexico and Central America and is made sweeter with honey.

8. *Matico* Tea: Native to Chile, Peru, Ecuador, and Colombia, it's used to treat ailments like a sore tummy after lunch and nasal issues when you get sick. Ann remembers this tea growing up, but she was never allowed to drink it. One Indigenous use is as a poultice: It is spread on cloth material and applied to skin sores to heal them.

You can find most of these tea flavors at specialty tea companies online and also on Amazon. Many towns have little apothecaries owned by a small business owner, and those are your best bets for discovering new tea flavors. Ann loves going into the tea shop in her hometown. It feels like she's visiting the little shop in the film *Practical Magic*, except this tea shop has the most wonderful herbs, spices, and tea mixes.

More uncommon and unconventional (hard to find) teas that are just as special include:

1. *Mamajuana* Tea: Originally from the Dominican Republic, this tea is a traditional tonic, made with herbs, roots, barks, and rum or wine.
2. *Guapinol* Tea: The guapinol, or "beauty leaf," is a tree that grows in Central, South America and the Caribbean that is sourced for its bark, fruit or resin. This has a mild, earthy flavor.
3. Quillai Tea: The quillai tree is originally from Chile. Its bark is used to make a tea that's slightly bitter and pungent. Because of its frothing qualities because it contains saponins, the bark is also used to make shampoo.
4. *Tilo* Tea: You may know this one as "linden" or "tilia." This tea has a flowery flavor and is known for its calming, relaxing effects.
5. *Pata de Vaca* Tea: Literally meaning "Cow's Foot," the *pata de vaca* is a tree native to Brazil, Argentina and Paraguay. Its leaves are used to make an herbal tea with a slightly sweet, herbal taste.
6. *Palo Azul* Tea: The palo azul tree is native to Mexico and Central America, and the tea made from its bark has a subtle woody flavor.
7. *Borojó* Tea: This tea or juice is made from the fruit of the *borojó* tree, a tropical rainforest tree native to Colombia, Panama, and Ecuador. The tea tastes fruity and almost tangy.

8. *Chañar* Tea: This tea, from Argentina, Bolivia, Chile, and other parts of South America, has a fruity flavor and scent that's said to be good for respiratory support. The ripe fruit can also be fermented to make an alcoholic drink.

9. Chaparral Tea: Originating in the southwestern United States and parts of Mexico, and made from the creosote bush, a desert shrub, this herbal tea has a strong medicinal taste.

10. *Uña de Gato* Tea: The woody *uña de gato* vine (Uncaria tomentosa), is native to the Amazon rainforest and other tropical areas in South and Central America, and its bark and roots are used to make a bitter, earthy-flavored herbal tea. Not to be confused with the other "Uña de Gato" (Uncaria guianensis).

One of the richest sources of herbal knowledge from your Indigenous ancestors are herbal documents that are called by a specific "codex name." One in particular is called the *Badianus Manuscript* or the Codex Barberini, or *Libellus de Medicinalibus Indorum Herbis* (*Little Book of Medicinal Herbs of the Indians*). This is a very important historical artifact that details the medicinal plants used by the Aztec people. This text is one of the earliest written and illustrated manuscripts from the New World, written by Indigenous physician Martin de la Cruz and translated by Juan Badiano in the sixteenth century. It's made up of about 78 pages, with 180 illustrations of plants and their Nahuatl names, along with their medicinal uses. If your family is from Mexico, it's very likely that your ancestors used some of these plants to help heal their families.

Plant mixtures are laid out based on medicinal use, and maladies like gout were said to be cured by a mixture made from the bush known as *piltzintecouhxochitl*. Plants were mixed and were prepared using methods like maceration with swallow's blood, and applied on the body. There are remedies for everything you can think of—even one to help people who were "struck by lightning."

One of Ann's most satisfying routines has been trying a unique new herbal tea each month. Her "tea research" consists of first finding lists of herbs and their benefits online or in a book. She then goes searching for herbs on Amazon or Etsy. If she can't find them there, Ann usually goes to her local tea and herbal shop. If she can't find them here, she does a longer search for websites that sell rare and exotic teas.

You might also want to learn how to blend teas, and create your own special flavors with your favorite aromas or select them for their medicinal uses, like to support digestion. It's also cost effective because you're buying ingredients in bulk, so the teas you make can last you for a long time. If you want to learn the techniques, go to Ann and Christina's website, senoraera.com.

Radical Señora Gardening Secret #6:
Go all in like your great-grandmother

If your grandmother had a *huerto* or a *ranchito*, there is a high possibility that she had her own flock of chickens that fed the family. Chickens aren't thought to be native to Latin America, and they most likely arrived with the Spanish in the fifteenth century. However, there is some recent data that suggests there were chickens in the Americas before the European invasion. This means your Indigenous ancestors may have had chickens, too. So how do we coop like a señora?

Ann's family garden has expanded into a more robust *huerto*, where she and her husband have a food garden, fruit trees, and chickens. She is planning on getting bees, too, but for now that's where they plan on stopping. Don't feel like you have to keep expanding. Watching those YouTube homesteaders, Ann often feels like she is not doing enough, so how dare she call herself a gardener when she just has X number of beds and no animals? Early on she and her husband decided they really didn't want the added responsibility or cost of more animals, and so they are sticking to just chickens and some guard dogs. You don't need to go all out. It's about whatever makes you feel good.

You may also want chickens. There is nothing more delicious than eating fresh eggs or more earthy than collecting them each morning. So, what do you do if you want chickens? Consider what Ann went through and did during her own coop adventures, but you'll want to listen to the professionals, like Kathy Shea Mormino, the author of *The Chicken Chick's Guide to Backyard Chickens*. There's a lot of chicken misinformation online, so you'll want to make sure that in addition to getting ideas from hobby farmers, you also seek out books and courses from the experts.

If you have some space (and don't have an HOA), you'll need five things to get started.

1. A secure chicken coop: You can never get "too" secure. At first, Ann was tempted to go and buy a starter coop from a big-box store, but these are usually really flimsy structures and won't protect your flock. You'd be surprised at how strong and smart predators are. Some, like raccoons, can even open coop latches. In the end they went with a mom-and-pop maker of chicken coops in San Diego, Mellott Chicken Coops, because the coops are handmade, weather resistant, and predator proof. You'll want to

avoid things like chicken wire and being too loosey-
goosey with the structure, because you need to make
sure your chickens are safe, healthy, and happy—and
not coyote food...yes, even if you live in the city.

2. Feeding and watering gadgets: You'll want to grab
   feed systems that are specially built for chickens, so
   that you add food once a week and they're all set.
   One key thing is to be sure the food and water are
   tall enough to be able to avoid mice, which will
   come calling, let me assure you of that.

3. Bedding: Pine shavings are preferable because you
   can do what's called the layering method, which is
   excellent for waste management and keeps the
   coop fresh and clean. Whatever you decide, the
   bedding has got to keep the coop dry, because as
   Kathy Shea Mormino stresses in her book, moisture
   breeds bacteria.

4. Chicken materials: You'll want to get high-quality
   food, which ideally gives your chickens all the nutrition they need. The type of food should match
   their age ranges, because younger chickens need different types of food than those that are already egg
   laying. You'll want oyster shells, which act as vitamins, and a "chicken first-aid kit" with things like
   wound spray, electrolytes for animals, a thermo-
   meter, and any emergency supplement your local
   vet recommends. Some people don't advocate for
   this, but make sure your chickens are vaccinated
   against certain viruses. You can lose an entire flock if
   one gets sick. And it's not pretty! Ann has lost entire
   flocks to one awful disease called Marek's.

If you're not sold on keeping chickens but still want to step up your *ranchito* game, there are less time and money intensive activities, like canning and fermentation, which will allow you to preserve foods like your great-grandmother may have. It could be as simple as pickling cucumbers or red onions—from your garden or the farmers' market—to create the most delicious pickles you have ever tasted. Fermentation projects are fun, and you really only need mason jars, a big pot of water, and simple accessories to handle the jars in the boiling water. You can buy a simple kit off Amazon, one that has everything you'll need to start canning.

You already know about the benefit of growing your own food, but there are added bonuses to making things from the herbs and vegetables you grow. There's the sense of connection to your homelands and the spiritual connection to your ancestors, the joy of learning things and knowing that you'll likely be passing this cultural knowledge on to your descendants, helping keep long dead traditions alive. You'll have a sense of accomplishment from making things, which is particularly useful during stressful times, when you need to take your mind off things. You'll feel stress relief and an overall sense of well-being because when you concentrate, there is an element of mindfulness that is almost meditative.

One of the most obvious benefits—if you get good at creating and growing things—is that you may actually save some money on grocery bills if you plan things out properly. You'll also like the fact that you and your loved ones are eating more delicious and nutritious food. Curiously immersing yourself in the skills that were lost over the past century, using them all to your advantage, then teaching them to the next generation will give you such a gratifying feeling.

Radical Señora Gardening Secret #7:
Plant your homeland's harvests

You may remember some of your favorite flowers in your grandmas' gardens or the trees in great-grandmother's *huerto*. Some of the botanicals from our homelands can be grown in various hardiness zones in the US. Actually, growing these exotic veggies, fruit trees, nut trees, and flowers may be difficult, because the zones may not exactly match up with the environment needed, and you may, for instance, have a cold blast that will kill the hardiest harvest.

As was mentioned before, it's been Ann's dream to grow avocados, lucumas, and chirimoyas in her orchard, because these are the fruits she remembers from her great-grandmother's *huerto*. Her hardiness zone is similar to that of her ancestral town in Chile, but the frost that they get in her zone is cold enough to kill the hardiest lucuma tree. Her one avocado tree that came with their house is struggling and hasn't given any fruit; however, the avocado trees outside her town seem to be thriving. It really is a big puzzle that you'll have to figure out and solve. All the fun will be in researching, planning, and matching up the hardiness zones between your city or town and your family's hometown. If your trees or bushes don't grow, you still got a crash course in the botanical knowledge of your señora ancestors.

When starting to cross-check hardiness zones, just Google "X hardiness zone versus Y hardiness zone" and you'll get a few websites that will give you an idea of how two zones interact and match up. You'll also need to know the temperatures, frost dates, hottest days, and frost days.

To get you started, here are some ideas about veggies, nut trees, and fruit trees native to Latin America that can also be planted in parts of the United States. You can download a quick planting guide created by Ann and Christina on their website, senoraera.com.

1. Avocado (*Persea americana*): Zone 10. Native to Mexico and parts of Central and South America, avocados can be grown in southern regions of the US, particularly in California, Florida, Hawaii, and Texas.
2. Tomatillo (*Physalis philadelphica*): Zones 5–9 as annuals, and zones 10–11 as perennials. Native to Mexico and parts of Central America, these guys can be grown in many parts of the US, particularly in those states with a warmer climate.
3. Papaya (*Carica papaya*): Zones 9–10. Native to tropical regions of the Americas, including Mexico and Central America, papayas can be grown in southern regions of the US, particularly in Florida, California, and Texas.
4. Pineapple (*Ananas comosus*): Zones 11–12. Native to South America, particularly Brazil, Argentina, and Paraguay, pineapples can be grown in southern regions of the US, especially in Florida and Hawaii.
5. Guava (*Psidium guajava*): Zones 9–12. Native to Mexico, Central America and northern South America, guavas can be grown in southern regions of the US, particularly in Florida, California, and Texas.
6. Passion Fruit (*Passiflora edulis*): Zones 9+, but it has been known to grow in zones as cold as 5. Native to South America, particularly Brazil, Paraguay and northern Argentina, passion fruit can be grown in warmer regions of the US, particularly in Florida, California, and Hawaii.

7. Macadamia Nut (*Macadamia integrifolia*): Zones 9–11. Native to Australia and parts of Oceania but also found in Central and South America, macadamia trees can be grown in Hawaii and certain regions of California.

8. Cacao (*Theobroma cacao*): Zones 11–13. Native to the Amazon Basin, spanning Colombia, Ecuador, Peru, Venezuela and Brazil, cacao trees can be grown in South Florida and Hawaii, although they require specific conditions and care.

9. Peruvian "jungle" peanut (*Arachis hypogaea var*): Zones 10–12. This pinstriped nut, native to Peru and Ecuador, is a very old variety of peanuts. It is said to be excellent for making peanut butter.

10. Roselle (*Hibiscus sabdariffa*): Zones 9–10. This is native to Africa, but widely cultivated in Caribbean and Central American. You can make tea, other drinks, jams, and syrups from roselle flowers. They taste kind of like cranberry.

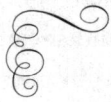

CHAPTER 8

The Señora Home

Reusing, Repurposing, and Creating a Zero-Waste Household

WHEN ANN AND her family arrived in the United States, a new movement was becoming popular: environmentalism. One day, while at the supermarket checkout not too long after arriving in the US, the cashier gave her the kid's version of a book called *50 Simple Things You Can Do to Save The Earth.* After having her parents translate it for her, she was floored, and not because the book was earth shattering, but because—back then in the late 1980s—some of the "simple things" the book suggested were things they already did back in her homeland. Their normal, ancestral ways of living were considered "groundbreaking" here in the United States.

Using kitchen towels instead of paper towels was common for the ancestral señoras of her family. "So much waste—and so expensive!" they would have said about paper towels. The tried-and-true multipurpose kitchen towel, with dainty little paintings of flowers, was always the trusted sidekick, helping the señora clean messes, dry the dishes, and pick up a hot pan.

The amount of waste our civilization is creating is a critical issue that's also acutely affecting our homelands. The amount of trash being thrown into our ancestral lands–specifically old clothing and plastic–has become a global environmental and social problem. Chile, for example, has become a massive dumping ground for what's called "fast fashion" from all over the world. Tons and tons of clothing arrive in ports, where they are taken to be resold farther inland. What's not sold is then taken to landfills in the Atacama Desert, a breathtaking region between the Cordillera de la Costa and the Andes Mountains and one of the most scientifically important geographic regions in the world.

After being dumped, these textiles release chemicals into the soil and the groundwater and emit greenhouse gases, which contribute to climate change. This practice can also lead to microplastics entering our food chain and ultimately ending up inside human bodies.

Researchers have consistently found that toxic microplastics are ending up in everything–including inside us. They end up in the water that we drink, the seafood we eat, and even in the air that we breathe. Some researchers have found that microplastics can even cause cellular damage, inflammation, oxidative stress, and disruptions in the gut microbiome, though the research is still out.[1] There doesn't seem to be any way around avoiding all plastic in your life, but you can limit the amount of exposure. The website Dialogue Earth says that over the past twenty years, plastic production has doubled to nearly five hundred million tons. This is predicted to increase by *anywhere from 66% to potentially tripling* in the coming years.

Only 9 percent of plastic is recycled, with 12 percent ending up being burned. The rest is sent to landfills or ends up in your local environment, which pushes global greenhouse emissions higher.[2]

The United Nations has placed the plastic problem on its radar, to try specifically to deal with "waste colonialism," which means how other countries are dumping their garbage on our homelands. Much of the world's plastic ends up in Mexico, where toxic chemicals have been leaching into its land and its people for many years.

One way to create less garbage on a personal level is to have more of a "zero-waste" lifestyle, where your goal becomes to reduce the amount of stuff that you use every day.

Christina and Ann took this concept seriously as they built their beauty line. They wanted their products to create as little waste as possible, because the beauty industry has a major trash problem. They purposely avoided using plastic bottles and instead chose glass, which can then be recycled by most city waste programs. The paper their boxes used was fully compostable, which meant anyone could add them to the compost bin in their garden—where they would eventually break down and end up in garden beds—or toss them into a recycling bin. Their goal was to create a product that didn't end up in some landfill.

Ann had never really thought too much about this issue until she met her now good friend Janine, an eco-pioneer and founder of the environmental organization GreenWave, who currently lives in Costa Rica and is third-generation Mexican-American. She taught Ann so much about the importance of using less plastic, avoiding single-use products, and recycling. It never really hit home for Ann until she had a family, because she saw how much waste they were generating.

Christina took the no-waste philosophy into her personal life and made it a mission to completely stop buying fast fashion. Instead, she buys statement pieces that are higher quality, made with better materials, and thus won't be thrown away after a year. Many of these pieces are so timeless that they'll become family heirlooms for generations. She has also become a minimalist shopper. She doesn't shop a whole lot and avoids buying things "just because." Less Amazon and H&M and more from mom-and-pop boutiques and high-quality brands.

The señoras of the past were also what we would now call minimalists. They didn't do "shopping hauls," like your favorite Instagram influencers, or have four Amazon boxes arrive every other day, like some of us do. They used just what was needed in the home and made the rest themselves. They didn't do this to "save the earth" but to save money, because goods were expensive back then in Latin America, and so massive shopping sprees just weren't common.

How did we turn into such a consumerist culture? Over the past century, factories began producing products more cheaply, making things more accessible to everyone. Global marketplaces, too, meant we could get things much cheaper abroad than did previous generations. Postwar suburban living (your grandmother's era) made people want to buy more cars and household goods. Malls became the epicenter of families' lives.

The products your great-grandmother used were very simple and often homemade. If the señora didn't make the product herself, then it was likely made by the shopkeeper or the señora down the block. Common items were multipurpose, which meant they could be used for many different tasks. For example, the soap she used for washing the laundry was a combination of oils like olive oil and animal fat, or animal fat and ash, and could also be used for washing the dishes. A similar type of soap, but with slightly different ingredients, could be used for the body, face, and even hair.

Today's zero-waste gurus are sharing the ideas of señoras from all around the world, whose homes were zero-waste wonderlands. How so? Señoras were pros at creating a circular economy. First, they had no need for packaging, since the items they made and used in the home were easily stored in the pantry, inside linen bags. Second, many of the ingredients they used were just recycled from the kitchen, like when old cooking oil was used to make dish soap. Food scraps went to the chickens or the compost heap out back, and eggshells went into the soil. A señora's trash could fit inside a small bag compared to the massive trash bags of today. Collecting her food from the *huerto* out back or the *mercado* down the street meant a carbon footprint of zero. Glass bottles were reused to ferment and pickle vegetables, fish and meat from the deli were wrapped in newspaper, and that paper was eventually used for the fire out back. Everything had a purpose, and very little went in the trash.

You think recycling is a new concept, but it's far from it—as the señoras from your ancestral line did a very early form of recycling back then—it was just called something different. To this day, Ann's mom has fond memories of growing up in her family's hometown, where once a week, a man on a bicycle would ride down the streets of each neighborhood, collecting used paper, plastic bottles, and egg cartons.

Buying fewer things and going more DIY mean you'll be creating less trash, you'll have less clutter in your house, and you may even save some money. It's worrisome to think how much more trash we all make compared to our great-grandmothers.

Ann has another funny memory of moving here in the eighties. One of the first things her parents did here was to order a garbage bin from the city. They were bewildered when they received a bin that was the size of a person. Even in that decade, they were not used to generating so much garbage back home. She remembers her parents joking about the fact they would never have enough garbage to fill up that bin. Sure enough, within a few years, they were filling up that trash can as well as their neighbors. Nothing signals becoming more "modern" like bringing three of those giant ninety-five-gallon containers of trash out to your curb every Monday.

Interestingly, when Ann put into place at her home the stackable señora habits outlined in the wellness chapter—of eating fewer ultra-processed foods and more whole foods, and composting scraps—she found that her trash volume was slashed considerably. Her household went from putting out three people-sized trash cans to just one every week.

It's also easy to forget that your washing machine and dishwasher are relatively new innovations. Just like you are the last generation to probably remember what daily life was like before the Internet, your *abuela*'s generation was the last to remember what it was like to do the laundry and wash dishes manually in a house full of ten kids, a baby, some chickens, a bunch of dogs, and a cranky husband.

The señora's basic tool set included a washboard, soap, simple towels, and a sewing machine. Here's what her home may have looked like:

Tableros de Fregados

Your Indigenous ancestors washed their clothing on the rocks at nearby creeks. Señoras later washed clothing with a *tabla de lavar*, which was a washboard on which you would scrub your clothing. Then came the *escurridor*, a little hand-cranked machine with rollers that put your wet clothing through to squeeze out the water. The first electric washing machine, created abroad in 1908, arrived in Latin America in the 1960s.

She didn't have the modern powder or plastic pod detergent we have today or that your grandmother used. The multipurpose tool that was in every woman's tool kit was the quintessential bar of soap—*jabón*. This little bar had many different jobs to do; it helped the señora wash clothes and dishes and clean just about anything you can think of.

The Queen of *Jabón*

The multipurpose *jabón de aceite* was a bar of soap that was made out of just a few ingredients and usually included oil, an animal or vegetable fat or ash. It was used to clean everything around the home: clothing, dishes, furniture, stains, and more. This soap had fewer ingredients than today's highly synthetic kind, had zero smell, and was pretty ugly—it usually just looked like a lumpy white or beige slab. That smooth, perfect-looking bar of soap that corporations developed came much later. Every family had their own "secret" *jabón* recipe to make at home, meaning the soap didn't need any packaging. Later, señoras purchased *jabón* from their local store and likely used it for months, then repurposed it into another bar of soap.

The History of Soap and How It Came to Latin America

The history of cleanliness is actually pretty nasty. To the Spanish of the 1400s, being too clean and washing oneself with water in a bath were revolutionary ideas—and considered a corrupting practice. The Spanish were still feeling spicy from when the Moors had invaded them. Baths were a big deal to the Moors, and thus the Spanish associated baths with their former conquerors. In fact, Moorish baths had been destroyed by King Ferdinand and

Queen Isabella after they conquered Granada in the 1400s, and
Moors who converted to Christianity were restricted from taking
baths. Because the Moors were "clean," the Spanish decided they
just wanted to be "dirty" and proclaimed that it was "more Christian" that way.

The invention of soap was another turning point in the history of our señora home rituals. The earliest recorded type of
soap dates back to around 2800 BC in ancient Babylon, but one
of the oldest known types of modern soaps was made in the city
of Aleppo, where soap making involved olive oil and animal fat.
In her book *The Dirt on Clean: An Unsanitized History*, writer
Katherine Ashenburg notes that during the Middle Ages, "toilet
soap" was made out of olive oil in places like Marseille, Italy,
and Spain. Soap made in Castile was an expensive purchase,
and so it was primarily used in elite Spanish households. Folks
used soap with water, but sometimes they added herbs for medicinal purposes.[3]

Soap then made its way to Mexico and other parts of Latin
America, but it's hard to track the exact timeline. Early on, it is
known that a factory was built in Guayaquil, Ecuador, in which
soap was made from cow tallow and the ashes from herbs. Mexico's first soap factory was erected in Mexico City in 1575. This
soap, which was commonly used in Mexican households, may
have also included saponified *tequesquite*, a natural mineral salt.
Tequesquite is also known as *tequixquitl*, a Nahuatl word that
means "stone that sprouts." During the Aztec era, this ingredient had been sourced from Lake Texcoco in central Mexico.

Jabón de Castilla, or Castile soap, was another form of this
multipurpose soap and was used for body care as well as washing the laundry. It was introduced in Spain in the eleventh
century, and at that time monasteries also used it to clean their
halls. This soap was also called *Sapo hispaniensis* and was con-

sidered among the best in the world because it was made from olive oil, which made it more of an effective cleaning product.

In a 2023 article for the newspaper *Diario Las Americas*, writer Iraima Gomez Ramirez writes that these soaps were widely used for many years in ancestral homes throughout Latin America. But these soaps were not without their set of problems. They were unstable in cold water and also in hard water. That's why synthetic soaps were introduced. The first synthetic soap, called Persil, was created in Germany in 1906 by the company Henkel, and it was made of sodium perborate and sodium silicate. It was marketed as cheaper and more convenient for señoras.

During your grandmother's generation, US corporations like Procter & Gamble started taking market share in Latin America with products that were mass produced, cheaper, and easier to make, and were made up of a long list of synthetic chemicals, instead of the botanical, oil, and animal-based products of the previous generation. These modern-day developments turned the page on home cleaning: They allowed for everyone to have a more uniform standard of cleaning, but they also introduced a lot more waste.

There were several local personal care and home soap brands that retained market share even though they were competing with their US counterparts, and these were the señora's favorite cleaning supplies. Jabón Popeye, made with a glycerin base (initially with whale fat), was used to wash clothing by the señoras of Chile. It was created by an Italian immigrant in Chile, Miguel Maritano, who created soaps the old-fashioned way, cutting them by hand and then manually stamping each soap bar. Mexico's Fábrica de Jabón La Corona has made soap from natural ingredients and other products for the home for nearly a hundred years. Zote is an iconic laundry soap in Mexico, first made in the 1970s from natural ingredients, like beef tallow and coconut oil. It was used for laundry, personal hygiene, and sometimes even pest control. The soap is still produced at the Fábrica de Jabón La Corona in Ecatepec, a municipality in the State of Mexico. Rosa Venus–also called "Jabón Chiquito"–was a soap created in Mexico in the same factory during the 1950s, and its small size made it a more affordable and an effective competitor to global brands.

The soaps the señoras of the past used are now called "artisan" or "small batch" soaps and are sold at specialty retailers and by small beauty brands. This type of soap's high-quality ingredients often mean that these soaps are a bit pricier than so-called conventional soap and are perceived as a more elegant version of the soap that you might find at the grocery store. These will last you a lot longer and will be better for your skin than soap from a big corporate brand. Ann and Christina became so enamored of the history of soap and how tied it was to a señora's life, they decided to add soap products to Vamigas, called "Orchard Blends."

Here are Christina's and Ann's tried-and-true methods for keeping the señora traditions alive and well in the modern home:

Radical Señora Home Secret #1:
Go multipurpose or DIY

A Radical Señora keeps things simple with her cleaning routine, both for her own and her family's health, and also for the environment. Using fewer products in your home and reusing them will make you feel environmentally responsible and more in control around what goes in your body. Christina and Ann avoid using "extra" things during the laundry process, like fabric softeners and dryer sheets.

You don't really need those fake, synthetic fragrances in your clothing. You might use alternatives for the dryer, like wool dryer balls, or nothing at all. There are some very niche DIY things you can use, like soap nuts, which you can grab at any online marketplace. Soap nuts are the seeds of soapberries, which come from the lychee family and are native to India. You place five soap nuts in a muslin bag, add the bag to your washing machine, and turn on the water. You can reuse them until they start to fall apart. Keep in mind they'll stink like hell when you open them for the first time!

Grabbing good, natural artisan soaps for both body and face from any of their favorite beauty brands, although they are pricier than regular soap, is something Ann and Christina love to do. A more inexpensive alternative is Aleppo-style soap, which has been one of Ann's favorites. It is the world's oldest modern soap and was likely the model for the soap that was brought to the New World centuries ago. Its ingredients are good for sensitive skin and might include olive oil and laurel berry oil. These soaps are also much cheaper than any regular soap in the market, because they come in bulk, which means you'll be buying them at two dollars apiece, and they are very big, so they last a *long time*. Aleppo-style soaps will add a special element to your home. Their light, natural scents are a soothing alternative to the harsh chemical fragrances of conventional soap. They also look really beautiful on your bathroom countertop, and so they will be a favorite accessory for the guest bathroom.

There are certain ingredients that señoras of the past used in the home that you already have in your pantry, like vinegar, baking soda, beeswax, olive oil, and more. There are many ways you can use these ingredients in your modern kitchen, and you can get creative, too. Here are some easy, low-waste home tricks.

DIY DISHWASHER PODS: When Ann ran out of detergent once to use in her dishwasher, she found a recipe online that taught her how to mix 2 spoonfuls of dishwashing detergent with 2 spoons of baking soda. It didn't clean her plates as well as the usual chemicals, but it did the trick. She doesn't use it often, but it's a good trick to have on hand for occasional use.

DIY COOKING SPRAY: Ann consistently runs out of oil cooking spray, and it's the most annoying thing to her in the world when she wants to cook eggs quickly, so sometimes she makes her own. She adds olive oil or avocado oil and water to a small spray bottle and shakes. Her homemade spray is just as good as the expensive store-bought versions. Just make sure the oil doesn't get rancid.

DIY DISHWASHING SOAP: If you're ever in a pinch—or you want to become a dedicated "no-waste" señora—you can make dish-washing soap that you can also use as hand soap by combining your ancestor's favorite Castile soap, baking soda, Aleppo soap, and water in a bottle. You can even add essential oils, like citrus or lavender, if you want your dishes to smell good.

DIY FURNITURE POLISH: Remember the bottle of polish your grandmother would use to shine the coffee table and cabinets... and that strong smell of citrus? Those are chemicals used to mimic what señoras of the past used to shine the furniture, which was lemon. There are countless recipes online that you can follow to make your own furniture polish, like one with white vinegar, olive oil, and lemon. Others add coconut oil to beeswax to create a longer-lasting shine.

WHITE VINEGAR FOR EVERYTHING: Señoras use white vinegar for everything; it is very multipurpose, given its acidity, its natural antimicrobial properties, and its ability to neutralize bad smells. Add a bit of water to vinegar in a dish and use it as a spray to clean your microwave and deodorize your dishwasher and your garbage disposal. Add it to water and baking soda in burned pots and pans, bring the mixture to boil, and it will help you gets those pots and pans clean. Add a cup full to the toilet and watch it clean with the next flush. Use it as a stain remover on clothes. Create a spray to wash fruit and veggies. Seriously, it can be used for nearly everything you can think of.

These are just some of the ways you can create a more "no-waste" señora home and buy less stuff, while at the same time getting creative with ingredients you may have lying around in your pantry closet.

Radical Señora Home Secret #2:
Ditch single-use products

One of Ann's biggest pet peeves in the kitchen is single-use paper napkins and paper towels, because she grew up in a culture and at a time when these weren't used. Disposable paper products were invented by accident when in 1907 Arthur Scott, heir to the Scott Paper Company, used discards from the factory's toilet paper production as towels. The product, called the "Sani-Towel," was marketed as a sanitary alternative to the towel in order to stop the spread of germs in industrial spaces. The paper towels really took off for home use during the 1930s.

Paper towels began to be widely used by señoras in Latin America during the 1980s, 1990s and the aughts, due to a huge marketing campaign by global brands. Ann remembers that when she left Chile, paper towels were not a commonly purchased product. However, when she went back several years later, every señora's kitchen had them. The same goes for paper napkins. When Ann left Chile, she was using cloth napkins, and she came back to a land where everyone was in love with those annoying perforated white napkins.

It wasn't always like this. Señoras of the past used the simple kitchen towel for kitchen messes and cloth napkins for their meals. They avoided generating around twenty-five pounds of paper towel waste each year, and seventy-five pounds over three years, and you can, too, by simply buying a set of cute kitchen towels and cloth napkins at your local home goods store. Don't use those napkins just for special occasions. Break them out every day for your meals. They have the extra benefit of adding a little bit of style and aesthetics to your dining experience.

The use of single-use products might be slowing down. More and more people are talking about the end of single-use products and understanding the significance of the shift. Lately there has been a trend in zero-waste boutiques opening around the country, They are called refill stores and offer beauty and home cleaning products that are package free. You essentially go into the store and place your items in refillable bags or glass jars, which you bring back the next time your shop. It's a great concept that's just catching on, and you can find products that you'll totally fall in love with. Most of them are either made by indie brands, or home-made and high quality, and you don't have to pay for the box and bag, just what's inside. To find one near you, just do a search for "zero-waste shop + your city" and go have a look around. Some of Christina's and Ann's favorites are the Refill Shoppe in Ventura, California, the Nada Shop in Encinitas, California, and Sun Moon Rain in Santa Monica, California. Some refill shops, like Eco Now California in Orange County, have clothing swap days, when you can show up and trade your cute fashion—and take your señora era sustainable life to a whole new level.

Radical Señora Home Secret #3:
Mend things; don't throw them out

The last time your pants ripped, did you automatically throw them in the garbage and buy new ones? In the time of long-ago señoras, it was not common to throw clothing away. Instead, they mended things that ripped—even old socks. In fact, throwing clothing away was like a crime against nature. Just try throwing out a shirt in front of your grandmother—you'll hear a gasp that will envelop your entire house.

Your dress wouldn't have ripped as easily if it was made from higher-quality materials. Instead of buying fast fashion from places like Shein and cheap online shops or mall stores that buy bulk from overseas, buy clothing that's sturdier, so that you can keep wearing it for many years to come. After all, these types of marketplaces are always at risk of becoming more expensive due to new tariffs. Use a sewing machine or simple hand sewing kit to mend any tears in clothing. You won't be creating new garbage, and by extending the life of your garment, you'll be saving money. You also won't be supporting companies that could have terrible working conditions in their factories or are possibly exploiting their workers abroad, because this is one way to make clothing that's very cheap—by not paying a living wage to employees.

If you want to go one step further, you might ask the señoras of your family to teach you new sewing or embroidery techniques. You'll receive invaluable cultural knowledge, which you can then pass down to the next generation. Also, have you seen the incredible new sewing machines at your local fabric store? Go test one out. You'll leave the store drooling—and saving up your money to buy one.

Radical Señora Home Secret #4:
Air out your bedding before you wash

One of Ann's grandmothers did something that Ann always thought was odd. In the morning she would put on a hair tie and apron and turn on some music, and then the first task she'd do was take out some of the bedding and hang it up to air on the balcony. It didn't matter how cold it was: The bedding was always hanging out a window. Ann later realized it wasn't just her grandmother—señoras have been doing this since the Middle Ages.

Airing out bedding once a week is a time-tested señora practice that helps keep your bedroom feeling crisp and clean and smelling good, without having to resort to any chemical sprays. Sunlight also has antibacterial characteristics that may help to sanitize your bedding. What's more, by regularly airing out your bedding, you can preserve the fabric better and extend its lifespan.

Simply pull back the covers when you leave the bed and leave your bedding fully exposed for twenty to thirty minutes. If you really want to go full señora, then once a week you might hang the bedding on your balcony or over a wall on your back patio. It'll smell as crisp and fresh as though you had put it through a full cycle in the washing machine.

Radical Señora Home Secret #5:
Reuse like a Señora

From reusing the Christmas cookie tin to store her needles and thread to storing pots and pans in the oven, the señoras of the past were unsung heroes of recycling long before it was cool. You might reuse the jars that supermarket marmalade came in or pickle jars for your gardening adventures or to meal prep. Use old Tupperware to store old buttons or other small accessories or materials. Use egg cartons as seed starters for your garden. Use packing materials for starting your *asados* in the evening. Compost food waste using a kitchen or outdoor composter (just make sure to refrain from adding dairy or protein) and make your own soil or mulch for your garden. Use old clothing or old towels to make *trapos* to mop the floor or cut them up and sew pieces together to make tote bags. Use old wine corks or used coffee grinds to create mulch for your garden. These are just some simple things to do, but the possibilities to reuse old things are endless.

Radical Señora Home Secret #6:
Avoid Plastics Like the Plague

Avoiding microplastics was an important cultural moment in 2024, when loads of new research began to show just how potentially dangerous being exposed to too much plastic was to human health; it ends up in your brain, your gut, kidneys, heart and even your reproductive organs. Señoras of the past never really had to deal with this problem because plastic became popular in the 1950s, and even later in our homelands.

Easy ways to avoid it include avoiding plastic water bottles and instead using reusable stainless steel ones, swapping out your toothbrush for ones with natural ingredients like bamboo or plant materials, tossing plastic cups and plates from your kitchen cabinets, not using plastic utensils they give you for takeout, giving babies their food and milk in things made out of glass or stainless steel, and so much more.

Christina and Ann began to avoid using too much plastic in their own homes, especially around their little ones. This meant using toothbrushes that were not made out of plastic (usually bamboo), and getting rid of everything in their kitchen made from plastic, and swapping it with glass. That meant no more Tupperware containers, and instead all glass all the time. This sounds really hard—and it is because many household items are made of plastic. But the benefit will outweigh the extra work.

⟿ Notes ⟿

CHAPTER 1: STEPPING INTO YOUR GREAT-GRANDMOTHER'S ERA

1. Luis Noe-Bustamante et al.
2. Corey Keyes
3. Dr. Yasmin Davidds
4. Lauren Mora and Mark Hugo Lopez
5. Latoya Hill and Samantha Artiga
6. Paul Taylor et al.
7. https://www.forbes.com/advisor/business/pto-statistics/
8. Michael Grothaus
9. UnidosUS
10. Tricia Hersey
11. Alicia Nuñez et al.

CHAPTER 2: HUSTLE CULTS TO SEÑORA ERA

1. Lucy Pérez et al.; Kelly Goldsmith et al.
2. Kelly Goldsmith et al.
3. Lauren Mora & Mark Hugo Lopez
4. Stephanie Horan
5. Kip Davis and Ingrid Carrete
6. Joelle L. Martinez
7. Christina Montoya Fiedler
8. Dr. Mariel Buqué
9. Lisa A. Keister and Brian Aronson
10. Aki Ito

11. Aaron Zitner
12. Pete Grieve
13. Servet Yanatma
14. Deloitte
15. Thomas Curran
16. Edward C. Chang et al.

CHAPTER 3: WORK LIKE A SEÑORA

1. Maytal Eyal
2. Jessica Stillman
3. Cal Newport

CHAPTER 4: A SEÑORA THROUGH THE AGES

1. Encarnación Pinedo, *Encarnación's Kitchen*
2. Susan Migden Socolow
3. Jane Landers
4. CUNY, Dominican Studies Institute
5. CUNY, Dominican Studies Institute
6. Sonya Lipsett-Rivera
7. Reina Gattuso
8. Encarnación Pinedo, *El cocinero español*

CHAPTER 5: FOR SEÑORAS IN THEIR WELLNESS ERA

1. CDC, National Center for Health Statistics
2. *Lancet*
3. John M. Ruiz et al.
4. Lewina O. Lee et al.
5. Dan Buettner
6. Frank Filocomo
7. Michael Norton
8. Northwestern Medicine
9. Mayo Clinic Staff
10. Sandra Aguilar-Rodríguez
11. Marion Nestle
12. US Department of Health & Human Services
13. Olga Kornienko et al.
14. Derek Thompson

15. Robert Waldinger and Marc Schulz
16. Rhaina Cohen
17. Agnaldo Garcia et al.
18. Faith Popcorn
19. Robert D. Putnam
20. Socolow
21. Linda Poon
22. Christoph Zangger
23. Pew
24. Catherine E. Milner and Kimberly A. Cote
25. Ran D. Goldman
26. Anahad O'Connor
27. Karen Weintraub
28. Aditi Shrikant
29. disorders
30. Jonathan Haidt
31. https://news.sfsu.edu/archive/news-story/digital-addiction-increases
    -loneliness-anxiety-and-depression.html
32. https://www.researchgate.net/publication/268230174_Hearth_and
    _Campfire_Influences_on_Arterial_Blood_Pressure_Defraying_the
    _Costs_of_the_Social_Brain_through_Fireside_Relaxation
33. World Health Organization

CHAPTER 6: FOR SEÑORAS IN THEIR CLEAN BEAUTY ERA

1. Rebecca Fett
2. Ruth B. Lathi
3. Greta Stieger
4. https://time.com/6255795/toxic-stress-life-expectancy-how-to-reduce/.
5. Breastcancer.org
6. Stuart Bondurant et al.
7. USDA
8. USDA
9. (Half of US cosmetics contain toxic chemicals, the study says)
10. Tamarra M. James-Todd et al.
11. Zorimar Rivera-Núñez et al.
12. Ami R. Zota and Bhavna Shamasunder
13. Lily Martin et al.
14. Adelinda A. Candeias and Edgar Galindo
15. Barbara E. Mundy

16. Josue Esteban Calderon Sanchez
17. Paola Ochoa Pacheco et al.
18. Rebeca Chamorro and Yvette Flores-Ortiz
19. Isabel C. Quiñones et al.

CHAPTER 7: FOR SEÑORAS IN THEIR GARDEN ERA

1. Alvaro Huerta
2. Gabriel R. Valle
3. Tania González-Rivadeneira and Radamés Villagómez Reséndiz
4. Christopher Ingraham
5. Madeline Flahive DiNardo et al.
6. Morgan Kelly
7. Donald R. Davis et al.
8. Brett L. Markham
9. Harvard T.H. Chan School of Public Health

CHAPTER 8: THE SEÑORA HOME

1. Huixia Niu
2. Mélissa Godin
3. Katherine Ashenburg

Bibliography

Aguilar-Rodríguez, Sandra. "Cooking Modernity: Nutrition Policies, Class, and Gender in 1940s and 1950s Mexico City." *The Americas* 64: no. 2 (2007): 177–205.

Ashenburg, Katherine. *The Dirt on Clean: An Unsanitized History.* North Point Press, 2008.

Bondurant, Stuart, Virginia Ernster, and Roger Herdman, eds. (Committee on the Safety of Silicone Breast Implants, Institute of Medicine.) *Safety of Silicone Breast Implants.* National Academy Press, 2000.

"Average PTO in the US & Other PTO Statistics." *Forbes Advisor.* Accessed March 7, 2025. https://www.forbes.com/advisor/business/pto -statistics/.

Buettner, Dan. *The Blue Zones: Lessons for Living Longer From the People Who've Lived the Longest.* National Geographic, 2008.

Buqué, Dr. Mariel. *Break the Cycle: A Guide to Healing Intergenerational Trauma.* Dutton, 2024.

Candeias, Adelinda A., and Edgar Galindo. "Cognitive Aging: Why We Need Creativity to Increase Cognitive Preservation." *Health Psychology Report* 10, no. 4 (2021): 257–65.

CBS News. "Half of US Cosmetics Contain Toxic Chemicals, Study Says." *CBS News* (June 15, 2021). https://www.cbsnews.com/news/cosmetics -toxic-chemicals-us/.

CDC, National Center for Health Statistics. "Life Expectancy in the US Dropped for the Second Year in a Row in 2021." *National Center for Health Statistics Newsletter* (2022). https://www.cdc.gov/nchs/ pressroom/nchs_press_releases/2022/20220831.htm#:~:text=For%2 0Immediate%20Release%3A%20August%2031%2C%202022&text=That %20decline%20%E2%80%93%207.0%20to%2076.1,life%20expectancy %20since%201921%2D1923 (accessed February 3, 2025).

Chamorro, Rebeca, and Yvette Flores-Ortiz. "Acculturation and Disordered Eating Patterns among Mexican American Women." *International Journal of Eating Disorders* 28, no. 1 (2000): 125–29.

Chang, Edward C., Jameson K. Hirsch, Lawrence J. Sanna, Elizabeth L. Jeglic, and Cathryn G. Fabian. "A Preliminary Study of Perfectionism and Loneliness as Predictors of Depressive and Anxious Symptoms in Latinas: A Top-Down Test of a Model." *Journal of Counseling Psychology* 58, no. 3 (2011): 441–48.

"Claire's Stores, Inc., Announces Voluntary Recall of Three Make-Up Products." *US Food and Drug Administration announcement* (March 11, 2019).

Cohen, Rhaina. *The Other Significant Others: Reimagining Life with Friendship at the Center*. St. Martin's Press, 2024.

CUNY, Dominican Studies Institute. "After Years Residing in Seville, a Freed Black Woman from Santo Domingo Missed Her City (1575)." *CUNY Dominican Studies Institute Newsletter* (August 19, 2024). https://dsi.ccnydigitalscholarship.org/dsi-blacks-in-america/exhibits/show/first-blacks-in-america/trial-21.

Curran, Thomas. *The Perfection Trap: Embracing the Power of Good Enough*. Scribner, 2023.

Davidds, Yasmin. *Graciously Assertive: How Becoming a Better Human Makes You a Better Leader*. Moorehouse, 2024.

Davis, Donald R., Melvin D. Epp, and Hugh D. Riordan. "Changes in USDA Food Composition Data for 43 Garden Crops, 1950 to 1999." *Journal of the American College of Nutrition* 23, no. 6 (2004): 669–82.

Davis, Kip, and Ingrid Carrete. "Hispanics Are Gaining Wealth in America." *Ipsos* (October 24, 2022): 1–6. https://www.ipsos.com/sites/default/files/ct/publication/documents/2022-10/2022_10_04_Hispanics_Wealth_Davis_Ipsos.pdf.

Deloitte. "Advancing Workplace Well-Being." *Deloitte Insights*. Accessed March 7, 2025. https://www2.deloitte.com/us/en/insights/topics/talent/workplace-well-being-research.html 2023.

Dialogue Earth. (June 15, 2023). https://dialogue.earth/en/pollution/371082-as-plastic-piles-up-in-mexico-waste-pickers-bear-the-burden/.

Eyal, Maytal. "Self-Silencing Is Making Women Sick." *Time*. (October 3, 2023). https://time.com/6319549/silencing-women-sick-essay/.

Fett, Rebecca. *It Starts with the Egg: How the Science of Egg Quality Can Help You Get Pregnant Naturally, Prevent Miscarriage, and Improve Your Odds in IVF*. Franklin Fox, 2023.

Fiedler, Christina Montoya. "Latine Families Are Learning to Leave Hustle Culture Behind." *Parents* (May 29, 2024). https://www.parents.com/parents-latina-magazine/latinx-families-are-learning-to-leave-hustle-culture-behind/.

Filocomo, Frank. "Are Americans Losing Their Sense of 'Belonging'?" *National Review* (May 11, 2023). https://www.nationalreview.com/corner/are-americans-losing-their-sense-of-belonging/.

Flahive DiNardo, Madeline, Laura DePrado, Nicholas Polanin, and Joel Flagler. "Enabling Gardens: The Practical Side of Horticultural Therapy." Cooperative Extension Fact Sheet FS1208. New Jersey Agricultural Experiment Station, Rutgers (July 2013). https://njaes.rutgers.edu/fs1208/.

Popcorn, Faith. *The Popcorn Report: Faith Popcorn on the Future of Your Company, Your World, Your Life.* New York: Doubleday, 1991

Galván, Astrid. "Federal Judge Temporarily Halts Texas Law Allowing State Arrests of Immigrants." *Axios* (February 29, 2024). https://www.axios.com/2024/02/29/texas-immigration-border-law-lawsuit-ruling.

Garcia, Agnaldo, Julia Sursis Nobre Ferro Bucher-Maluschke, Daniela Marisol Pérez-Angarita, and Fábio Nogueira Pereira. "Friendship in Latin American Social Comparative Studies." *Interpersona: An International Journal on Personal Relationships* 10: no. 1 (2016): 1–12.

Gattuso, Reina. "The Chocolate-Brewing Witches of Colonial Latin America." *Atlas Obscura*, January 27, 2020). https://www.atlasobscura.com/articles/were-there-witchhunts-in-south-america.

Godin, Mélissa. "As Plastic Piles Up in Mexico, Waste Pickers Bear the Burden."

Goldman, Ran D. "Honey for Treatment of Cough in Children." *Canadian Family Physician* 60, no. 12 (2014): 1107–10.

Goldsmith, Kelly, Caroline Roux, and Jingjing Ma. "When Seeking the Best Brings Out the Worst in Consumers: Understanding the Relationship between a Maximizing Mindset and Immoral Behavior." *Journal of Consumer Psychology* 28, no. 2 (2017): 293–309.

González-Rivadeneira, Tania, and Radamés Villagómez Reséndiz. "Home Gardens in Latin America: Wild Foods in the Mesoamerican Ekuaro of P'urépechas, Mexico and the Andean Chakra of Kichwas, Ecuador." *Ethnoscientia* 7, no. 4 (2022): 119–41.

Grieve, Pete. "Americans Work Hundreds of Hours More a Year Than Europeans: Report." *Money* (January 26, 2023). https://money.com/americans-work-hours-vs-europe-china/.

Grothaus, Michael. "These Are the Best Flexible Jobs with Good Salaries in America Right Now. Most Aren't in Tech." *Fast Company* (January 24, 2024). https://www.fastcompany.com/91016143/best-jobs-2024-good-salaries-flexible-wfh-indeed-list.

Haidt, Jonathan. *The Anxious Generation: How the Great Rewiring of Childhood Is Causing an Epidemic of Mental Illness.* Penguin, 2024.

Harvard T.H. Chan School of Public Health. "The Nutrition Source." Accessed February 4, 2025. https://nutritionsource.hsph.harvard.edu/.

Hersey, Tricia. *Rest Is Resistance: A Manifesto.* Little, Brown Spark, 2022.

Hill, Latoya, and Samantha Artiga. "COVID-19 Cases and Deaths by Race/Ethnicity: Current Data and Changes Over Time." *Kaiser Health News* (2022).

Horan, Stephanie. "Fastest-Growing Jobs for Hispanic and Latino Americans–2021 Study." SmartAsset (October 11, 2021). https://smartasset.com/data-studies/fastest-growing-jobs-for-hispanic-and-latino-americans-2021.

Huerta, Alvaro. "Barrio Wisdom: To Survive the Coronavirus, Americans Must Learn from Chicanos." *L.A. Taco.* March 26, 2020.

Ingraham, Christopher. "Gardening Boosts Your Mood as Much as Some Kinds of Exercise, Study Says." *Washington Post*, May 15, 2020. https://go.gale.com/ps/i.do?id=GALE%7CA624002353&sid=sitemap&v=2.1&it=r&p=AONE&sw=w&userGroupName=anon%7Ea2afb10&aty=open-web-entry.

Ito, Aki. "How Hustle Culture Got America Addicted to Work." *Business Insider* (January 23, 2022). https://www.businessinsider.com/hustle-culture-got-america-addicted-to-work.

Jadad-Garcia, Tamen, and Dr. Alex Jadad. "Toxic Stress Load Is the Biggest Barrier to Living Longer. Here's How to Reduce It." *Time*, February 14, 2023. https://time.com/6255795/toxic-stress-life-expectancy-how-to-reduce/.

James-Todd, Tamarra M., Yu-Han Chiu, and Ami R. Zota. "Racial/Ethnic Disparities in Environmental Endocrine Disrupting Chemicals and Women's Reproductive Health Outcomes: Epidemiological Examples across the Life Course." *Current Epidemiology Reports* 3, no, 2 (2016): 161–80.

Keister Lisa A., and Brian Aronson. "Immigrants in the One Percent: The National Origin of Top Wealth Owners." *PLOS ONE* 12, no. 2 (2017). https://journals.plos.org/plosone/article?id=10.1371/journal.pone.0172876.

Kelly, Morgan. "Sowing Seeds of Happiness: Emotional Well-Being while Home Gardening Similar to Other Popular Activities, Study Finds." *Princeton Environmental Institute Newsletter* (May 10, 2020).

Keyes, Corey. *Languishing: How to Feel Alive Again in a World That Wears Us Down.* Crown, 2024.

Kornienko, Olga, David Schaefer, Thao Ha, and Douglas A. Granger. "Loneliness and Cortisol Are Associated with Social Network Regulation." *Social Neuroscience.* 15, no. 45 (2020): 1–13.

Lancet. "The Hispanic Paradox" *Lancet* 385, no. 9981 (2015): 1918.

Landers, Jane. "Founding Mothers: Female Rebels in Colonial New Granada and Spanish Florida." *Journal of African American History* (2013): 7–23. https://www.journals.uchicago.edu/doi/10.5323/jafri amerhist.98.1.0007

Lathi, Ruth B., Cara A. Liebert, Kathleen F. Brookfield, et al. "Conjugated Bisphenol A (BPA) in Maternal Serum in Relation to Miscarriage Risk." *Fertility and Sterility* 102, no. 1 (2014): 123–28.

Lee, Lewina O., Peter James, Emily S. Zevon, et al. "Optimism Is Associated with Exceptional Longevity in 2 Epidemiologic Cohorts of Men and Women." *Proceedings of the National Academy of Sciences of the United States of America* 116, no. 37 (2019): 18357–62.

Lipsett-Rivera, Sonya. *Gender and the Negotiation of Daily Life in Mexico, 1750–1856.* University of Nebraska Press, 2012.

Lynn, Christopher Dana, "Hearth and Campfire Influences on Arterial Blood Pressure: Defraying the Costs of the Social Brain through Fireside Relaxation." *Evolutionary Psychology* 12, no. 5 (2014): 983–1003.

Markham, Brett L. *Mini Farming: Self-Sufficiency on ¼ Acre.* Skyhorse, 2010.

Martin, Lily, Renate Oepen, Katharina Bauer, et al. "Creative Arts Interventions for Stress Management and Prevention–A Systematic Review." *Behavioral Sciences* 8, no. 2 (2018).

Martinez, Joelle L. "The Growing Influence of Latino Millennials in Today's Workplace." *Fast Company* (March 11, 2024). https://www .fastcompany.com/91053534/the-growing-influence-of-latino-mil lennials-in-todays-workplace.

Masci, David, and Michael Lipka. "Where Christian Churches, Other Religions Stand on Gay Marriage." *PEW Research Center Newletter* (2015).

Mayo *Clinic.* Staff. "Exercise and Stress: Get Moving to Manage Stress." *Mayo Clinic*, November 4, 2021. https://www.mayoclinic.org/healthy -lifestyle/stress-management/in-depth/exercise-and-stress/art -20044469.

McFarling, Usha Lee. "The 'Hispanic Paradox' Intrigues a New Generation of Researchers Determined to Unravel It." *Stat* (September 14, 2023). https://www.statnews.com/2023/09/14/hispanic-paradox-life-expectancy-research/.

Milner, Catherine E., and Kimberly A. Cote. "Benefits of Napping in Healthy Adults: Impact of Nap Length, Time of Day, Age, and Experience with Napping." *Journal of Sleep Research* 18, no. 2 (2009): 272–81.

Mora, Lauren, and Mark Hugo Lopez. "Key Facts about US Latinos with Graduate Degrees." *PEW Research Center Newletter* (October 3, 2023). https://www.pewresearch.org/short-reads/2023/10/03/key-facts-about-us-latinos-with-graduate-degrees/.

Mundy, Barbara E. *The Death of Aztec Tenochtitlan, the Life of Mexico City.* University of Texas Press, 2015.

Nestle, Marion. *Food Politics: How the Food Industry Influences Nutrition and Health.* rev ed. University of California Press, 2007.

Newport, Cal. *Slow Productivity: The Lost Art of Accomplishment Without Burnout.* Portfolio, 2024.

Niu, Huixia, Shaojie Liu, Yujie Jiang, et al. "Are Microplastics Toxic? A Review from Eco-Toxicity to Effects on the Gut Microbiota." *Metabolites* 13, no. 6 (2023). https://pmc.ncbi.nlm.nih.gov/articles/PMC10304106/.

Noe-Bustamante, Luis, Sahana Mukherjee, and Jens Manuel Krogstad. "A Majority of Latinas Feel Pressure to Support Their Families or to Succeed at Work." *PEW Research Center Newletter* (May 14, 2024). https://www.pewresearch.org/race-and-ethnicity/2024/05/14/a-majority-of-latinas-feel-pressure-to-support-their-families-or-to-succeed-at-work/.

Northwestern Medicine. "Health Benefits of Having a Routine: Tips for a Healthier Lifestyle." *Northwestern Medicine Newsletter.* Updated December 2022. https://www.nm.org/healthbeat/healthy-tips/health-benefits-of-having-a-routine#:~:text=An%20effective%20routine%20can%20help,emotional%20well%2Dbeing%20and%20energy.

Norton, Michael. *The Ritual Effect: From Habit to Ritual, Harness the Surprising Power of Everyday Actions.* Scribner, 2024.

Nuñez, Alicia, Patricia González, Gregory A. Talavera, et al. "Machismo, Marianismo, and Negative Cognitive-Emotional Factors: Findings From the Hispanic Community Health Study/Study of Latinos Sociocultural Ancillary Study." *Journal of Latino/a Psychology* 4, no. 4 (2016): 202–17.

O'Connor, Anahad. "The Claim: Gargling With Salt Water Can Ease Cold Symptoms." *New York Times*, September 27, 2010.

Pacheco, Paola Ochoa, Rafael Castro Pérez, David Coello-Montecel, and Nancy Pamela Castro Zazueta. "Quality of Life in Older Adults: Evidence from Mexico and Ecuador." *Geriatrics* (Basel) 6, no. 3 (Sember 16, 2021). https://www.mdpi.com/2308-3417/6/3/92.

Pérez, Lucy, Bernardo Sichel, Michael Chui, and Ana Paula Calvo. *The Economic State of Latinos in America: The American Dream Deferred*. (McKinsey & Company report, 2021). https://nalcab.org/wp-content/uploads/2021/12/McKinsey_the-economic-state-of-latinos-in-america-full-report_Nov-2021.pdf.

Pinedo, Encarnación. *El cocinero español* [The Spanish kitchen]. E. C. Hughes, 1898.

Pinedo, Encarnación. *Encarnación's Kitchen: Mexican Recipes from Nineteenth-Century California*. Edited and translated by Dan Strehl. University of California Press, 2005.

Poon, Linda. "Why Won't You Be My Neighbor?" Bloomberg (August 19, 2015). https://www.bloomberg.com/news/articles/2015-08-19/why-americans-are-less-likely-to-interact-with-their-neighbors-than-ever-before.

Putnam, Robert D. *Bowling Alone: The Collapse and Revival of American Community*. Simon & Schuster, 2000.

Quiñones, Isabel C., Sylvia Herbozo, Alissa A. Haedt-Matt. "Body Dissatisfaction among Ethnic Subgroups of Latin Women: An Examination of Acculturative Stress and Ethnic Identity." *Body Image* 41 (2022): 272–83.

Rivera-Núñez, Zorimar, Pahriya Ashrap, Emily S. Barrett, et al. "Personal Care Products: Demographic Characteristics and Maternal Hormones in Pregnant Women from Puerto Rico." *Environmental Research* 206 (2022). https://www.sciencedirect.com/science/article/abs/pii/S0013935121016777.

Ruiz, John M., Patrick Steffen, and Timothy B. Smith. "Hispanic Mortality Paradox: A Systematic Review and Meta-Analysis of the Longitudinal Literature." *American Journal of Public Health* 103, no. 3 (2013): e52–e60.

Sanchez, Josue Esteban Calderon. "El cabello como un problema estético en la invasión de América." *Cuadernos del minotauro* 4 (2006): 9–34.

Shrikant, Aditi. "Youth Suicide Rates Rose 62% from 2007 to 2021: 'People Feel Hopeless,' One Recent Grad Says." CNBC (December 5, 2023).

https://www.cnbc.com/2023/12/05/youth-suicide-rates-rose-62per
cent-from-2007-to-2021.html#:~:text=During%20the%20last%20two
%20decades,seven%20of%20them%20by%20suicide.

Socolow, Susan Migden. *The Women of Colonial Latin America (New Approaches to the Americas)*. 2nd ed. Cambridge University Press, 2000.

Stieger, Greta. "BPA Substitutes and Chromosomal Abnormalities." Food Packaging Forum (September 17, 2018). https://foodpackaging-forum.org/news/bpa-substitutes-and-chromosomal-abnormalities.

Stillman, Jessica. "A Psychologist's Scary Warning to Women Leaders: Being a People Pleaser Is Making You Physically Sick." *Inc.* (November 27, 2023). https://www.inc.com/jessica-stillman/a-psych ologists-scary-warning-to-women-leaders-being-a-people-pleaser -is-making-you-physically-sick.html.

Taylor, Paul, Mark Hugo Lopez, Jessica Martínez, and Gabriel Velasco. "When Labels Don't Fit: Hispanics and Their Views of Identity." *PEW Research Center Report* (April 4, 2012). https://www.pewre-search.org/race-and-ethnicity/2012/04/04/when-labels-dont-fit-his panics-and-their-views-of-identity/.

Thompson, Derek. "Why Americans Suddenly Stopped Hanging Out." *The Atlantic* (February 14, 2024). https://www.theatlantic.com/ ideas/archive/2024/02/america-decline-hanging-out/677451/.

UnidosUS. "Latinos Are Among the Most Burdened in Student Loan Debt. Here's How Advocates Say That Can Be Alleviated." *Unidos-US Newsletter.* (August 17, 2022). https://unidosus.org/progress -report/latinos-bear-the-brunt-of-the-countrys-1-7-trillion-in -student-loan-debt-heres-how-advocates-say-that-can-be-allev iated/#:~:text=UnidosUS%20has%20been%20part%20of,%2C%20im-proving%20income%2Ddriven%20orepayment%20(.

US Department of Health & Human Services. "New Surgeon General Advisory Raises Alarm about the Devastating Impact of the Epidemic of Loneliness and Isolation in the United States." US Department of Health & Human Services press release (2023).

US Food and Drug Administration. "Hair Smoothing Products That Release Formaldehyde When Heated." (October 15, 2024). https:// www.fda.gov/cosmetics/cosmetic-products/hair-smoothing-pro ducts-release-formaldehyde-when-heated.

Valle, Gabriel R. "The Past in the Present: What our Ancestors Taught us about Surviving Pandemics." *Food Ethics* 6, no. 2 (2021): 1–12.

Waldinger, Robert, and Marc Schulz. "What the Longest Study on Human Happiness Found Is the Key to a Good Life." *The Atlantic* (January

19, 2023). https://www.theatlantic.com/ideas/archive/2023/01/har
vard-happiness-study-relationships/672753/.

Weintraub, Karen. "Can Being Cold Make You Sick?" *New York Times*,
February 23, 2018.

World Health Organization. *Global Status Report on Alcohol and Health*.
Geneva: WHO Press, 2014.

Yanatma, Servet. "Average Working Hours in Europe: Which Countries
Work the Longest and Shortest Weeks?" *Euronews* (July 22, 2023).
https://www.euronews.com/next/2023/07/22/average-working
-hours-in-europe-which-countries-work-the-longest-and-shortest
-weeks#:~:text=Among%20men%2C%20the%20shortest%20aver
age,the%20EU%20at%2041.7%20hours.

Zangger, Christoph. "Localized Social Capital in Action: How Neighbor-
hood Relations Buffered the Negative Impact of COVID-19 on
Subjective Well-Being and Trust." *SSM – Population Health* 21
(March 2023). https://www.sciencedirect.com/science/article/pii/
S2352827322002865.

Zitner, Aaron. "America Pulls Back From Values That Once Defined It,
WSJ-NORC Poll Finds." *Wall Street Journal*, March 27, 2023.

Zota, Ami R., and Bhavna Shamasunder. "The Environmental Injustice
of Beauty: Framing Chemical Exposures from Beauty Products as
a Health Disparities Concern." *American Journal of Obstetrics &
Gynecology* 217, no. 4 (2017): 418–22.

Zubair, Ujala, Muhammad K. Khan, and Muna Albashari. "Link between
Excessive Social Media Use and Psychiatric Disorders." *Annals of
Medicine and Surgery* (2023) 85, no. 4: 875–78.

❦ Acknowledgments ❦

WE'D LIKE TO thank our families, those who are both here and no longer with us. We're particularly indebted to the señoras of our families, Carmen Luz and Elizabeth, who helped us become the señoras we are today, as well as to our incredible ancestral doñas in Chile, Mexico, and Portugal—Mercedes, Margarita, Elsie, Vera—and our great-grandmothers Maria and Virginia.

We would also like to thank our husbands, Don Matt and Don Benjamin, and our fathers, Don Zuen and Don John. To the tiniest members of our families, Margaux and Valentina, may you grow up into powerful, strong señoras and conquer the world. And our gratitude goes to our brothers and sisters and *primos* and *tíos*, too, *obvio*! We also want to thank Leticia and the Dafina/Kensington team for giving us a chance.

This book goes out to everyone who has been part of the growth of Vamigas and to our fifty thousand plus Señora Era TikTok community, especially our beta readers, whose perspectives we are so grateful for.